NOTES

ON THE CAUCASUS

By WANDERER

London

MACMILLAN AND CO.

1883

CONTENTS.

CHAPTER I.

CHAPTER II.

CHAPTER III.

DESCRIPTION OF TIFLIS.

CHAPTER IV.

RAMBLES IN GEORGIA.

CHAPTER XI.

CHAPTER XII.

SPORT IN CIRCASSIA AND THE CAUCASUS IN GENERAL.

CHAPTER XIII.

THE CAUCASUS.

CHAPTER I.

Introductory Remarks and Political Retrospect—The Army of the
Caucasus.

THE Caucasus is by the Russian Government officially
divided into Cis-Caucasia and Trans-Caucasia. By
the former the steppes north of the main chain of
mountains are indicated; the latter designation in-
cludes the provinces of Georgia, Mingrelia, Imeritia,
on the west, and of Russian Armenia, Erivan, Shusha,
Shirvan, etc., to the east and south of the sierra.
The whole area consists, roughly speaking, of a
conglomeration of mountains intersected by streams
and rivers, sometimes cutting their way through
the hills, at the bottom of deep gorges, sometimes
widening into broad open valleys.

The Caucasus is divided across its centre from
east to west by the rivers Koura (Cyrus) and Rion
(Phasis), running respectively into the Black and
Caspian Seas. These rivers, on account of rapids
and other obstructions, are only navigable for a certain distance from their mouths; but their valleys,
especially that of the Koura, into which the Araxes

falls, become broad plains as they approach their embouchures.

Though an exclusively alpine country for the most part, the Trans-Caucasian ranges are not precipitous, but a sort of wide undulating downs, forming in many parts large plateaux elevated from 3000 to 5000 feet above the sea-level. Great variety of climate exists: on the steppes of the Kouban and Terek rivers north of the main chain are fertile, well-watered prairies, covered in spring and summer with a luxurious vegetation, and overhung by closely-wooded mountains. A little farther south is the province of Shirvan and the Mogan steppe, a burnt-up salt waste, uninhabitable during summer on account of snakes, heat, and malaria, and a bleak desert during the winter months.

The country, again, towards the embouchure of the Rion is, during great part of the year, a semi-tropical swamp, subject to deadly fevers; while south of it, along the Turkish frontier, are dry, healthy uplands, cool in summer, and with a Canadian winter.

As regards general topography the Caucasian provinces may be said, roughly speaking, to present a vast "quadrilateral," defended on its flanks by seas, marshes, and deserts, and on its front and rear faces by mountain ranges of great height and breadth.

Much of the low-lying country of Georgia itself is subject to malarious fevers, prevailing in parts where, from the dried, burnt-up appearance of the soil, one would not expect them. Disagreeable north-east winds often blow with great force winter and summer, producing sudden changes of temperature by no means conducive to health ; in fact, the climate of Georgia, *i.e.* of the valley of the Cyrus, may be described as consisting of alternations of heat and cold, varied by wind and dust, with occasional spells of very fine weather.

That of Imeritia and Mingrelia is in summer semi-tropical, but they have occasionally very severe winters, which kill all but the hardiest trees and shrubs. The upland plateaux of Russian Armenia are pleasant during the summer, when the thermo-meter in Tiflis often stands at 100° Fahrenheit in the shade, but are bleak and frozen wastes in winter.

Three-fourths of the land area of the Caucasus being, from scarcity of water, saltness of the soil, and the emigration of the greater part of the mountain population to Turkey, uncultivated, its grain-producing powers are limited. Labour is dear, and colonisation confined to communities of German and Russian peasants.

The Russian middle class seem to have little or no turn for industrial or commercial enterprise, their education apparently militating against the qualities required for pioneering.

The population may be roughly divided into Christian and Mahometan, or Tartars, as the latter are usually called. The Christians consist of Armenians and Georgians, the Mahometans of Persians and Lesghians. The Circassians and Tchettchentz, who formerly inhabited the mountains on the Black Sea

coast, and along the main chain above the Terek, etc.,
many of whom still remain on the northern slopes,
are only nominally Mahometans.

The Armenians, who have become—outwardly at
any rate—much Europeanised of late years, possess
the pushing business aptitude which rarely fails to
ensure success in commerce.

They have long monopolised the trade of the
Caucasus, and are at present rapidly permeating the
army and civil services. They are clever and intelligent, often speaking several languages, and are gradually extending their commercial operations into
Europe. The Georgians are less avaricious, but more
indolent.

Many of the better classes of the natives, both
Christian and Mahometan, after attending college and
passing their examinations, now enter the Government service, civil or military, in which latter especially they often attain high rank ; the policy, first
inaugurated by Prince Worowzoff, of detaching the
nobility from their estates and encouraging them, by
bestowing titles, decorations, etc., to seek employment
under Government, has done much to Europeanise
the country.

The Russian language is now fast becoming the
language of the country, and will take a traveller
almost anywhere, enough being understood even in
remote villages to procure him what he wants. Among
the educated classes French is very widespread, and
is, next to Russian, perhaps the most useful, though
both German and Turkish are widely spoken. In

some parts of the country Turkish is the most useful language of any.

Anterior to the sixteenth century the Caucasus had always formed part of Persia, either actually or nominally, according to the resources and prestige of the various regnant dynasties, Ghaznevides, Seljooks, Khaureznians, and Tartars, which have supplanted each other in that anarchical empire, have ruled over Asia Minor and Central Asia from the Black Sea to Bokhara, and the Mediterranean to the Indus, and have disappeared, leaving scarcely a memory behind.[1]

It must not be supposed that the Persians "held the Caucasus" as the Russians hold it, or as we hold India. They governed according to the nature of the country, the character and habitats of the various rude robber tribes and races which form the population. Over some of these their rule was tolerably assured ; over others slight, approaching to nominal ; over others, again, completely *nil ;* which policy is the secret of Oriental domination, and the reason why Asiatics will always in the long run prefer an Asiatic *régime,* for all its despotism, etc., to European forms of government. The first, though hard to bear at times, is elastic—sometimes severe, sometimes hardly

---

[1] As the Persian poet says—

"Kuja an Feridoon, Zohak o Djem,
Shahan Arab, o Khosrouan Agem."

Where are Feridoon, Zohak, and Giamschid,
The Kings of Arabia and Emperors of Persia ?

It will perhaps some day be asked—Where are so and so, and so and so, Kings of England and Emperors of India.

felt at all. The second is unvarying, monotonous, and leaden.

Under the Persians the eastern districts of the country—viz. Shirvan, the Caspian provinces, Erivan, and the Araxes valley, the plateau of the lesser Caucasus, Georgia, and Kakhetia—were governed either by Persian "khans" or tributary (hereditary) Georgian princes; while the mountain tribes—Daghestans, Svanetes, Ossetes, Circassians, etc.—managed their own affairs, consisting of tribal wars with each other, slave-hunting, and predatory razzias on the low country, in complete independence. Things went on thus, comfortably enough, until the suzerainty of the Persians was seriously menaced by the Turks towards the close of the sixteenth century.

The Osmanli, who were then (1575 to 1600) at the *apogée* of their power, after invading and overrunning the Caucasus as far as Derbend on the Caspian Sea,[1] garrisoned and held Tiflis, Erivan, and the valley of the Koura, including the highlands and elevated plateaux between it and Kars; but they soon found, as the Russians have found subsequently, that holding the Caucasus was an expensive business, and, after a series of bloody campaigns (often cited by historians as the commencement of their decadence), agreed to a "demarcation of frontier," which lasted, with slight modifications, to Paskievitch's campaign in 1829.

Towards the end of the last century the Russians, who had conquered the Crimea, and thus became pos-

---

[1] Their dominion at this date extended from Derbend, on the Caspian, to Algiers, and from Baghdad to Buda Pesth in Hungary.

sessed of the great "debatable ground" extending
up to the foot of the northern face of the Caucasian
sierra (then inhabited by various warlike nomadic
tribes, including Kalmuks, Turkomans, Nogais, revolted Cossacks, etc.), commenced intriguing in the
Caucasus itself by setting the Georgians and other
soi-disant Christian races against the Persians (just
as they set the Bulgarians against the Turks a few
years ago), and with the same result.

The Georgians refused to pay tribute, and revolted.
Aga Mahomed Khan, then Shah of Persia, marched on
Tiflis to coerce them: "atrocities" ensued; the Russians
"intervened" to "protect" the Christians, and have
stopped there (A.D. 1800) ever since, much to the
disgust of the "protected," who foolishly believed that
"Roosky" was interposing "pour l'amour de Dieu,"
and would go away after he had arranged matters.

The Russians, once settled at Tiflis, after a couple
of campaigns (1806 to 1810)—in which they annexed
Zanga (Elisabetpol) and the Caspian provinces, and
(1826-27, in which they took Erivan and the Araxes
valley, down to the present Russo-Persian frontier)
finally drove the Persians from the Caucasus, and
having about the same time taken Goumri (Alexandropol) and Akhaltsik from the Turks, and suppressed
their fortresses on the Black Sea littoral—turned their
attention to the complete subjugation of the hitherto
unconquered mountaineers, which had been in con-
templation, and indeed carried on intermittently,
since the commencement of their occupation in 1800.

The first thing undertaken was a war with the

Ossetes to secure the Dariel Pass, after which a long struggle went on with varying success with the Lesghians on the east and the Circassians on the west, until both finally succumbed, after thirty years' fighting, in 1862.

It was now the time to advance farther south in "High Asia;" accordingly the Central Asian campaigns came off, in which Tchernaieff, Kauffmann, and Skobeleff distinguished themselves by subjugating Tashkend, Khokand, and Bokhara; advancing the Russian standards in Central Asia to the frontiers of China and the Hindoo Khoosh; ultimately (in 1873) occupying Khiva; the warlike Tekke and Salor Turkomans, the main strength of the nation, being held in check by a Caucasian force disembarked at Krasnovadsk on the Caspian.[1]

Then came the Turkish war of 1877 and 1878, by which Batoum, Kars, Ardahan, and a large slice of territory as far as the Soghanli range, was added to Russian domination, and their influence over Persia

---

[1] It being notorious that these unprofitable territories were not only acquired at a loss, but that their maintenance causes, all told, a deficit in the Imperial budget of something like £5,000,000 per annum, it follows that they must have been occupied with some definite object, and in pursuance of some fixed plan for ultimately recouping the coin invested, more especially as the Russian *militaires* who contrive the annexations are the last people in the world to entertain humdrum notions of peaceable public (or private) enterprise, or of slowly acquiring wealth by improving the produce or agriculture of a country and developing its natural resources. The Russian civil administration has not even yet effected anything of the sort in the Caucasus,—a fine country, possessed of every natural advantage, which they have now had eighty years in their possession,—or indeed anything to speak of in Russia itself.

by the suppression of the Kurdish insurrection and
the cession of Khotour, firmly riveted and consoli-
dated, followed by the crushing defeat and complete
subjugation of the remaining (independent) Turkoman
tribes by Skobeleff in 1880-81, which has carried
them to the Afghan frontier.

As their next move will probably carry them to
our (N.W.) frontier, perhaps some distance beyond,
a short notice of the army of the Caucasus, by which
the above feats were mainly performed, may not be
superfluous.

The army of the Caucasus is variously composed
and commanded. For many years the Caucasus was
a sort of penal settlement, whither turbulent and
insubordinate officers of all ranks were relegated, as
were also political " suspects," not considered culpable
enough to be sent to Siberia ; it was also a sort of
" foyer " (and is now to a certain extent) for adventurers of all nations, sometimes commercial, but
chiefly military. Officers from every nation in Europe
are consequently found in its ranks, in addition to the
Asiatic element of Armenians, Tartars, Georgians, and
other Caucasians, who form a numerous and valuable
contingent, thoroughly acquainted, as most of them
are, with Turkish and other Oriental languages.

The policy of the Russians is not to raise separate
corps and regiments of Asiatics, as we do in India,
but to employ Asiatic officers, who are on a footing
of perfect equality in every respect with Russian
militaires, and can rise, equally with them, to the
highest positions.

This system has its advantages in preventing mutinous combinations and possible *émeutes*, but presents the drawback of a want of solidarity and *esprit de corps*, also being one cause of the jealousy, pique, and hostility which prevails, sometimes causing serious *contretemps* on active service.

The rank and file of the " regulars " is Russian, with numerous Poles, and some Russo - Germans, Jews, and Russian Tartars intermixed. In the dragoons (also Russian) are many Caucasian Tartars.

They have very few parades, and absolutely no pipe-clay ; a company or two is paraded daily during the summer months for rifle practice, under the adjutant and musketry instructor, and the corps is assembled once a month for muster ; the rest of the time the men do much as they choose, and usually either work at trades, selling the product of their industry at a sort of market which is held every Sunday in the bazaar of the town, or hire themselves out at so much per diem to private individuals as porters, labourers, etc.

As the men receive no pay from Government— nothing, in fact, beyond their uniform—and a very inferior ration of bread and soup per diem, the army may be said to be to a very great extent self-supporting. The fighting strength of the army of the Caucasus (without the reserve) may be taken to be from 60,000 to 70,000 effective men, or about that of our European garrison in India. The reserve would raise it to about 120,000, and the levies of irregular Georgian and Imeritian cavalry and infantry, which are called out in war-time, to perhaps 30,000 more. Every military cantonment comprises a military (reservist) colony (attached to it), to which every soldier, after completing his term of service (five years), can retire, demand his plot of land, and marry, so that these settlements are extending yearly, and materially strengthen the Russian hold of the country.

To the above available army of 150,000 men, or thereabouts, must be added the Cossacks, not the least valuable portion of it in a military point of view, who are computed to be able to turn out 50,000 horsemen,—perhaps, for Asiatic campaigning, the most useful existing cavalry, taking them all round, in the world.

The Cossacks are domiciled in the fine " steppes," or prairies, on the northern slope of the Caucasian sierra—magnificent plains of unlimited extent, covered during the spring and summer months with rich verdure, and offering grand facilities for horse and cattle breeding.   These are dotted over with Cossack " stanitzas," or villages, densely populated, and owning large droves of horses and cattle ; and from them are recruited the numerous Cossack corps on duty throughout the Caucasian provinces, as well as those forming the " cordon " which is kept up along the sea-coast and the Turkish and Persian frontiers, from Kertch to Batoum, and thence inland to the Caspian Sea.

The Cossacks are armed and equipped in complete Tcherkess [1] fashion, found by long experience to

_____
[1] Circassian.

be the best possible "costume, arms, and accoutrements" for irregular cavalry, and accordingly never
altered.[1] They carry a long but light Berdan carbine
of small bore, mounted after the pattern of a Lesghian
rifle (short straight stock, no trigger guard, knob
trigger), and slung "sideways" by a leather rheim (a
great advantage while riding, as it sits close to the
back), with felt or fur "khilak" or "ghilaf" (guncover)
to protect it from rain or dew, which saves an
immensity of trouble in the way of cleaning and
polishing. A single long pistol is also carried, a
falchion sword (*i.e.* a sword with no guard or cross
hilt) suspended from a shoulder strap, and a long
two-edged dagger or "khinjal" worn at the waist, in
front.

Their uniform is the long close-fitting Circassian
choga with cartridge cases on the breast (worn over
an "alkaluk" with high stand-up collar), a "bashlik"
or hood, and cap or "papak" of white, gray, or black
sheep-skin, thickly wadded, to keep off the sun in
summer, the cold in winter, and sabre-cuts at all
seasons. Long boots complete the "get-up," and last
but not least the "boorka," or large felt horseman's
cloak, which, when not in use, is rolled up and fastened by long leather rheims behind the saddle. The
whole equipment, developed as it was by the Cir-

[1] Our military authorities, sempiternally smitten with a mania for
"tights," have of course long ago "done away" with the picturesque
and useful costume (the old Persian dress) formerly worn by Indian
irregulars, which, being very much in the same style as the Cossack
uniform, was perfectly adapted for the exigencies of long and serious
campaigning.

cassians, who have been untold centuries on the war-
path, is admirably calculated for campaigning and
rough work,—of which fact, always adopting it as I
did while in the mountains, I had ample proof.   The
" boorka," or big felt cloak (which envelops the horse's
croup as well as the rider), keeps him, in addition to
the " bashlik" or hood, dry from head to foot in the
roughest weather.

Three of these cloaks, spread on sticks or
switches planted in the ground, " wigwam fashion,"
will make a warm waterproof little tent, big enough
for three or four men, in which a fire can be lit.

The Cossack (or rather Circassian) saddle is composed of a wooden tree, something the shape of a pack-
saddle, with a broad woollen cushion, tightly stuffed,
as a seat.   It is placed over three or four thick
" numdahs " or felts.   It has three girths, not placed
one over the other, as with us, but apart.   The first
girth draws, as with us, behind the forearm; the
second, or rear girth, across the horse's short ribs,
opposite his stifle joint; the third, which is the one
over the saddle which keeps the cushion in place
(with a thin " rheim " across the pommel and cantle,
as in a Persian saddle), draws across the centre of the
horse's belly.   They also use a light crupper and
breastplate.

This saddle is, as I have often experienced, ad-
mirable for rough mountain and forest work, for
ascending and descending steep hillsides and rocky
precipitous paths ; giving a firm, steady seat, while it
has the great advantage, that being a " pique " saddle,

furnished with strong "rheims" or thongs of raw
hide at pommel and cantle, one can attach anything
to it.

In effect it must be something exceedingly "hot
or heavy" which it will puzzle a Cossack to transport
at a pinch. Such articles as half a bullock, for instance, or a live sheep, or a couple of lambs, will be
speedily negotiated; while it is no uncommon incident to see a Cossack or Cossacks, each with a heavy
pole several inches in diameter and 18 or 20 feet in
length on each side of the horse (one end attached to
the saddle, the other trailing on the ground, perhaps
the ground ends loaded up with boughs and brush-
wood), when constructing a standing camp is in
question.

The Cossack bridle is, after the Asiatic pattern,
a strong single snaffle, knotted up short with a long
tail or end, and is far the best and most convenient
for a light "irregular" horseman, having many
advantages.

Their horses, as may be imagined, are rough unkempt animals, but at the same time stand any
amount of hard work and short commons. Bred on
the steppes, and running loose till four or five years
old, they are hardy as bears, and look not unlike
those animals so far as their coats go, which in winter
are often three inches in length. They may be seen
at this season rolling in the snow in the middle of
severe storms apparently enjoying themselves, or
scratching up the drifts with their fore feet to get a
bite of withered herbage. Only geldings are used on

service. The Cossacks do not lose time in breaking
them in. When four or five years old they are driven
in from the steppe, "corralled up," saddled, bridled,
and mounted; any animal which shows signs of vice
or gives trouble is promptly lassoed, thrown, and laid
into by four or five Cossacks with staves and cudgels,
who hit him with all their force wherever they can
get a blow at him, over head and flanks ; when released, half-stunned, and half-strangled with the
lasso, he is trembling all over and completely
cowed; he is then immediately saddled, bridled,
mounted, and "bucketed about" for an hour or
two, after which discipline he usually remains quiet
for life.

It is incredible what the horses of the steppe,
who are all of Mongol extraction, can stand in the
way of ill-usage and general endurance.

I have often seen Cossack horses in summer, when
there are always swarms of great gadflies on the
steppes, quietly grazing with the blood running down
their ribs and shoulders from the bites of several of
these insects, one alone of which would drive an
English horse wild.

It is well known that the Nogai Tartars, who
inhabit portions of these steppes towards Astrakhan,
used in the old campaigning and plundering times to
possess horses which would travel four or five days
continuously with only a handful of fodder once in
eight or ten hours, and a drink of water once in the
twenty-four, and were trained in the following
manner :—

They were not worked till rising seven or eight, at which age they were caught, saddled, and loaded with sacks of earth or sand; at first the sack was the weight of the rider, viz. 10 or 11 stones. This was gradually increased daily till they carried 20 or 22 stones, under which weight they were every day walked or trotted for seven or eight miles, the ration of food being diminished as the weight was increased.

After eight days they gradually decreased the weight until the sacks were empty, also decreasing the food, till at last, for two or three days the horse got absolutely nothing, except that they tightened the girths. This lasted for three weeks. On the twenty-first day they worked them hard till they sweated, then unsaddled and poured buckets of ice cold water over them. The animals were then picketed to pegs in the "maidan," allowed to graze, and given every day a little more rope.

The Tartars admit that this training used to kill about five horses out of seven (as it well might), but aver that an animal that had passed the ordeal would stand *anything*, and was a " fortune to a man."

This training was of course an epitome of what the horses actually had to go through on their plundering expeditions and campaigning. Travelling for days with next to no feed, swimming through half-frozen rivers, carrying great sacks of loot, retreating across waterless deserts, etc.

The Cossacks marry early, but their wives always

remain at the "stanitzas," which are consequently, especially when a campaign is going on, usually over-populated with females. Many of them, having a strain of Circassian or Tchettchentz blood, are very good-looking.

Though not "cavalry" in the European sense of the word, the Cossacks are excellent at scouting, skirmishing, foraging, and living on a country at free quarters, and, like all good "irregulars," "very bad to run away from," usually giving no quarter.

There are Cossack Horse Artillery, six-pounder batteries of six guns each, which at a short distance, from the number of horsemen who accompany each gun (none of whom ride on the limbers, and consequently quite hide the pieces from view), look like troops of cavalry. They go over any ground, and did excellent service during the war.

The qualities of the Russian infantry soldier are well known. He will go anywhere (under competent commanders) on black bread and water; will undergo fearful hardships without complaining, or at any rate without mutinying; and though wanting to a certain extent in "dash" and *élan*, possesses a dogged courage which, joined to his physical endurance, makes him a formidable adversary.

The Russian Field Artillery, now composed of Krupp steel breechloading guns (nine-pounders) is exceedingly good. The officers, like all in the higher branches of the Russian service, possess superior attainments; the privates are picked men, well-drilled; and the batteries (of eight guns each) excellently

horsed and equipped. They have also mountain
batteries of small steel guns similar to ours, but no
screw pieces as yet.

The native levies raised in time of war of irregular
cavalry and infantry, Georgians, Imeritians, Svanetes,
etc., are nowise inferior to the Russian regulars;
for though not possessing their steadiness, they have
more *élan*, and are excellent guerillas, superior to
the regulars for the mountain campaigning, bush-
fighting, and outpost work on which they are
ordinarily employed.

CHAPTER II.

Caucasian Mountaineers : Circassians, Abkhasians, Svanetians, Ossettes, Daghestans, etc.

CIRCASSIA is a country lying along the eastern shore of the Black Sea for a couple of hundred miles, between Anapa (close to Kertch and the Sea of Azov) and Gagra, where Abkhasia commences. It divides the Black Sea from the Kouban and Kabardian steppes, and is in the shape of an isosceles triangle ; the sierra and subjacent mountain range, comparatively low, narrow, and undulating at its northern extremity, becoming broad, lofty, and precipitous as it trends south and south-east, until towards the Abkhasian boundary it reaches an altitude of 10,000 to 12,000 feet and a continuous breadth of 100 miles or thereabouts.

Circassia, which is perhaps the most beautiful mountain country in the world—a rich soil, splendid forests of oak, ash, chestnut, walnut, beech, and other exclusively European timber, fine clear mountain streams and rivers full of trout and other fish—is now uninhabited, with the exception of a few insignificant stations and posts along the coast, populated mainly by horse-stealers, loafers, and drunkards from various parts of the Caucasus (chiefly Mingrelia), many of whom have permanently made their native towns and villages too hot for them.

The Circassians, who were originally a brave manly people, living in a sort of republic, much given to raiding upon their neighbours and each other (more apparently with the object of keeping up war-like habits and general efficiency than for the loot obtained, which was often of trifling intrinsic value), after heroically supporting nearly half a century of incessant warfare with Russia, were finally blockaded and starved into submission.[1]

They then decided, sooner than live under Russian domination, to quit their country and emigrate to Turkey, where land, rent free, and other advantages, had been promised them by the Government. When it is considered that the immediate effect of this re-solution was virtually to reduce the whole population to beggary, the repulsion felt by Asiatics towards

---

[1] Mountaineers being on an average better men "all round" than lowlanders,—better walkers, riders, and marksmen, more abstemious and hardy, all which qualities tell enormously in warfare—are, when fighting on their own ground, equal to three or four times their number of ordinary troops. The Russian generals only succeeded in subduing the Circassians, Lesghians, Tchettchentz, etc., by reckless prodigality of men, by severe continuous blockading, and by employing other war-like mountaineers against them, joined to disunion among the tribes, some of whom were always refusing to co-operate when great advantages might have been gained. With all this, it took them half a century and more to subjugate the Circassians. I was told on good authority while in Circassia that it had cost the Russians 20,000 men from first to last to subdue a single valley (Sachu) about fifteen miles in length, whose entire population could not have exceeded 1000 to 1500 fighting men at the highest estimate.

"civilising Russian influence" may be adequately estimated.

The Circassians not being a commercial people, very few of them, and those only nobles, possessed any coin or specie. Their land, which was their principal source of subsistence, of course went at once for nothing; their cattle, horses, etc., they were compelled to part with for whatever the Russians or the Armenians, who accompanied the Russian force of occupation, chose to offer—a horse worth 300 rbs. being sold for 15 or 20 rbs., a cow worth 30 rbs. being sold for 5 rbs., etc.

But this was not all. The accommodation for these unfortunate people in the vessels on board of which they embarked for Trebizond and Varna was entirely insufficient. Men, women, and children from the mountains in the interior, totally unaccustomed to the sea, were crowded into spaces barely adequate to a third of their number; consequently thousands died, stifled by bad air and misery, on the passage.

On their arrival in Anatolia no arrangements for their reception had been made by the Ottoman Government; consequently they had to encamp in inclement weather in the open (on the sea-shore, or wherever they could get permission), and, being penniless, thousands more died of starvation, disease, and exposure.

Altogether two-thirds of the population of Circassia are computed to have perished during this exodus. Some of the chiefs committed suicide from despair, riding into the sea mounted and armed and drowning

themselves; others, collecting their adherents, took to
brigandage, finding it the only way to get anything
to live on; others went into service with pachas (many
of the girls entered Turkish harems); and the remnant
finally settled down on the lands which, after delays
innumerable, were at length provided for them by the
Government. Meantime the Russian Government,
which from first to last had spent some millions of
money—it would hardly be safe to say how many—
and some hundreds of thousands of lives in subjugating their country, has done nothing whatever with
its acquisition.

Russian peasants, who detest mountains and forests
(and have besides plenty of land and to spare at
home), will not emigrate to it. The few Moldavians,
Greeks, and Germans who came at first on the
strength of representations made to them by Government agents, usually left or leave after a year or two,
finding Russian governmental promises "all cry and
little wool;" in fact, the only "increase" is that of
the wild hogs, bears, and wolves in the forests, which
are yearly showing improved census returns.

The *sites*, even of the former villages (all built of
wood), are rapidly becoming completely indistinguishable from the surrounding jungles, and would, indeed,
long have been quite so were it not for the fine
orchards of the former inhabitants; the apple, pear,
walnut, and cherry trees of which still remaining,
though sadly broken and mauled by bears, dimly
indicate once flourishing and well-populated locations.

A more striking instance on a large scale of the

"Fiunt solitudinem pacem appellant" would be difficult to discover either in ancient or modern records
of such feats.

I once asked a well-posted Russian gentleman,
with whom I was on tolerably intimate terms, and
who was (as usual with educated men in Russia)
ready enough to criticise official measures, what he
considered the object of the Russian Government to
be in perpetually annexing non-paying territory at
considerable expense both in acquiring and holding
the same.   He said he took the objects to be—first,
the keeping up of "prestige," so as to be always on
the winning hand ; secondly, the "tchinovniks"[1]
and army, individually and personally, often gain by
the process ; thirdly, there is a theory that land now
unoccupied in Asia will some day, by the natural process of over-population going on in Europe, become
of considerable value; in fact, that Europe will have
to come begging to us for land.

However, I am digressing.

Having passed upwards of a year in Circassia, I
had good opportunities of seeing what the country
was like, and of ascertaining the actual results of
Russian occupation.   The Emperor and grand dukes
have large estates, or rather large tracts of choice land,
in the country, which they have made themselves presents of.   So have also all the military commandants
and *militaires* in civil employ (there are few regular
civilians there).   Numerous grants along the coast

---

[1] Tchinovnik, a government employé, lit. a person of "rank,"
which the word "tchin" signifies.

have been purchased by wealthy Russian gentlemen, merchants, and speculators, most of whom have never even visited their possessions.

On none of these grants, with one or two exceptions, has anything been done ; many are entirely uninhabited—not a hut or a shed built on them.

The stations, Cossack posts, etc., are supplied with provisions by sea from Odessa and the Crimea. No roads have been made, or any harbours or port accommodation ; yet the Russian occupation, or rather annexation, dates from 1863, and is now consequently an affair of nearly twenty years' standing.[1]

The excuse for this is, that in the event of a war everything along the coast would be destroyed by the Turks or English ; but in reality Circassia is a " white elephant," about which the Russian Government (not being a commercial or colonising one, and finding no population ready to its hand to screw money out of by custom-house and other recognised devices of *vol organisé*) cannot trouble itself, and therefore just leaves alone to get on how it can ; while the local authorities, who, like other people, must live, and whose official salaries are quite inadequate for this purpose, having no other resources, recoup themselves out of the subsidies allowed by the imperial budget for roadmaking and other " improvements."

The Circassian " commonwealth," *i.e.* while the

---

[1] At least half the " stations," " cantonments," and settlements marked on the Government maps of Circassia have no existence ; the only pretence for them being that at the first annexation of the country detachments were encamped at these spots, etc.

Circassians were a nation or people, was, like those of other independent mountain tribes still or lately existing in the Caucasus, grounded on a basis of complete personal equality, and to a certain extent on community of property.

The population was divided into three ranks or castes, viz. chiefs, gentlemen retainers, and peasants ; but they had no king, and, except in time of war, no accredited authority or rulers. If a chief, for instance, chose to organise a raid, his retainers could refuse to accompany him. At the same time, if he returned with booty, any of his clan had the right to ask for a portion of the spoil, or choose some of it, but were bound in return to supply the chief with any provisions, forage, clothes, etc., he might demand. If the chief went on a campaign against a *foreign* enemy, his retainers and clansmen were obliged, under pain of eternal disgrace, to follow him into any danger, and obey him implicitly.

Retainers and clansmen could own slaves and serfs, but not the chiefs ; but the serfs, at the same time, had the right to quit any master whom they were not content with, and to choose another ; while clansmen and retainers who did not "get on" with their chief, could, in like manner, leave him and join another.

The three ranks never intermarried. Peasants were not allowed to wear coats of mail, and fought on foot. Personal independence was carried to such a pitch that sons were not supposed even to obey their parents.

National questions were deliberated on and decided by a sort of "Congress" or Parliament, presided over by the oldest chief. There were two houses or "chambers," that of the chiefs and that of the retainers, answering to Lords and Commons.

The "proceedings" were conducted with dignity. Each "house" had its spokesmen or orators, and deputations frequently passed from the one to the other.

Prisoners taken in war were the property of the captors, and could be sold, but were usually in the meantime well treated.

A man could sell his wife and his daughters, and very often did so, with the full consent of the females, who rather looked forward to going to Constantinople or Trebizond and becoming perhaps wives of a pacha or some Turkish dignitary. Brothers, on the decease of the father, could sell their sisters.

Offences were punished by heavy fines, or by ignominy.

The Circassians were supposed to have been, at some very remote period, nominally converted to Christianity, just as they were nominally converted, towards the close of the eighteenth century, to Islamism. They were actually, however, and are, if anything at all, intelligent and tolerant pagans.

They possessed certain sacred groves, and "deotas" or shrines, and used a sort of occasional worship, supposed to propitiate local divinities, procure good weather for the harvest, good luck in expeditions, etc., which very closely resembled that of some of the

Indian mountaineers, if, indeed, it was not identical, as it doubtless was originally.

It is certain that they were not real Mahometans, so long as they remained in the Caucasus at least. I was much amongst them while in Circassia, there being one village near Ardiller, recently re-established by a Russian commandant,[1] with some of the men of which, who were good "shikarees," I made several excursions. I never saw them repeat the "namaz." Once when a number of Circassians were assembled by the "popo-cheetel," or military commissioner of the district (on the occasion of some "abrêks," or outlaws, who had been in the mountains for nine years, living by hunting and occasional brigandage, giving themselves up), there was present a Turkish "hadji" from Trebizond, and two or three other Anatolian Mahometans, much considered by the Circassians, having always traded to the country before Russian occupation. The hadji and the other Turks regularly prayed, with great solemnity, night and morning. Three or four of the outlaws would join them—I suspect out of complaisance. The rest of the Tcherkess would sit smoking and looking on at the devotions, some of them openly making fun of it, rather scandalising the Christians of the party by their unconcealed irreverence.

I have been somewhat diffuse on this head, for the reason that the religious "notions" of the Tcher-

[1] The men of this village were Tcherkess from the northern face of the chain above the Kuban steppe, some of whom remained at the time of the exodus; all from the south-west slope and Black Sea shore departed.

kess closely coincide with those of all the nominally
converted (but in reality pagan) mountaineers of the
Caucasus, such as the Abkhas, Svanetes, Ingouch, etc.
None of them ever had any *written* "scriptures," and
a tendency to disbelieve in regular forms of religion,
and to go in for "luck" divination, and old-established
"deotas" and fetiches, is prevalent throughout.

The Tcherkess, besides being warriors, were capital
craftsmen, excellent hunters and trappers; in fact,
"good men" all round.

The arms, saddlery, and accoutrements fabricated
by the Circassians and Tchettchentz were the best of
their kind in the Caucasus, all others being inferior
copies of their patterns. They possessed a first-rate
breed of mountain horses (now extinct), very clever
on rocky and difficult ground, and, though small,
stout and untiring.

The Abkhasians are second-rate Circassians—all
the bad qualities of the latter and few of the good.
As courageous and reckless, perhaps more so, but
more treacherous and *rusé*, and altogether less to
be depended upon. They have the credit, and always
had, of being capable of anything.

The Tcherkess left their country in a body sooner
than live in subjection to Russia, and none who left
have returned.

Some of the Abkhas did the same, but others
could not make up their minds, and agreed to become
Russian subjects. Being at any rate nominally Mahometans, the Russian authorities stipulated that, as
a preliminary, they should become Greek Christians,

to which they consented, and were baptized a hundred at a time by immersion in a river.   This was in 1866. Shortly afterwards General Cogniard, governor of the newly-annexed territory, arrived with his staff and bodyguard of 100 Cossacks, with the object of making a settlement, arranging the land boundaries, imposts, and general jurisdiction.

A grand assembly of chiefs and their followers was convened for this purpose, but during these *entrefaites*, several of the leading *émigrés*, dissatisfied with the reception they had met with from the Turks, had returned from Trebizond and begun taking part in the proceedings.   The upshot was that, finding the "sense of the meeting" was hostile to Russian ascendency, they "raised the crowd" on the Governor, officers, and escort, who were all (with the exception of one or two Poles) barbarously massacred.[1]   After this they attacked Sookhoom Kaleh, which is about thirty-five miles from where the revolt took place, but ineffectually, being short of ammunition, and the weather, which was very tempestuous, being against them.   They then, on the approach of reinforcements from Gouriel, dispersed.   The ringleaders fled to Turkey, the rest again submitted, and again rose in insurrection during the late war.   Most of them departed with the Turks when they evacuated Sookhoom Kaleh.

---

[1] The General, taking into account that he was in the midst of 2000 or 3000 of the wildest ruffians in the Caucasus, had certainly made imprudent speeches and utterances, and issued uncalled-for regulations ; one mandate, forbidding the Abkhasian women to wear "pyjamas," was especially injudicious, and, seeing that the practice prevails extensively in civilised countries, perhaps absurd.

About a thousand of these, however, *again* returned in the year 1881, and after enduring fearful hardships, under which many of them succumbed (the Russian authorities refused to allow them to land and they were re-embarked, to be landed at a village on the Anatolian coast, which turned out and fired upon them), have been permitted to resettle.

The country of Abkhasia quadrates with the character of its former population—rough, difficult of access, and forbidding. Immense mountains of 8000 to 9000 feet, rivers running in gloomy gorges overhung by dense pine forests, and funereal box and yew; a dangerous iron-bound coast, overhanging the sea at a great elevation, the waves washing the base of the precipices which form it—are the leading features. Here and there in the interior are picturesque glens and open valleys, and high up on the main range are magnificent upland pastures.

Bears, wild pigs, and roe-deer are, as in Circassia, tolerably plentiful, while chamois and ibex are to be found on the higher ranges.

Containing, however, as it does, numerous "abrêks,"[1] especially since the war, Abkhasia is not a country that the ordinary tourist—if he knew what he was about at least—would care to visit. Next to the Abkhasians and Tcherkess, proceeding eastward, along the main chain, are the Svanetes, inhabiting the upper valleys of the Ingour and Tskenisquali rivers, near their head-waters in the main sierra.

e, the Svanetes of the Ingour, are

means an outlaw or brigand.

almost the only complete mountain tribe now existing
in its normal state, apart from Russian influence.

Inhabiting a rude country, very difficult of access,
the Imperial Government has left them pretty much
to themselves; they accordingly are probably much
what they were 1000 years ago, a race of "wild
warriors," untouched by modern civilisation, a sort of
ancient republic regulated by petty chiefs and elders,
with the vendetta in force, and every man armed
keeping his house.

They practise infanticide as regards *female* children to a considerable extent, probably to prevent
over-population, females not being now, as formerly,
saleable articles. They are a tall, fine race, and the
women, who are handsome, are free and easy in their
manners, thinking it a disgrace not to have a few
"followers."

The Svanetes are good shots and hunters, good
armourers and general craftsmen. They often descend
to Mingrelia and Imeritia, bringing cloth, leather, and
other produce, which they barter for copper plates,
iron pots, piece goods, salt, etc.

The Russian Government (at Kutais) shortly before the war, conceived the notion of putting a tax on
the spirits (a sort of whisky) manufactured by the
Svanetes, and of generally entering into "closer relations" with these mountaineers. Accordingly, a
"political," accompanied by three assistants and a
doctor, was sent to make a tour of the valley with a
view of arriving at an understanding on the subject.

He and his party had got about half through the

country when a discussion took place at a village in which they had put up for the night, respecting the supper and accommodation prepared for the party by the headman, which the "political," who seems to have been an injudicious style of individual, asserted "was not fit for dogs," with other abuse. This passed off for the moment, but during the night the whole party was murdered.

The "political" not returning, and rumours of foul play reaching Kutais, a force was despatched to inquire into the matter, and bring the offenders to justice.

As the column marched along, the mountaineers turned out of their respective villages, armed as usual, and grouping themselves on the knolls and eminences commanding the rude pathway, silently watched the Russian infantry defile past.

On arriving at the village where the assassinations had taken place, the officers at the head of the column were hailed by a group of Svanetes on a bluff about a hundred yards above the road, amongst whom they perceived four or five personages in full uniform, whom they naturally took for their missing friends.

This, however, turned out to be a sort of practical joke on the part of the Svanetes, who, thinking it would be fun to surprise the Russians, had got themselves up "for the occasion" in the clothes of the assassinated political and his subordinates. This at least was the "turn" which Russian officialdom gave to the "incident." It was, however, in all probability an artfully-planned move, with a view, by enraging the Russian officers, to precipitate a conflict, when the whole valley would have risen and surrounded the column, which, like the unfortunate politicals, might have "remained" in it.

If this was their expectation, however, they were disappointed, the matter being arranged amicably, I believe, by a fine. I could never hear that any one was punished for it; no officials in the world, by the way, are cleverer at "forgiving and forgetting" than Russians, *i.e.* when policy dictates.

It was the eve of a big war, as both the Svanetes and the officials well knew,[1] and a mountain campaign, always undesirable, would then have been least of all convenient. The religion of the independent Svanetes is, like that of the Tcherkess, a sort of paganism, with a slight dash of Christianity. They have some ancient churches, now converted into "deotas" or shrines, and adorned with chamois horns, looking-glasses, and other native offerings.

They live in low stone houses, built half under ground in the sides of hills, and roofed with earth. Immediately north of Svanetia is the great peak of Elborouz, the most lofty of the Caucasian chain. It is, however, like other Caucasian peaks, not difficult of access to practical mountaineers, being "done" without much trouble by Mr. Grove's party in 1874, and

---

[1] It is noteworthy that the struggle with Turkey, or rather with Turkey and England (for we were looked upon as *certain* to join the Turks), was known by all classes to be imminent for at least a year before it broke out. It was common to hear a Tartar or Georgian, when annoyed by some "Jack in office," say openly, "Wait a bit: the English and Turks will soon be here."

again in 1876 ; also by Mr. Freshfield's in 1878 ; though never, as far as is known, previously ascended.

East of Svanetia are the Bassians, a Tartar race (on the northern slope of the chain), and some other domesticated tribes of mountaineers (on the south side), depending on the government of Kutais. Their country is now traversed by a good road, which, following the valley of the Rion, crosses the main chain to Wladikavkas and the Kouban. East of these again lies Ossetia, comprising the large segment of the sierra lying between the valleys of Kakhetia and Dushet in Georgia, and the Tchettchentz and Lesghian countries on the north and east.

The Ossetes are a fine manly race, of perfectly fair complexion *teinte vermeil*, supposed by many to be of European origin. Some think they are descendants of a party of crusaders, who are said to have come north in returning from the Holy Land, and to have settled in the Caucasus.

There have been always traditions, of very old date, connecting certain Caucasian tribes with the crusaders ; but these legends have probably originated from the fact of the "types" of these tribes, Circassian, Tchettchentz, Ossete, etc., being identical with the European. This, and their having been once Christianised, would have led old travellers unacquainted with their language (which does not bear out the analogy in the least) to suspect European origin. It is more likely, in my opinion, that the present European races derived *their* origin (in very remote prehistoric times) from the Caucasus, and that they afterwards adopted the language of the Aryans.

All modern research goes to prove that the Aryans, a central Asiatic race, were ahead of the rest of the world in arts, arms, and civilisation; in which case they would in all probability invade the white barbarians of Europe, as they did the dark ones of India, or as the Romans did the Gauls, ending by imposing their language and institutions on the conquered. No traveller can fail to be struck by the identity of type of Caucasian mountaineers (especially where free from foreign admixture) with that of Europeans.

The Ossetes, naturally brave and warlike, fought long and obstinately with the Russians for the possession of the Dariel Pass (the ancient "Pylæ Caucasiæ"), the Khyber of the Caucasus, through which now runs the "route militaire de Georgie," in those days, and virtually now, the only practical communication across the chain.

Hard by the military road, about half way to the crest of the pass, from its opening at Wladikavkas, lies a huge boulder, fallen from the gloomy precipitous crags above, still called "Yermolofsky Kamen," or "Yermoloff's Stone," under which that general, who conducted the campaigns against the Ossetes, is said on one occasion to have concealed himself from the victorious mountain men, who were furiously pursuing a routed Russian column down the valley.

The Ossetes, who were always good orthodox Christians, now form perhaps the most civilised

mountain community of the Caucasus. Many of the
better class enter the imperial service, civil or military.

Eastward of Ossetia are some small tribes, the
Ingouch, Touchi, Karaboulaks, etc. The Touchi
are mountain Georgians, but the Ingouch and Karaboulaks originally formed part of the Tchettchentz
nation. The Tchettchentz, however, became Mahometans (nominally at least), while the Ingouch remained pagans. These latter are curious, being
perhaps the only white heathens extant, who have
retained very ancient pagan observances (probably
anterior to Druidical rites and Hindooism) to the
present day.

They have, or had, a short time ago, no notion
of a Supreme Being; their religion, like that of the
Himalayan hill-men before the introduction of Hindooism, consisting in the worship of certain remarkable sacred rocks (or "deotas"), which they called
"yerdas," and before which they sacrificed.

On the occasion of a funeral the relatives of the
defunct had the right to demand sheep for this
purpose, and were never refused. The mutton, after
sacrificing, is eaten in common at a sort of "wake."
They have silver fetiches or household gods, of no
particular shape, to which they make "pooja," to
procure rain, children, etc.

All the Tchettchentz were also formerly of this
religion. These sacred rocks or "yerdas" served
as courts of justice, to take a false oath "before
the rock" being a thing unheard of. They have no
officiating priests or sacrificers.

The Ingouch have great personal pride and determination of character. Forty or fifty years ago, when slavery was an institution in the Caucasus, and people purchased servants, male and female, from the mountaineers (as now in Central Africa), Ingouch slaves were excessively rarely met with, they either refusing to be taken alive or committing suicide.

An Ingouch whose ideas of *meum* and *tuum* were confused being detected by some Russian soldiers at Wladikavkas in the act of driving off a cow, was so severely beaten that, though he contrived with great difficulty to reach his village in the mountains, he shortly afterwards died. His remaining brother, taking his rifle, ammunition, and some millet in a bag, set out alone to avenge his death. Arriving by bypaths in the vicinity of Wladikavkas, he took up a position before daylight among the rocks on the hillside, and watched till he saw a Russian soldier at a convenient distance from the lines. After stalking and "dropping" his man, which, being a good shot, he rarely failed in doing, he cut off the ears of the Russian, and made for the mountain, where he offered them up on the tomb of his brother, and again returned to prowl round the outposts. In this manner he, in the course of a few months, managed to "pot" three officers and fifteen privates, a tolerable "bag" for one man, armed only with a flint rifle and inferior (home-made) powder.[1]

[1] This may seem incredible to people unacquainted with mountaineers and mountain warfare, but is nevertheless true. Many similar exploits during the long wars with the Tcherkess, Lesghians,

The Ingouch are polygamous, being allowed as
many as five wives. On the death of a man his son
or sons succeed to his wives, with the exception of
their actual mothers.

The history of the Tchettchentz is much that of
the Circassians. After many years of severe intermittent warfare with the Russians, they gave in.
Some left the country; but most of them, I believe,
remained and settled down as Russian subjects.
Beyond the Tchettchentz country, stretching east-
wards to Derbend, Temir Khan Schoura, Petroffsk,
and the Caspian Sea, are Lesghistan and Daghestan,
containing many different tribes and dialects. Nearly
all are Soonni Mahometans. The Lesghians submitted after Schamyl had surrendered at Ghonuib;
but many revolted in 1877 during the Turkish war,
and being eventually put down, a great number,
some say 15,000 families (but I suspect 15,000 souls
would be nearer the mark), were transported to
Siberia, *i.e.* they were settled on land near Oren-
bourg. Much of the country, however, remained
quiet. The Lesghians and Daghestans, unlike the
Circassians, Tchettchentz, and Abhkasians, are orthodox
Mahometans, praying pretty regularly, frequenting
mosques, and making pilgrimages to Mecca. They

Ossetes, etc., could be cited. There was a standing order during
these campaigns against smoking at night while going the rounds of
the sentries or while on outpost or picket duty, officers being often
killed or wounded while lighting a pipe or cigarette by mountaineers
who had crept up in the darkness to within a few yards. Following
these "abrêks" up is dangerous work, even by daylight, their object
often being to draw pursuers into an ambuscade of their comrades.

are big heavy men, with a strain of Mongol blood, more Turkish in character than the Western races, more steadily industrious, practical, and *rangé*. They are sharp traders and business men; many of them are well-to-do merchants; others work at trades, chiefly as armourers, silversmiths, coppersmiths, etc., in the towns of the Caucasus. An extensive manufacture of carpets and rugs of fine quality is carried on in Daghestan and the Lesghian country, whence, indeed, the Tiflis bazaars are principally supplied. Much of this eventually goes to Europe; also lambskins of fine quality (Astrakhan), wool, walnut burrs or loupes, raw silk, etc.

CHAPTER III.

DESCRIPTION OF TIFLIS.

Tiflis society—Public amusements—Baths—Manners and
customs, etc.

TIFLIS is a considerable town, partly European, partly
Asiatic, built along the river Koura or Cyrus, in a
hollow between barren hills. It is situated in about
as inconvenient a position as could possibly have been
chosen to construct a capital city in, more especially
as there are fine open plains on each side of the river
a mile higher up.

The reason of this is that certain hot mineral
baths, situated in a narrow gorge, below steep mountains, being much appreciated by the Georgians and
Persians, who, like all Northern Asiatics, detest cold
ablutions, the original town formed itself around
them.

To the original Asiatic town the Russians have
added a European one,—much better built, by the
way, than the majority of Russian cities *chez eux*,
being largely planned by foreigners, and constructed
by Greek and Persian masons. Tiflis, which already
～   area it did at the com-
ɩ⁀ʋproving and pro-

gressing yearly. It has four fairly good hotels (French), two large clubs, a theatre, and racecourse, and three public gardens, besides numerous German beer gardens, and suchlike. It is already in communication by railway with the seaports of Poti and Batoum on the Black Sea, and will very shortly be linked with the Caspian.

The foreign element—as those great men our newspaper correspondents put it — is well represented, specimens of most, if not all, European and many Asiatic nations being always on hand.

In the cafés of the European portion the traveller will discover French, Italians, Germans, Austrians, Poles, civilised Armenians, Greeks, etc., and occasional Servians, Moldavians, Hungarians, Turks, and Syrians; while in the caravansaries of the native town he will, if he chooses to take the trouble and can talk Turkish, find no difficulty in unearthing representatives of most Northern Asiatics, Khorassans, Persians, Turkomans, Kirghiz, Kalmuk, and Nogai Tartars, and even occasional Khivans, Kokhandes, and Afghans. Of Europeans, next to Russians, Germans muster strongest, next come Poles, then French, Italians, and last English, who, though they have designed and executed most of the public works, railways, etc., are least common of any.

The society of Tiflis is composed of the staff of the Viceroy, on which officers of high family and rank are always to be found serving; of the civil authorities, the governor, vice-governor, judges, municipal councillors, etc.; of the local nobility (the Georgian

princes and their families); of the officers of the
general staff, most of whom are, professionally and
socially, very superior men; lastly, of wealthy con-
tractors and merchants, chiefly Armenians, and the
officers of the various line regiments.

As might be expected, there is not much " solidarity " in Tiflis society. People are friendly enough
outwardly when they meet, and do not sit glaring at
each other without speaking unless formally introduced (as Englishmen do in clubs and elsewhere);
yet Russians somehow usually dislike Germans;
Germans dislike and affect to despise Russians; both
hate Armenians, and the feeling is reciprocated.

Poles, again, hate and despise Russians, Germans,
and Armenians,—everybody, in fact, often including
each other individually. Mahometans in the Russian
service often keep aloof. The Georgians are, I think,
the most tolerant, and on the whole get on best with
everybody.

To foreigners, especially if matinal in their habits,
Tiflis society presents the drawback of being too
exclusively nocturnal.

Polite Russians—and Tiflis is Russianised—rise
from 10 to 11 A.M., drink tea, smoke a cigarette or
two, and go to their offices, where they do a great deal
more smoking and chatting, and a little work, returning
home about 2 or 3 P.M. to dine. After dinner—sometimes a lengthy affair—they sleep, many of them
actually undressing and going to bed till 6 or 7 P.M.,
when they arise, and have evening tea, which, with
smoking and talking to visitors who drop in, brings

them on to 9 o'clock, when it is time to go out for
the evening (either to a club or a private party),
where dancing, conversation, and card-playing goes
on always till 12 or 1 o'clock, often till 3 or 4 A.M.
The upshot is that a foreigner who wishes to be "in
the swim" must adopt Russian ways, and this, for a
man who cannot sleep after 7 A.M. and is accustomed
to breakfast early, and get through his work in the
morning, means an entire change of habits.

Nor is this all, for much of the procrastination and
dawdling of Russian officials is notoriously owing
to their way of making amusement a primary and
business a secondary consideration; and this the
intelligent foreigner will find is contagious.

The result is that few foreigners mix much with
Russians; those who do often finding reason to repent
having done so.

The above *façon de vivre*, strange to say, does
not seem to interfere so much with military as with
civil efficiency.   Russian *militaires* are not much
troubled with parades, discipline, or "duty" generally.   Parades, if held at all, are arranged for the
evening, or are held under the adjutant (almost always
some hard-working officer without interest, not in
"society," who does all the work of and virtually
commands the regiment), while the swell colonel and
his field-officers are flirting, card-playing, or asleep—
it would be wrong to say "never putting on uniform,"
for Russian officers are rarely out of it, but never
seeing the regiment except on field-days and gala
occasions.

This peculiarity, by the way, of being perpetually in uniform, is one of the standing " shams " peculiar to Russia.   Not only actual *militaires*, but all sorts of subordinates, doctors, telegraph clerks, railway employés, etc., who have nothing to do with the army, wear swords and showy uniforms ; all which, catching the eye of a " tourist," leads him to gather that Russians are a tremendously warlike lot, always in harness, devoted to their profession, etc., whereas the very reverse is nearer the mark.

However, to return to our *moutons*, viz. Tiflis society, clubs, and card parties.   The clubs are in reality " casinoes," frequented by ladies, at which dancing goes on every evening, and at which occasional grand balls and big dinners are held.

The " swell " club is the Kroojok ; next comes the Armenian Club, which, to a stranger, is the more interesting of the two.

The Kroojok is a public assembly room, frequented by people in good society (though not the *crême*), such as may be met anywhere with no particular *cachet*.

The Armenian Club is, on the other hand, a *type du genre*, where specimen cards of all the Asiatic races in the Caucasus, male and female, may be met and studied, and where Asiatic dances and music alternate with polkas, mazurkas, and waltzes.

Cards, supper, and drinking also go on, and much characteristic conversation and interesting information respecting the country is to be heard and acquired. *to*   *any amount* of pronounced d-eyed Georgian and

Armenian beauties, naturally the great attraction to the younger *habitués*.

The German colony is a long wide street on the left bank of the Koura, leading to the Moostahid Gardens, the grand parade, the racecourse, and railway station.

It is used as an evening promenade for riding and driving. It is lined on each side by houses and gardens. This is a good place to see the aristocracy of Tiflis on a fine evening in spring or autumn; in the summer they are all away at country houses or in the mountains.

A military band plays twice a week in the Moostahid Gardens, which is a well-laid-out pleasure-ground (in the Persian style) on the side of the river (it originally belonged to a Persian mufti or moostahid, hence the name).

A phaeton will take you there and back from the town for a rouble.

The museum at Tiflis is well worth a visit, especially for archæologists. The ethnological and natural history departments are also well represented.

The whole place is under the care of Professor Radde, a German savant of high attainments, research, and perseverance, who has travelled much in pursuit of science, not only in the Caucasus but in most parts of the Russian empire.[1]

The Asiatic town commences on the east side of

---

[1] Literary men visiting Tiflis should make the acquaintance of the talented Professor Bergé, the Government historian, keeper of records, etc., a man of great and varied information, and one of the first Orientalists of the day.

the Erivansky Ploshad or square, in which are situated
two of the principal hotels, the bank, general staff,
and other buildings of note. In this square a daily
market is held, which, however, except on Sundays,
is over by 11 A.M., or thereabouts.

Leaving the square, you find yourself in the
Armenian Bazaar, or quarter, a long narrow street,
gradually descending to the river, in which are long
rows of jewellers', silversmiths', furriers', armourers',
and native tailors' shops, etc.

You can here purchase a complete Caucasian "rig
out" either of the Lesghian or Tcherkess fashion:
choga, alkaluk, shulwal, papak (or fur cap), and
bashlik, all complete, with arms and accoutrements,
sword, dagger, and pistol (which latter is best replaced
by an English revolver), for about 100 roubles, or a
£10 note, which, if you intend knocking about the
country for any time on horseback (the best way of
seeing it), is no bad get-up for the purpose, being the
best yet invented for camping out and "roughing it"
in—at least to my mind.

It will save your European clothes, which you can
wear in the towns. You will never—i.e. if you wash
your face and hands, which can generally be done—
look dirty or untidy in it; whereas you will look like
a loafer after a week in the mountains in European
ordinary costume; while for sleeping in comfortably
it is unequalled. Even to Alpine Club men the above
costume would be valuable, kept in the baggage as a
change at night; and I am confident that if Messrs.
Grove, Moore, or Freshfield revisit the Caucasus, and

adopt my suggestion, they will thank me for the hint. You ought, however, if you wear it habitually, to talk Russian or Turkish.

While on the topic of dress I may add, for the information of travellers who may intend visiting the Caucasus, that the most effective equipment they can possibly *take* there, is, in addition to the usual travelling dress, either a uniform (if entitled to wear one), or a full-dress evening suit of superfine black, with everything to correspond, and a tall hat.

Every Russian official, notwithstanding his easy manner, is a martinet at heart in the matter of etiquette; and in Russia, either a uniform or a dress coat is *de rigeur* in calling upon or visiting officials, even by invitation, *the first time.* They will pass over the omission, will assure you it is of no consequence, not expected of travellers, etc.; but they nevertheless feel it, and will never be so cordial as if you had called in correct *tenue.* And they are, it must be admitted, logical from their point of view: it is the custom of the country, and though the official himself may not care about the infraction, putting it down to insular ideas, etc., his subordinates and domestics will (as he knows) look upon it as a sort of slight put upon him, and as a breach of the *convenances,* which feeling will not help the visitor.

Besides, they argue that if *they* were travelling in foreign countries they would carefully abide by the prevailing etiquette (as they indubitably would), and therefore naturally think Englishmen should not be above doing so.

It must not be supposed that I mean to inculcate the traveller's carrying a dress suit or uniform all over the country (up Ararat or Kasbek, for instance); but if he wants to make himself agreeable, he should certainly wear one when calling on dignitaries or accepting invitations to dinner, etc., *in the towns*— wherever, in fact, a portmanteau can be easily carried. It is just complying with these observances which will raise him in Russian estimation; and on this the whole success of his journey may depend.

Beyond the Armenian Bazaar, and close on the river, which is here very deep, running between narrow scarped works of considerable height above it, and crossed by two bridges close together, is a sort of covered bazaar or bozestein, the great mart for piece goods and Manchester fabrics, passing through which you emerge on to the Tartar Maidan, the old Turkish market-place, beneath the ruins of the fortress, built by Mustapha Pacha in the sixteenth century, when Osmanli for a time ruled the Caucasus.

In the centre of the place is a long painted pole, used as a flagstaff. These poles (still used for the same purpose in our camps and cantonments in India) denoted in the immense Turkish and Tartar camps of former days the bazaar or market, forming landmarks in the wilderness of tents, baggage, camels, and arabas, to which the country people coming in with provisions could direct their steps.

Here the traveller can add a pair of "khoorjens" or carpet saddle-bags (all prices and qualities) to his equipment, and afterwards crossing the bridge to the

Persian caravansary can buy a "boorka" or felt cloak [1] (without which he will find himself badly off in the mountains). Any amount of Asiatic saddlery, very good of its kind, is here available. A "nukta," or headstall and rope, is absolutely necessary, and a Cossack whip is advisable. A strong Asiatic bridle, ending in a long single thong and loop, will be found both more useful and more convenient than the European double affair.

Recrossing the river by the lower bridge, a few yards farther on, immediately below the Avlabar fortress prison (a sort of Bastile, on a precipice over-looking the stream), you pass the only mosque in Tiflis, an unpretentious building with a blue minaret, and, turning to the left, reach the regular "Tartar Bazaar," leading to the baths. Here is always a motley crowd, struggling and scrambling along the narrow street, which, in wet weather, is a slough of black mud. Extraordinary stinks assail the nostrils, and you are jostled by divers barbarians ; besides running a good chance of being knocked down by camels, mules, donkeys, etc., all heavily loaded and driven rapidly along. Strings of waggons, mounted travellers in batches, Cossacks, and post-carts also often crowd up the roadway, the sides of which are flanked by Persian eating-houses and cook-shops. After night-fall the unwary traveller runs some risk of having his saddle-bags cut from his saddle, this particular "little game" being a speciality of the Tartar Bazaar.

· At the "Hummams" natural mineral springs of

---

[1] These are supposed to be the "chlamys" of the ancients.

hot water, just not too hot to bear, a good bathroom with antechamber or dressing-room can be had for one rouble the hour (twenty minutes is quite enough for most people). Attendance—*i.e.* shampooing in ortho-dox fashion, is charged extra—as are soap and towels.

You engage the bath for the time above specified ; if you remain over it, you pay for another hour. Two people (or half a dozen, for whom there is plenty of room) pay no more than one. Cold fowls, bottles of wine, and other accommodation of *cabinets particulars* can be procured by ordering and paying for the same.

There are divers curious *historiettes* connected with these baths, most of them, however, too Rabelaisian for print.

It was here that Lieutenant Z——, a Russian officer of high connections and good family, a few years ago killed a cabman for refusing to drive the lieu-tenant and two lady friends (also of high family, who had been to a ball, and afterwards visited the baths) to the Moostahid Gardens, where they proposed to pass the remainder of the evening (it was about 3 A.M.) *al fresco.*

The lieutenant was court - martialled for this breach of discipline, and condemned to Siberia, escap-ing, however, eventually, having influential friends, with a year's close arrest in the main-guard (where he used to give *petit soupers*) and degradation to the ranks. He, I believe, recovered from this latter in-fliction during the late war.[1]

---

[1] As did Lieutenant B——, the young man who snatched away a chair on which the late Emperor was leaning during a ball at St.

I once heard a Russian officer, *apropos* of this
"incident," insist that it was all the cabman's fault,
and that the lieutenant was not to blame; as thus,
Z——, said he, very properly struck the cabman (for
refusing to drive him, and for insulting the ladies who
were with him, by using opprobrious language) with
his fist. The cabman retaliated by brutally seizing
Z—— and trying to throw him down. Z—— being in
uniform, this was a gross outrage to the cloth, which
he was justified in avenging on the spot.

After being duly steamed, soaped, shampooed, and
soused with cold water (of which there is a cistern
in each bath), the visitor can take a cup of coffee
at a neighbouring Tartar dukan, where, if he talks
Turkish or Russian, he may often hear of a good horse
for sale; or he may inspect the wine cellars, a street
or two of which are adjacent to the maidan,—very
uninviting - looking dens, containing, nevertheless,
immense stores of superior local vintage; or he may
visit the Persian caravansary, and overhaul the carpets of divers makes from Daghestan, Khorassan, and
Turkomania, which he will find there; or the silversmiths' shops.

As might be expected from the heterogeneous
population inhabiting the labyrinths of obscure dens

Petersburg; making matters worse when he perceived his mistake by
exclaiming: "Pardon, your Majesty; I thought it was only *some general
or other.*" The Emperor, saying, "I will teach you to respect
generals," ordered him to do duty as a private in the Caucasus; in
which position he, however, was socially and materially almost as
well off as before, dining at the best hotels, attending balls, shooting-
parties, etc., and well received everywhere, in the best society.

and alleys, often quite underground, of the Asiatic town, stabbings, affrays, robberies, and abductions are by no means rare occurrences. There is, I believe, however, more "robbery with violence" outside Tiflis than in the town itself, which, all things considered, is efficiently policed.

There is generally a robber or two of mark in Georgia in addition to the Tartars and Toorks of the steppes, who, though not professionals, being often men of substance (though nomadic), as cattle-drovers, will make a *coup* now and then if the spoil is likely to repay the risk of the venture.

The last celebrated brigand was Tatoo Salokidze, who was hung at Tiflis in 1880. He was of good Georgian family, but being always "wild," took to the road, and had for several years "flashed the muzzle" on the routes between Tiflis and the frontier. He was at the head of a small band, and owned to twelve or fifteen deaths.

I once met him in a small dukan near the old Turkish fortress of Dzellal Oghli, in which I had put up for the night on my way from Alexandropol, just before the war. I had no idea, of course, at the time who he was; and it was not till after his execution that, happening to purchase a photograph of him and one of his comrades, taken in jail, with fetters on, I recollected his stern, rather melancholy countenance.

I did not go to see him turned off.

Tatoo often came into Tiflis. In 1878 he and a "pal" killed a shopkeeper in the most fashionable street in the town, near the Grand Duke's Palace,

about six o'clock in the evening, afterwards walking
quietly off.   For this murder two innocent men, who
were arrested the same evening by the police for being
mixed up with some trifling scuffle, were executed.
Tatoo afterwards shot a policeman dead in the Tartar
Maidan, who had attempted to arrest him as he was
stepping into a public vehicle, afterwards driving
coolly off.   He was captured near Kars, I believe,
while sleeping in a wine-shop.

With regard to the chance of being robbed while
travelling in the Caucasus, I do not think that there
is much danger,—certainly not more than in Sicily,
Calabria, Albania, and other wildish countries where
people travel; but precautions are indispensable.   It
all depends, like everything else of the sort, upon how
you go to work, and what sort of a man you are.   I
have myself travelled, often quite alone, all over the
Western Caucasus and the southern provinces, also in
Circassia, and have been twice to the Caspian, besides
frequent journeys in the mountains and forests round
Tiflis, and have never been attacked, though it was
often prophesied that I should be.   I took care always
to be well mounted and armed, and (if in a likely
place to be "bailed up") kept ready.

I believe that robbers, unless very "hard up," will
not attack a well-appointed horseman who looks as if
he could use his weapons (and this they can tell at a
glance), guessing that he has probably little more than
his horse and arms about him, and will not "part"
easily.   "Hawks," as the old proverb says, "winna
pick out hawks' een."

CHAPTER IV.

RAMBLES IN GEORGIA.

TRAVELLING in the Caucasus is rarely pleasurable at any season; autumn is the best time for travelling in moderate discomfort, *i.e.* travelling in moderate discomfort on horseback, which, to my mind, is the only way of seeing anything of a country. Once out of sight of Tiflis, which, built as it is in a hollow, you

very soon are, you might be, for any sign of European life discernible, in Mesopotamia, Afghanistan, or
Bokhara; wide wastes of treeless hill and plain burnt
up in summer and frozen in winter, great open tracts
of arable land, no enclosures, the flat-roofed villages
nestling in hollows and ravines ; in summer tremendous heat, in winter the dry nipping air of Persia or
Central Asia.

You can, it is true, get your padrojna (or purwana
for post-horses), and, subject to divers delays, drawbacks, dust, and dirt, bowl along, or rather shake along
(for the vehicles are springless), over a post-road at
any season of the year, being duly packed in your
wooden conveniency and duly shot out of it here and
there along the route, at the mercy of the smatritels
or stationmasters, who will horse you on according to
their good pleasure—the said pleasure depending
mainly on your proficiency in Russian soft sawder
and impromptu liquoring up; for tips from a foreigner,
unless very judiciously administered through a third
party, they often scorn.   And, in fact, if there is any
pressure on the road, any big wigs travelling with
Crown padrojnas or a flight of trading Armenians,
they often really cannot supply horses, and you are
in for twenty-four hours of some miserable dog-hole
full of fleas and dirt.   The post-roads, again, usually
lie along hot valleys or over dusty sandy plains, where
the heat in summer rivals that of the Punjab, its post-
house discomforts leaving those of the five rivers far,
far behind in intensity.   The astute and wary traveller will therefore do well to mount his powerful

gelding from the Cossack plains, and, with well-stuffed
saddle-bags, a companion similarly equipped, and both
well armed, work his devious way over hill and down
dale as he best can.   He will thus at any rate make
sure of a cool route over grassy upland and through
forest glade, where green leaves and clear streams compensate for short commons and inferior lodgings, while
he will daily come across scenes and scenery, glimpses
of ancient life and picturesqueness undreamt of in the
philosophy of post-cart travellers.

After this fashion, accompanied by an English
lad born in the Caucasus, I started from Tiflis at the
end of August, for a ramble towards the south.
Although Freddy had hardly ever been outside
Tiflis, and knew nothing of geography, he was a
smart boy, and talked Georgian and German as well
as Russian, and as I, in addition to Russian, could do
Turkish and French ; we had five languages between
us, enough for ordinary purposes even in this polyglot
neighbourhood.   Getting to horse by 6 A.M., we left
Tiflis by the Kodjor road, mounting the barren hill for
seven or eight miles without incident, except that after
the fifth or sixth mile a queerish feel in the head told
me unmistakably that a touch of my old acquaintance,
intermittent fever, was coming on. Guessing, however,
that the heat and dust of Tiflis would not be likely to
improve matters, I pushed on, and crossing the Kodjor
ridge (leaving the sanitarium about three miles on
the right), descended the eastern slope and made for
Elizabethal, one of the large Suabian colonies or bourgs
which have been established some sixty years now, in

various directions round Tiflis; like all of them, it is in a flourishing condition; its well-built German granges with high gable ends, extensive outhouses, barns, and stabling, contrasting as strikingly with the low flat-roofed half-underground Georgian villages round it, as the steady-going, hard-working, always employed inhabitants contrast with the slouching loafing Georgian peasants. Each of these colonies has a solidly-built church and a Lutheran minister, and the people are, take them altogether, the most respectable in the Caucasus. Passing the colony, we struck across the open country by a *cutcha* road for two or three miles, till we came to a water-mill in a valley amongst large walnut trees. Here were very extensive orchards and vineyards belonging to the colony, stretching for a mile or more along the left bank of the stream, which, descending from the Ak Boulak mountain, turned the mill and irrigated the garden ground beyond.

Here I felt so uncomfortable, together with the sun, which was very powerful, and increasing fever, that I concluded to halt, though we were not above twenty-five versts, or eighteen miles, from Tiflis, and consequently not more than half a moderate day's journey. Entering the enclosure we accordingly off-saddled under the shade of the walnuts, and picketed the horses to eat grass. I lay down, and towards evening felt slightly better, though not by any means well; having, however, had the precaution to bring some blue pill and colocynth along with me, I took a strongish dose of each and awaited the result. The mill, owned by a German, was doing a great business, as most of the neighbouring Georgians brought their corn to be ground there; there were also one or two Armenian traders from Tiflis, come to purchase fruit.   The grapes were just beginning to ripen, and the Germans complained much of a certain Armenian village (possessing two conspicuous churches) on the opposite slope of the valley, the inhabitants of which, they said, were in the habit of regularly robbing the vineyards and orchards by night, often coming armed, in bodies of four or five or more.   They were, they said, a rascally bad lot, and had shot one of their " choukeedars " or watchmen through the body the year before.   There was a large Greek village farther up the valley, with whom, and with the Tartar villagers lower down, they said they got on very well—in fact, with every one except the Armenians, who, by their account, were, as Artemus Ward said of the Injuns, "pizen, wharever found." Towards evening a couple of stout fellows, armed with double-barrelled guns, which they discharged at a mark, and then carefully reloaded with heavy charges of slugs, mounted guard at our end of the gardens ; they were relieved every three hours during the night by others, and patrolled steadily for 300 yards up and down, below which point another beat commenced, and so on to the end of the vineyard.   They warned us to look carefully to our horses.   Such is the Caucasus; the fact being, that crime virtually goes unpunished, the rural police and magistrates often conniving at, or being regularly in league with, thieves and rob-

bers ; convictions, besides, from hard swearing being
next to impossible.   Each class of the community has
its own methods of " conveying."   The educated
Armenian, who is nothing if not civilised, goes in for
polite European stealing, for fraudulent bankruptcies,
dealing in false notes, robbing insurance offices, etc.
The Georgian " industrial" burgles, cheats at cards,
or steals horses after a rude and primitive but often
profitable fashion; while the Tartar, thinking "nobly"
of looting as a species of war, affects the " High
Toby " " flash the muzzle " style of plunder, considering garden robbery and suchlike as low mean business,
quite beneath a man whose ancestors followed Shah
Abbas and Nadir Shah.   Cattle stealing on a large
scale—1000 sheep or a herd of bullocks at a haul—
from a rival " aoul " with whom he is at loggerheads, is
his little game, or " bailing up" Armenian " fat chuffs"
and " bacon-fed knaves," the backs of whose waist-
coats and the lining of whose caps disgorge store of
twenty-five rouble notes, legitimate spoil, the product
of peculation and cheating.

We started about 8 A.M. next morning, I feeling very weak and seedy, and mounted the opposite
hill, leaving the pious Armenian village on the left,
and striking across a sort of upland for a couple of
hours, which had been recently reaped, came to a
Tartar village, on the edge of the deep rocky cañon
formed by the Chram river.   Crossing this after a
prolonged rest and halt at the bottom under some
walnut trees, hard by a fine vineyard and irrigated
garden, we arrived about 5 P.M. at the large Ger-

man colony of Ekaterinfeldt, in a valley of the
wooded mountain spurs which fringe the great central
plateau of Georgia.   Passing through the great bourg,
with its long double street of houses and courtyards
all crammed with harvesting, we emerged at the far
end and went on up the valley for a mile, till we
reached a vineyard and garden-house belonging to a
Georgian nobleman, Prince Baratoff, where the care-
takers, a couple of Tartars and a Georgian, finding I
knew the "kniaz," consented to lodge us for the night.
After safely housing the animals—always the great
point (for though *you* may camp out without danger,
if well armed, your horses always run great risk of
being stolen if not put inside somewhere)—we spread
our boorkas, or large felt cloaks, in the garden by the
stream and went to sleep.   Next morning, shortly
after sunrise, I had a severe attack of ague, followed
by a hot fit of fever, necessitating taking up my quarters in the garden-house, where I lay for several
hours in considerable discomfort ; however, after some
hot tea, about noon it passed off, and I was able to eat
part of a fowl that the Tartars, who, as usual, turned
out rattling good fellows, had prepared.   About 4
P.M., finding myself much better, we got the "quads"
ready and struck across country for Ak Boulak, or
Bailey Klootch, as the Russians, who have changed
many of the native names, call it, a large cantonment
and military settlement on the mountain, about ten
miles off, where I thought I would remain for a day
or two; but, after reaching and crossing the intervening
plateau, a broad flat, covered with long grass and thorny

jungle, whence we could see the cantonment on the ridge, and the old Tartar fortress on the opposite side of the river, we suddenly found ourselves arrested by the precipitous cañon of the Chram, across which we could find no way of getting without making a detour of several miles. We therefore, as darkness was already setting in, returned by another road to Ekaterinfeldt. There we put up in the "gostinitsa," or inn of the place, which, being kept by a Russian landlord, was of course dirty, and the beds "inhabited;" however, bringing some Persian powder to the front, and spreading our cloaks over the mattresses by way of an abattis, we managed to keep the enemy off till towards morning, when we arose and, saddling the horses, were once more *en route*. Working up the valley again we crossed just below Prince Baratoff's garden, and began gradually to ascend the opposite wooded mountain, whence we had a fine view of the immense fertile vineyards and orchard gardens which surround the colony, its pretty church, etc. The track wound gradually up a hollow in the sloping mountain, through dense underwood of hazel, cornel, blackthorn, and other European jungle. When near the top of the ridge we encountered an armed cavalcade of Georgians, on approaching whom I was suddenly hailed in French, much to my surprise. However, I speedily recognised a young "kniaz," whom I had met early in the spring in Kakhetia. He was much amused at having at once recognised me (both of us being in Tcherkess costume) before I recognised him, and invited me to his country-seat (which was not far off), as these hospitable fellows always do. After thanking him and promising to look him up on my return, if I passed that way, we parted.

Crossing the ridge shortly afterwards, we descended into a picturesque valley, surrounded on all sides but the north, where it debouched into the plain, by precipitous densely-wooded mountains rising to 3000 or 4000 feet. Here was an ancient monastery and church in ruins, destroyed, like all the ancient churches in Georgia, by Timour, and a Georgian village, with the usual watercourse, vineyards, and orchards. Farther up the valley at the opening of the gorge, up which the road wound, was a small but flourishing German settlement.

On entering the gorge, which was very narrow, and confined by steep overhanging crags, we met some mounted Kizilbash, who told us it was six hours or thirty miles to Kara Kilissa.[1] Five or six versts beyond we came to some extensive and well-built iron-works with three or four blast furnaces, but deserted and doing nothing. These were established by Government about ten years ago, and a vast deal of coin laid out on them; their history seems to have been much that of the Kumaun Ironworks in India.

The valley still continued a regular gorge, closely shut in on each side by steep hanging woods of beech, oak, ash, and other European forest trees. We kept steadily ascending, meeting only a Georgian muleteer

[1] Kara Kilissa means in Turkish "the black church." There are many Kara Kilissas and Kizil Kilissas (red church) in the Caucasus and Asia Minor, the names often belonging to places where no church now exists.

now and then for ten or twelve miles, and after a halt
for breakfast at a stream where there was some grass,
finally emerged on the open near the summit about
4 P.M. We passed two or three deserted post-sta-
tions, this being the most direct route to the Turkish
frontier. The Russian Government, before telegraph-
ing was established, used to have riding couriers on
this line, which was in bygone days a much - frequented route. Many an Osmanli army in the Turko-
Persian wars of the sixteenth and seventeenth centuries has marched along it.[1]

At the summit of the pass the air, though there
was no wind, struck cold and keen, the elevation
being 4000 feet at least above the plains below. A
lot of Tartar "yailaks," or summer encampments,
were scattered about, and herds and flocks of fat-
tailed sheep, goats, and cattle, tended by scarlet-
robed Tartar women and girls, were grazing everywhere. We had to climb 1000 feet higher by a steep
winding track to gain the crest of the range, which
took us an hour more, and then to wind down the
other side for half the same distance. The forest had
now entirely disappeared; nothing but open undulating down and grassy plain was visible for miles and
miles, dotted now and then with an Armenian village
or Tartar "aoul." Much of the standing barley crop,

---

[1] It was used as an alternative route. In this manner Hassan
Pacha, returning from victualling Tiflis, escaped from Simon, the
Georgian prince, who was awaiting him at the dangerous pass of
Tomanis, on the then usual line, by Dzellal Oghli. Since the Russians
constructed the present post-road by Delijan, both routes have, except
as bridle-paths, been abandoned.

though it was the end of August, was yet green, and hay-making was being actively carried on.

About 6 P.M. we reached the Armenian village of Ish Tepe, a mile and a half short of Kara Kilissa, where, as we found there was a tolerable dukan (or grog-shop and store), we determined to halt for the night. The Armenian villages of these elevated plateaux are all on one model, built three parts underground, to resist the intense frost and biting winds of winter. The houses are all flat roofed and buried in earth mounds, so that at a short distance a village looks like a collection of "tummacks," or large mole heaps. In fact, were it not for the huge piles of cow-dung fuel, made into bricks a foot or more square, and stacked fifteen or twenty feet in height, and the great hay-ricks, for winter consumption, you would hardly remark them at all. As it is, as soon as snow covers the ground, which it does in October (lasting till April), it is a most difficult thing to "spot" a village at half a mile distance; and were it not for the ceaseless barking of the dogs, one would constantly fail to do so. The interior of these villages is a regular ramification of houses and small *cul de sacs*, without order or regularity; a door opening here, another there, a sort of human ant-heap; no end of complicated underground passages, dimly lighted by holes from above like a Turkish "hammam," or not lighted at all; for the rest, lots of strapping women and girls, lots of fowls, sheep, cattle, pigeons, cow-dung blocks, new-mown hay, boosa, refuse, and dirt of all sorts. We entered the cavern

which represented the grog-shop, after seeing to the
horses, and I was smoking a chibouque and consulting
the dukanjee about having a fowl sacrificed, when
there entered, in ragged Tcherkess uniforms, a couple
of the greatest ruffians (and I have seen a few) that I
ever set eyes on, both armed to the teeth, with revolver, sword, and khinjal.   One was a Cossack, the
other looked like, and I suspect was, a renegade
Tartar or Lesghian, but said he was an Armenian, a
dangerous rascal, with an evil eye and hook nose,
who looked, and no doubt was, capable of anything.
He was half drunk, and immediately began asking
all sorts of questions as to who I was, where from,
where going, what for, and so on, and bullying all
round.   They were road guards or " chappars," as a
rule the greatest rogues in the country, being often
themselves *ci-devant* assassins and highwaymen, and
always more or less in league with criminals.   The
worst was that, never dreaming of a row in an
Armenian village, I had, as is usually done, just 'previously given my " arms and accoutrements " to the
dukanjee to stow away behind the counter, to ensure
their not being stolen or tampered with.   Asking for
them again at that particular moment would have
looked queer, and besides would have probably pre-
cipitated a shindy ; for, as I knew, the rascals would
have been certain to endeavour to seize on and ex-
amine them, ask what I gave for them, and the like.
However, putting, as the French say, " a good face
on a bad game," I told him, in answer to his questions, that where I was going was none of his busi-

F

ness, and continued outwardly calm, but inwardly
perturbed, considering if matters got more unpleasant,
whether I should be able to clear the counter at a
bound and grasp my revolver, with a view to potting
them across it.   The renegade, who was by far the
greatest scoundrel of the two, kept ordering and
swallowing tumblers of vodky supplied (gratis) by the
landlord ; drawing his dagger occasionally, which was
over half a yard in length, and making passes with it
at the stomachs of the dukanjee and others. He eyed
me keenly at intervals, and I could see was calculating
whether it would pay to arrest me on suspicion, with
a view to getting me to offer him a bribe—a favourite
dodge of these gentry. He loudly proclaimed that
he intended to pass the night there, although on
arrival he had said he was going on directly.   A
happy thought striking me, that the horses had not
been fed, I ordered the barley, and presently strolled
out, to see them littered down in a big cavern which
answered for a cattle-shed : this turned out a good
move, as, shortly after my return, which I purposely
delayed as much as possible, he and his friend departed, much to my relief, as a row with these fellows,
whatever the upshot, would have spoiled the whole
journey.

   We passed an uncomfortable evening, as a lot of
peasants tumbled in by ones and twos after nightfall,
and began haggling with the dukanjee about necessaries.   They kept buying and eating water-melons,
which, being brought up from the low country, are
here considered a luxury, sitting the while on the

counter, which, dirty enough before, they made a regular pigsty of, with rinds, juice, melon seeds, etc., and all talking at once.   Those who were not stuffing, made me uncomfortably nervous by buying kerosene oil, which was drawn off from a large hogshead (standing against an open barrel of naphtha) into tin pots, pans, etc., lighted candles being held within an inch or two of the fluid as it ran from the tap by the dukanjee's man to see they did not get more than they paid for; he and the purchasers meanwhile carrying on conversations and arguments with people at the other end of the shop, so that I was in perpetual fear of the groggery catching fire.   However, by about 10 P.M. they cleared off, and we got a modicum of sleep.   I roused up the dukanjee at 4 A.M., as they said we could make Alexandropol by evening if we started early and rode all day.   Getting to horse by 5 P.M., and passing Kara Kilissa and Shah Nazir, two Armenian villages, we struck across the great plain, once the bed of a lake, reaching, after about five hours' brisk riding, the great Tartar "yailak" of Kara Agatch.   Kara Agatch means the "black tree"[1] in Toorki; and perhaps there once was a tree here, but there is not a vestige now even of a bush.   There is an old masonry pillar, or conical landmark, which denotes, I believe, what was the frontier fifty years ago, since when it has been twice moved on.   The whole plain, wherever the grass had not been preserved for hay-making, which was going on vigorously, was covered by grazing herds.   A long ascent

---

[1] Or black wood.

to the summit of a divide, marked by broad cairns of
gray stones, and much winding about for several
hours among spurs and ravines on the far side, all
bare and treeless, brought us, towards evening, to the
brow of a mountain, from whence the great rolling
plain, at either end of which stand Kars and Alexandropol (Gumri), displayed itself before us, and seven or
eight miles more down a gradual slope saw us entering
the latter city, and speedily housed in a caravansary
at thirty kopeks per diem for a room and ten kopeks
for the horses. We had enough of it for one time,
having done seventy-five versts since daybreak, and
been in the saddle at least twelve hours. However,
some tea freshened us up, and water, hay, and barley
did ditto for the horses, who, by the way, in these
countries are very rarely off their feed, whatever the
distance traversed.

Next morning we inspected the town and bazaar,
which, taken *en masse,* seemed much the same half-
finished, dirty, dilapidated hole as it was in 1877.
It was now, however, by no means so lively or full of
people as during the war, for to say nothing of the
military, many of the townspeople have since then
emigrated to Kars, and the newly-acquired territory.
I observed, however, not a few handsome new stone
houses scattered here and there, the result of commis-
sariat contracts and successful " nobbling" during war
time converted by the wily Armenian into brick,
stone, and mortar, which he wisely considers as a
safer investment than an illimitable paper currency.
The usual scramble for allotments of land, vacated

villages, and Government grants which ensued whenever a fresh "grab" of territory is effected by the
Imperial Government, had, I was informed, been
going on, and was still, though rather damped of late
by certain "formalities," in progress. No sooner does
the Russian Government annex new territory in Asia,
than there is a rush and scramble on the part of the
original Mahometan population to clear out, and
another on the part of the enterprising Armenian, or
rather Russo-Armenian, to get in. The rush, or rather
both rushes, are encouraged by a paternal Government, whose functionaries prophesy great things about
to come to pass, now that freedom, civilisation, and
enlightenment are to take the place of oppression,
barbarism, and ignorance. Land, on nominal terms,
road contracts, bridge building, and barrack building
ditto, all sorts of advantages are offered to the enterprising investor and settler. Popular enthusiasm
rises to fever-pitch ; the well-posted Armenian, who
talks every language, and is down to every move, sees
his way to making a pot of money, and "goes for"
the new territory like a starved mouse at a piece of
cheese. Whole villages get under weigh, and move
off with their household gods, while Russian capitalists
in Moscow, Kief, and Odessa form companies to buy
up all available land, trusting that it will shortly
double or treble in value.

Strange to say, there is no apparent hitch ; the
lands are made over to the applicants without any
undue obstruction or delay, the viaticums (without
which nothing, as everybody knows, can be got done

in any civilised country) hinted at being extremely
modest. The Government officials, however, take
care, while handing over the lands or grants, and
allowing improvements, buildings, and agricultural
operations to commence, not to be in too great a hurry
about completing the transfers, or signing the "mere
matters of form" which give a legal title, which is fair
enough, as the occupiers never pay down the purchase
money in full, or at any rate are never compelled to
do so. This eventually turns out to have been a
prudent delay, as somehow or other, after a year or
two of bustle and speculation, somebody suddenly dis-
covers that the sales of land have been grossly irregu-
larly conducted ; that no end of rules and regulations
have been infringed and uncomplied with. Articles
to this effect begin to appear in the local prints, and
representations are made in high quarters, which
result in a "ukase," suspending till further notice all
sales of land in the department of so and so, and
ordering an inquiry into the circumstances of all previous sales up to date. Somebody else next finds out
that additional "informalities" have attended the
departure of the previous occupants, the Turks and
Mahometans who left, or prepared to leave, for Turkish territory (many of whom are still hanging about,
being mostly completely ruined), that they have been
unfairly treated and unduly hurried, and suggests that
it would be a "great and generous idea" to invite
such of them as will "elect to be faithful subjects of
the Emperor" to return and reoccupy their lands.
The net is now dropped and the "haul" ready,—

nothing to do but to pull steadily on the ropes. The Greek, Armenian, and other speculators who have been buying up, squaring subordinates, and rejoicing over bargains, and the peasants who have sold off their property elsewhere and come several marches with wives, families, cattle, tools, and household utensils, to settle down (at the invitation of officials) in vacated territory, are blandly informed that the Imperial Government intends to reconsider the whole question ; that it has reason to believe that the Mahometan population have been most unfairly treated ; that those who wished to emigrate have neither received an adequate price for their land, nor sufficient time to sell it in ; that they have petitioned the Imperial Government to be allowed to return, and that the Imperial Government, as no titles have yet been issued, is in fact disposed to permit them to do so ; that the inviting and allowing Russian subjects from other provinces to come and purchase land, settle down, etc., was most unauthorised and irregular conduct on the part of Governor Brownesoff and Commissioner Jonesoff, who are accordingly reprimanded and removed (they do not go, however ; and when they do, you hear subsequently that they have been promoted) ; that, in fact, the late sales must be considered null, and undergo examination by a committee.

This being settled, and a sufficient time allowed for the pæans of the local prints over the wisdom and clemency of the Imperial Government to make due impression on foreigners and the uninitiated, the real business commences and the coin drops in.

The committee, composed of B., J., and Co., sits
steadily; all who pay remain; those who cannot or
will not are, as per ukase, removed and replaced by
such of the former proprietors as will stand something
to get back their property.   After B. and J. have in
this manner disposed of, say a third, of the vacated
territory, and thus accumulated a sufficient independ-
ency, they are "promoted for distinguished services,"
and a fresh lot take their places.

The ukase about "suspension of sale of lands" is
now cancelled, and on they go again.   There is to be
no mistake this time, all plain sailing, and in come
the bargain-hunters; or if they stay away the lands
are reported after a year or two as unsaleable, and a
proposal made, and strongly supported by the press,
to make grants of them to deserving officers for
"meritorious services in the field."   Somehow or
other the richer, more influential, and better paid the
officer, civil or military, the bigger and more valuable
is the grant of land he always contrives to secure for
"meritorious service," even if he has never seen a
shot fired, or has run away on hearing the same;
while you meet plenty of poor devils, who have been
in the thick of every campaign for the last thirty
years, *with* first-rate testimonials, but without a
square yard of land, or a rouble in their pockets, and
no apparent chance of getting either the one or the
other.

We remained one day at Alexandropol, to rest the
horses and ourselves after the previous day's heavy
march.   It being a "prasnik," or Russian holiday,

seven or eight Russian soldiers, fine-looking fellows, who had determined on a drink, came and took a room adjoining a grog-shop at the far end of the caravansary courtyard. Having laid in a store of vodky, they began as usual about 7 A.M., singing songs, while one of them played a violin, and all went on harmoniously for about two or three hours, by which time, most of them being extremely "sprung," they began fighting and quarrelling, first in the room, then in the courtyard. It was astounding to see the coolness with which the two or three who were comparatively sober took very severe blows from the drunken ones in endeavouring to quiet them, without retaliating or losing their temper in the least, and did their very best to get them away from the populace (who had crowded in to see the "tumasha") without further tumult. After a great deal of uproar a guard came down with fixed bayonets, and marched them off. The Armenian rabble, who one and all detest the Russian soldier—mainly, I believe, *because* he is good-natured and forbearing—exulted over the spectacle, calling them pigs, dogs, etc. One of the sober ones, a tall handsome fellow, who was doing all he could to keep the rest quiet, and get them to leave, was struck severely on the mouth by an Armenian grog-shop keeper (whose dukan he had entered in pursuit of a drunken comrade who had broken away), his lips badly cut and one or two of his teeth knocked out. With soldiers of any other nationality there would have been a serious row between them and the mob.

Next morning we left, taking the Kars road across

the Arpa Chai, now spanned by a solid stone bridge,
built, as an inscription on it relates, in sixty-eight
days (in 1878) by Colonel Rarberg, an engineer
officer,—now, by the way, General of Division, and
Military Governor of the lately-annexed Tekke Turkomans. After a ride of eighteen versts through a rolling
country, dotted with Armenian villages and intersected by ravines, we got to a cluster of villages, viz.
Bash Kadikler, Karrack Darra, Kalderan, etc., the
headquarters and centre of the Russian army during
the summer and autumn of 1877, being the position
to which they retreated after the repulse at Zivin
and the raising of the siege of Kars by Mukhtar Pacha.
The Russians since the annexation have here established
a Dukabor village from the uplands. Dukabors are
a Russian sect something like Quakers or Quietists,
relegated to the Caucasus by the Emperor Nicholas in
1840. A bevy of maidens belonging to this village
in the valley-bottom, most of them decidedly good-
looking, were fording the river just as we rode up to it;
as the water was deep, being up to our horses' bellies,
the ford of considerable breadth, and as they took
good care not to wet their clothes, we had a rather
finer exhibition than you would get at the Alhambra
or Gaiety. Passing through the village, which,
like all those belonging to the Dukabors, was neat,
clean, and orderly, we left the post-road, and began
working up to the Russian position when facing the
Turks, reaching about one o'clock the site of the
Grand Duke Michael's headquarters in the centre of
the line opposite the Aladja Dagh (mountain), the great

and small Yagnis, the Avliar and Vizinkef, where the
last and decisive action was fought. The Russian
plan of the campaign was, as is well known, to invade
Anatolia at four different points, the four columns
subsequently converging on Erzeroum, while a strong
force besieged and blockaded Kars. It was undoubtedly well conceived, only it broke down in execution,
as many well-laid plans are apt to do. During the
autumn and winter of 1876-77 the Russians were
hard at work, furbishing up the army of the Caucasus,
supposed to be always ready for active service, but
which turned out not to be able, at short notice, to
put more than some 50,000 men of all arms in the
field, a force which was supposed, and ultimately
proved to be, insufficient for the business in hand.
Accordingly, immense efforts were made ; every possible battalion and corps of Cossacks was marched to
the front, new levies of native troops, horse and foot,
were called out everywhere, and by the end of the
winter they had, including reserves, some 100,000
men massed along the frontier, from Erivan on the
east to Ozurget and Sookhoom Kaleh on the Black
Sea.

One day previous to the declaration of war a
simultaneous dive was effected across the Turkish
frontier at four different points, viz.—

At Ozurget, making for Batoum.

At Akhaltsik, making for Ardahan.

At Alexandropol, making for Kars.

At Erivan, making for Bayazid.

Each column, after, as was confidently expected,

making a successful *coup* on the above fortified places of the enemy, was to converge through the country (driving the defeated Turks before them) on Erzeroum. The Ozurget column, under General Aglubjee, very strong in artillery, and preceded by clouds of native levies, defeated a Turkish force who held a position about ten miles in the interior, and making another march, took up unopposed a strong position at Koutsevani, facing the fortified lines of the Turks at Tzikinzeri, resting on the mountains and Black Sea, the right of which they, by constructing a road for artillery, set to work to turn.

The column from Akhaltsik stormed and took Ardahan (Ardahan was believed at the time to have been bought, and I believe there is little or no doubt of the pacha having been bribed to take no measures for its defence) and pushed on afterwards towards Olti. The headquarters camp, and column under the Grand Duke Michael and Loris Melikoff, advanced upon and invested Kars, and a strong column was forthwith despatched under Generals Loris Melikoff and Heimann across the Soghanli Dagh towards Erzeroum. General Tergukassoff, rapidly crossing the western spurs of Ararat from Erivan, fell upon Bayazid, which he captured and garrisoned, and immediately marched along the caravan road towards Erzeroum, defeating the Turks signally at Toprak Kaleh, Delibaba, etc. Everything went on swimmingly till the defeat, or rather repulse with heavy loss, of Aglubjee in his attack on Tzikinzeri, about the 18th, and the defeat and repulse of the Russians at Zivin

on the 25th of June, which two events completely
changed the face of affairs; the Russians, instead of
victoriously advancing and driving a demoralised
enemy before them, retired in a demoralised condition
themselves, or had to remain strictly on the defensive,
while the invasion became a complete fiasco, the
Czar's forces being rolled back or checked all along
the line.   The Turks even became themselves invaders, landing and taking possession of Sookhoom,
disgracefully abandoned by General Kratchenkoff
without firing a shot.[1]

[1] Of the four columns, it will thus be seen that one remained
stationary at Ardahan, a strong fortress; two were repulsed, repulses
equivalent to defeats; one was victorious, but, being left *en l'air*, was
compelled to retire, a move which General Tergukassoff, undoubtedly
the best general (and I believe the senior general) employed (in
Asia) during the campaign effected in a masterly manner.   He
not only retreated without loss, convoying at the same time several
thousand Armenian families in safety to the Russian frontier (who would
otherwise have been infallibly massacred by the Kurds), but he had no
sooner placed these people in safety than he faced about, and rapidly
advancing by forced marches on Bayazid, routed Ismael Koort Pacha,
who, with some thousands of Turks and Bashi-Bazouks, was besieging
the citadel, and relieved the garrison, with which he retired unmolested
to the Araxes valley.
    The two battalions, who, with some Cossacks, had retired into the
citadel at Bayazid, on the approach of Ismael Pacha, and the Kurds,
suffered fearfully.   The only water was a small rivulet in a deep
rocky gully outside the fort, very dangerous of approach, being commanded, and watched day and night by Kurdish marksmen, who
shot down nearly all who attempted to procure any.   This water was
besides, even if drawn, undrinkable, as the Kurds, who had massacred
the Armenian population of the town, many of them in sight of the
garrison, purposely threw the carcases, as well as those of numerous
horses, mules, and camels, into the stream above, so that it ran through
a mass of putrefying bodies.   Conditions of surrender were offered by
Ismael Pacha, which the commandant (a Russian or Russo-German),

Now was the golden opportunity; had Mukhtar Pacha, while advancing with his army and covering Kars (from before which the Russians on his approach retired in something very like a panic), boldly detached his cavalry by mountain paths to execute a raid into Georgia, it is not asserting too · much to affirm that he would have then and there finished the war in Asia. Indeed, from the date of the battle of Zivin (25th June) until the end of September, such a move would have answered at any time, as during the whole of that period the Russians remained simply on the defensive, any attacks that they made being mere demonstrations to conceal their weakness and deter the Turks from flanking movements. It is necessary, however, to give a short description of the arena on which the Turkish and Russian forces faced each other, more especially as on this ground and in the immediate neighbourhood much severe fighting

after many days of severe hardship, the men eating dead horses, dying of thirst, etc., proposed to accept; but in the councils of war held, surrender was always negatived by a majority of Tartar and Armenian officers, who, knowing the Kurds well, would not trust them. At last, matters reaching a climax of misery, the commandant one day, after a stormy discussion, proceeded to the rampart (accompanied by the council) with the intention of hauling down the flag. More discussion ensued, cut short by the commandant beginning to pull it down himself. He was pushed away by one of the opposition, who hauled it up again. A scuffle took place, during which the flag was again partially struck by the commandant and replaced. On his attempting it a third time a Tartar officer quietly drew his revolver and shot him dead, the flag remaining thenceforth undisturbed, until General Tergukassoff, a few days afterwards, relieved the garrison.

I never heard that any one was court-martialled for the business, and I *know* that Major S——, on whom the command subsequently devolved, acquired *very* great " credit."

has taken place in former centuries. Between Kars
and Alexandropol lies a rolling open country, ranges
of mountains on each side, about fifty miles long, from
end to end, and twenty broad, of an oval shape, con-
tracting towards either extremity. It appears level, but
is in reality much cut up with ravines and hollows,
though much of it is veritable plain of great extent.
Through this valley from end to end runs the Kars-
Alexandropol road. The valley, which runs east and
west, is bounded on the north side of the oval by the
high ranges and plateaux I have described as lying
between Georgia proper and Turkey in Asia, part of
which were at the time of the war Turkish and part
Russian territory.[1] On the south side of the oval lies
the Aladja Dagh running in an irregular chain of sloping downs and detached or semi-detached bluffs, from
Kars to close above Ani, a distance of, as the crow flies,
some eighteen miles. When the Russians raised the
siege of Kars they retreated about half-way down
the oval, to Bash Kadikler, Kurrukdara, etc., where
they formed their force into a line of posts stretching
diagonally across the oval from north-west to south-
east, or from Zaim and Arj Kala, near the foot of the
northern mountains, to the Kizil Tepe and Ani, at the
eastern extremity of the Aladja Dagh, a line of twenty
to twenty-five miles. Mukhtar Pacha, with a view
to covering Kars, occupied the ridge of the Aladja
and outlying bluffs of Vizinkef, the great and small

---

[1] This is the lesser Caucasus, already mentioned, called by the
ancients Montes Moschites, and by the old geographers, Mount
Periardo, etc.

above mentioned, when the Russians immediately
took possession, and getting up a battery bombarded
the Avliar and Turkish centre which they could command from its summit, as well as reconnoitre the
whole position.   The Turks, finding their mistake,
made desperate efforts to retake the post, storming
with determined bravery, but without success; in fact,
they lost heavily both in men and officers, getting a
taste of the dressing they had just inflicted on the
Russians at the small Yagni. Leaving the great
Yagni, we crossed in front of the Turkish centre on
the Avliar mountain to Hadji Vali, a large village on
the slope below the Aladja Dagh, about a mile above
Sabbatan, on the right front of the Turkish centre.
This was also the scene of determined fighting, as by
it the Turks made their descents into the maidan,
and by it the Russians used to attack, and indeed got
their artillery up to pound the Avliar on the day of
their victory.   We reached this point about sunset,
and, having done some forty-five miles since morning,
prepared to halt for the night.   The village, which
had been a Mahometan one, from which the faithful
had retired since the annexation, was now inhabited
by Greeks, who did not seem in a hurry to accommo-
date us; however, routing out the headman, I went
at him in Russian and Turkish, and got him to agree
to find us shelter.   After some conversation I found
that they belonged to the same tribe of Greeks whom
I fell in with last year near "Psalk," who came over
in Paskievitch's time (or rather whose fathers and
grandfathers did), after the war of 1829.   They

informed me that they had been invited to settle here last year by Government, and were now in the thick of a " squeeze," the Turks having been invited back again, and one Mahomed Beg, who was originally Kotwal, and others, having actually put in an appearance at the village. The Greeks had been warned officially to quit, and matters were looking blue. They had been informed that each family would receive five roubles indemnity for damages and loss of time (travelling 100 miles with all their property, rebuilding houses in villages, etc.), and this munificent offer did not much please them. They took me for an agent sent by Government to find out secretly what was going on, under pretence of seeing the battlefields, and I had a great deal of difficulty in disabusing them of the notion, which made them extremely voluble on the subject of their grievances, which they to the last impressed upon me. General Franchini, a man of the highest character and attainments, who was governor of Kars immediately after the annexation, and would have seen them righted, resigned last year and retired from the service, and the Grand Duke, having also left the Caucasus, they were *en l'air*. As they truly said : " It all depended upon money." I suggested squaring Mahomed Beg and Co., who I do not believe really wanted to come back, as no Turk can live, except under very exceptional and favourable conditions, as a Russian subject ; and I believe they intended to try this plan, the drawback to which was, that as it involved considerable " kudos " to a Russian official in charge of

newly-annexed territory, to be able to report that
the Turks in his, or rather belonging to his, district
are all longing to come back and become faithful
subjects of the Czar, His Imperial Majesty's said functionaries, by secretly offering tremendously favourable conditions, do sometimes manage to entice
villagers to return and (for a time) take up allegi-
ance; and this move might of course, as it was
early in the game, be contemplated in the present
instance.

Though busy with harvest operations, the Greeks
were hospitable; the women, who are strapping females,
both boiled our kettle for us and brought us cheese,
milk, and well-baked brown bread, so we got on well
enough. We took tea in the antechamber, or rather
" ante-cave," of the headman's house, and passed an
hour or two there listening to their yarns; but knowing that the enemy, who had been "feeling" us for
some time, must be in great force, I refused to sleep
there, and we removed our traps and cloaks outside,
one of the women spreading a large felt rug and a
thick hempen mat for us on the ground. Even as it
was, the enemy who had already "effected a lodgment" (Caucasian fleas, no matter in what strength,
never deliver the "general assault" until you have
turned in) gave us much trouble, and required as
usual a tremendous expenditure of ammunition. They
made a final rally on the "khoorjen" that served me
for a pillow. I could actually *hear* them bringing up
reinforcements; luckily the "powder" was new and
strong, and finding they could *not* stand it, they

gradually retreated, and I slept till the morning star
was well up on the horizon. The air, even at this
time of year, was cold and chilly towards daybreak
(though dry and healthy), and we were glad to get a
bowl of tea, after which, mounting our "quads"
(mine, from hard work, began to look very like one
of Jorrock's famous 25-pounders), we made for the
centre of the Osmanli position, the famous "Avliar,"
which we reached about 9 A.M.

The Avliar is a conical grassy hill or peak, rather
steep (you can just ride up it comfortably), rising
from the edge of the main ridge, and fortified with a
rifle shelter trench all round the summit and a 3-gun
battery. The Russians have lately erected a solid
stone monument, surmounted by a wooden cross on
it, with a slate let in for an inscription, but blank as
yet ; perhaps they are puzzled for an appropriate one,
unless indeed it records the number of men and
officers it cost them to force the position. I descended
from horseback, picked up a few fragments of shell
and a cartridge-case or two, and gazed around ; all
now was silent, peaceful, and deserted, where four
years ago was such stir, bustle, and *feu d'enfer.*
Nothing now to be seen or heard but a kite hovering
or a lark twittering.

I thought of my friend Dr. C. and of General
Kemball, whose hospitality I enjoyed at Baghdad in
1867, and regretted not having been with them
during the glorious three months, when these knolls,
crowned by scarlet fezzes, over and over again hurled
back the Muscovite assaults. In fact, the Russians

only carried the Avliar by absolutely crushing the Turks at that point by the fire of nearly one hundred field-guns concentrated on it, while another hundred were in action at different points of the line.

The Turks had about thirty-five pieces in action. As it was, the Grand Duke and staff never expected the assault to succeed, and remained at headquarters until an aide-de-camp from the front, tearing up about 3 P.M., informed His Imperial Highness that the day was won. There was then a wild rush to get to the front and share in the glory, but the Grand Ducal headquarters being unfortunately some eight miles as the crow flies from the scene of action, across rocky ravines, grass, stones, etc., through which impediments His Imperial Highness could not be hurried recklessly, they were " too late for the fair." Tradition asserts, however, that they were not going to be done out of their renown for all that; that General P——, *the* great-gun of the party, finding that the portion of Mukhtar's army cut off on the Aladja Dagh had surrendered to a certain colonel, and been disarmed before their arrival, and that the pachas and officers had all given up their swords, remarked that "this sort of thing" was "most irregular," and (after wigging the colonel) ordered the whole performance (as far as related to the pachas and officers' swords) to be "done over again:" the despatch subsequently forwarded to the Emperor informing the world that twenty-two battalions, eleven pachas, and so many guns, etc.,

had surrendered to General P——, who subsequently
received the cross of St. George, besides other more
substantial tokens of approbation, from a grateful
sovereign for his services. Such, however, is military life.

" Sic vos non vobis mellificatis apes."

From the Avliar, twelve miles south-east of Kars,
I rode slowly and mournfully along the ridge towards
the city, pondering, not only over the chances that
Mukhtar had missed, but the still more glorious
chances that *we* missed by not taking up the running in 1877. What a hand of cards our Government had then ; but, as usual, without playing it !
We shall never, I fear, have such an opportunity
again.[1]

West of the Avliar and to the left rear of the
small Yagni is Vizinkef, a strong position above an
Armenian village, acting as a support or reserve to
the great and small Yagnis, as two other posts, the
names of which I forget, about half a mile to its right,
did to the Avliar.

After inspecting Vizinkef we descended to the
Armenian village immediately below it, from which
there was a fine view of Kars (about six miles off,
across the end of the valley), with a largish camp of

[1] A British fleet in the Black Sea and 8000 men landed in Mingrelia, "properly handled," in conjunction with Dervish and Mukhtar,
would have compelled the Russians either to make peace or quit the
Caucasus. The fleet could, immediately after landing the troops,
have steamed across to Varna, sent the gunboats up the Danube, and
cut the communication of the grand army in Bulgaria (then besieging
Plevna).

exercise outside it.[1]   I was told by a Georgian nobleman or kniaz, whom I found at the village, that all
the local troops had been lately ordered in for inspec-
tion. The kniaz, who was from Kakhetia, and, I found,
knew plenty of people whom I knew also, was very
polite, as they always are. The Georgians are the only
native gentlemen, or what comes up to our idea of
such, in the Caucasus; they have always good manners.
Having fed the horses, for which the kniaz would '
not allow me to pay (indeed he pressed me hard to
pass the day with him and go on to Kars next

[1] Since Kars has been ceded the Russians have put the works in
thorough repair and constructed new ones communicating by galleries,
souterrains, etc. ; they are reported to have spent up to date some
three millions of roubles, and the fortress is now, doubtless, in first-
class order. Visitors are not allowed to go over the works.

The capture of Kars, which did not hold out long after the
defeat of Mukhtar on the Aladja, notwithstanding that it was well pro-
visioned and garrisoned, has been often attributed to treachery, but it
is probable that its commanders, deceived by their own spies, were
surprised. The Turkish staff, who had all along good information,
learned (which was the fact) that a general assault had been determined
upon at 4 A.M. of the 11th December, and made their dispositions in
consequence—their troops being ordered to be under arms by 2 A.M.
of the above date. In the meantime the Russian general, at half an
hour's notice, commanded the attack at 8 P.M. on the 10th, at which
hour the Turkish troops, having turned in in order to be fresh and
ready soon after midnight, were, with the exception of the ordinary
guards and pickets, mostly asleep and unprepared. Nevertheless the
resistance at the Kanly battery, the point first attacked, was very
obstinate. General Grabbe, two colonels, and other good officers being
killed in leading on the column, which, by all accounts, hung back at
first considerably. After this the Russians got in at other points.
The confusion was fearful, and continued till near morning, both sides
firing into the enemy or each other promiscuously. As day broke
numbers of fugitives outside the town were cut down by the Cossacks,
who as usual, gave no quarter.

morning), we remounted and retraced our steps,
passing close to the great Yagni, and again crossing
the debatable ground between the two positions to
Hadji Vali, where we made no stay, but, descending
to Sabbatan, passed close to and inspected the Kizil
Tepe or Red Hill, where one of the most daring
exploits of the war took place.

The Russian left, consisting of a division under
General Devell, was posted, as already related, opposite the ruins of Ani ; the centre of their army being
at Bash Kadiklar, Kulveran, and Bairaktar ; their
right on Arj Kala, Zaim, etc. ; thus they remained,
shifting about and skirmishing, till the end of September, making from time to time general attacks
or demonstrations all along the line, during one of
which they occupied (in July) with a battery and
two strong battalions, and shelter-trenched on the
side of the enemy, the Kizil Tepe, a small grassy
volcanic hill, steep sided, with a sort of crater (open
down the south-west face), situated to the left of their
centre, and rising some 150 or 200 feet above the
plain.   This hill, being at least six or seven miles, as
the crow flies, from the Aladja, and some four from
the Turkish advanced posts, had never been approached
by them, and the Russian officers holding it thought
themselves secure enough. However, Mehemet Capitan,[1]
who had seen a lot of service with the Turks, and was

---

[1] He was a Prussian ; the men, with whom he was very popular,
would never call him anything but " Mehemet Capitan ;" he was, however, a brigadier during the war, and, I believe, a pacha for some time
before his death.

about altogether the best man in Mukhtar's force, thought otherwise.

In 1876-77, when the Russians, having decided on " going in," were preparing for the campaign, raising everywhere native levies, horse and foot " volunteer," irregular cavalry (which latter received very good pay), and the rest, the politicals in Daghestan, anxious for approbation, invited the Begs of their districts to get up a corps of irregulars, and the Government, discerning that capital could be made out of the affair, if it could be shown that the Lesghian chiefs, so far from being disaffected as supposed, had voluntarily raised an " efficient corps of cavalry" and " conducted it to the seat of war," immediately closed with the offer. The "efficient corps" (consisting of the most fearful ruffians imaginable, mounted on ponies), every other man of which had been "wanted" for something or other—for it must be borne in mind that going on active service at that time of day got any one out of any scrape, no matter how serious— having, after sundry " difficulties," shootings, etc. (the officers were all Lesghians, and they marched by themselves), duly worked its way to the front, was sent on outpost duty, and at once, being to a man Soonnis, entered into close and friendly relations with the enemy.

They used to stroll into Mukhtar's advanced posts and pickets when they chose, being hospitably received, while the Circassians and Kurds put up with them in return whenever convenient ; the Turks, knowing that they were perfectly safe to tell them everything, and the Russians nothing, or rather "all that was required," encouraging the practice. It was mainly owing to these fellows' "first-rate information" that the Russian staff believed to the last that Mukhtar had 60,000 men or upwards on the Aladja, whereas Mukhtar had about 22,000, and used to pitch empty tents by day, and light grass and cow-dung fires by night all the time he held the position, to conceal his weakness.

Mehemet Capitan, being always at the advanced posts and pickets, and generally on the *qui vive*, speedily discovered from the "efficient" who lay opposite, and were nearly as much in his camp as in their own, that the Russians on the Kizil Tepe kept careless watch, trusting to the Lesghians who lay directly between them and the Turks. He therefore, Mukhtar consenting and approving, started one moonless night to beat them up, at the head of three trusty battalions, supported by a reserve of about the same strength under, I believe, Ali Pacha.

Passing close to the Lesghian camp, which, as per agreement, did not stir or fire a shot, they got over the six or seven miles in good time, reaching the Russian pickets at the foot of the hill about 3 A.M. An immediate alarm was given, but the Turks, rushing up the slope without a moment's hesitation, with shouts of "Allah!" were into and through the shelter-trenches before the hurriedly-aroused Rooskies could man them properly or open an effective fire ; all who were not shot or bayoneted being hurled down the opposite slope facing the Russian centre, which slope, and the slope facing the Russian left, the Turks, without a thought of fatigue, immediately set to work to make defensible.[1]

In spite of the iron-bound volcanic soil they worked with such a will that before noon they had a long rifle-trench on each side, and a double tier of pits below it.[2]

In the meantime, having cut off the left wing and turned the centre of the Russian army, they had caused a panic. A stampede into Alexandropol or, what was much the same thing, a complete change of front (which would have enabled Mukhtar descending in force to attack them in flank) were the first things proposed, and it is said received immediate official sanction. Indeed, the Grand Duke is reported to have *ordered* the first of these strategic movements to be executed, and to have been with difficulty persuaded to reconsider his decision. By daylight the whole centre was in confusion, guns being limbered, tents struck, baggage packed, and waggons loaded; orders given one minute, countermanded the next, and then given again, etc. Mehemet Capitan, whose quick eye had immediately grasped the situation, sent off messenger after messenger to Mukhtar, counselling a general assault all along the line, and demanding reinforcements with which at once to attack the centre; but Mukhtar hesitated, and the critical moment was lost.

[1] The Russians had of course made no defences, except to their front.

[2] The men in these lower tiers, from the steepness of the hillside, were, as it were, sitting on ledges, quite exposed to fire except from immediately below them.

The Russian commanders, bolder counsels ultimately prevailing, themselves attacked Mukhtar's left and centre; urgent orders were sent to General Devell to "hurry up" with his division from Ani, and the Kizil Tepe was assaulted on two sides by a couple of brigades, and heavily cannonaded by three batteries with a view to recapture. To no purpose, however; the Turks, though shelled and stormed till evening, declined to budge, and the Russians, having lost many men, returned to camp, leaving such of their wounded as had fallen close under the position to their fate.

Devell, who had had a row previously with somebody in the centre, on account of his advice (he is a good general) being overruled, simply refused to "hurry up," saying he could not move his guns, and remained quietly encamped; for which disobedience he was ordered off to act as second in command under Tergukassoff, who was watching Ismail Pacha from the Araxes valley.

It is true that had he obeyed, Mukhtar, who had eight or nine thousand men on the Aladja (the Turkish right), could, and probably would, have taken him in flank as he was struggling across the broken intervening country; and it was, I believe, this plea which saved General Devell (who now commands the local troops of all arms in the Caucasus) from being shelved for disobedience of repeated orders. The chance of catching Devell in flank as he made his way up to restore confidence in the panic-stricken centre was probably Mukhtar's motive for the operation. Had he done so, the rout of the whole Russian

army would, it is all but certain, have followed. Such
is war; the success or failure of the best-planned
schemes often depending on trifling incidents impossible to foresee, such as a personal quarrel or
the failings of individuals. It is said that General
T——e had been ordered two days before to reinforce
strongly, and "cover" the Kizil Tepe; I forget the
detail of the reinforcement, but it was a strong detachment of infantry and some guns. On the day before,
this officer, who belongs to one of the first families
in the Caucasus, and is fond of cards, was hard at
work after tiffin at his favourite pursuit, when his
orderly officer presented himself and reported that
the detachment had dined and were ready to, or had,
fallen in. It was very hot, and the general, not
feeling inclined at the moment to move out and
grill himself on a blazing volcanic peak, told the
orderly officer to wait. When it got cooler he had
got more absorbed in his rubber, and, after one or
two interruptions, ordered the men to be dismissed
and re-assembled at daybreak. Before daybreak the
Turks were on the hill.

An engineer colonel had been ordered, a week
previous, to run up some regular defences on the hill
"in case of accidents;" but this gentleman, being con-
vivially inclined of an evening, never as a rule felt up
to much till after lunch, when it was rather late in
the day to begin; he had therefore sagaciously "post-
poned" fortifying the post in question.

To look at the Kizil Tepe, it seems perfectly
incredible that any troops could maintain them-

selves on it against heavy shelling, to say nothing of
repeated well-directed infantry attacks; yet nothing
could force the Turks out of it; they eventually
evacuated it of themselves, finding nearly a month
later on that the Russians were getting up reinforcements, and fearing to be cut off. What a contrast,
my dear friends and brethren in arms, does this present to our Majuba Hill business.

The Turkish leader, Mehemet Capitan, was not
brought up to military service, and had never passed
an "exam." of any sort in his life—was in fact just
the sort of man that would be denounced by your
strategical pundits as "a mere adventurer," "not
to be trusted," etc. His men were mostly peasants,
taken six months before from their villages, without any musketry instruction and next to no drill,
dressed in rags and badly rationed; without as much
"spit and polish" amongst the lot as would be considered requisite for a single full private of H.B.M.'s
army—for one solitary "Thomas Atkins." They
were likewise as destitute of Staff College professors
to control their movements and lead them on to
scientific victory as were our benighted Indian troops
in the glorious days of Clive, Lake, and Ochterlony.
Yet these fellows marched seven or eight miles by
night over broken ground, surprised and gallantly
stormed an entrenched position held by equal numbers,[1] fortified it on two sides in a few hours, under the

---

[1] The Turkish battalion's *actual strength* averaged 250 to 300.
A Russian battalion (on service) *ought* to be 840, but is 500 to 600,
sometimes 400 to 500.

most difficult conditions, and held it for weeks against the Russian army.[1]

Had he prepared for it beforehand, the moment of the Kizil Tepe surprise and panic might have been profitably employed by Mukhtar in effecting a raid into Georgia.   During the confusion a flying column might have been despatched across the plateau north of Kars without the Russian headquarters knowing anything of the movement for, in all probability, three or four days.   Three or four days' smart marching across the uplands would have brought the raiders to the fashionable sanitarium and watering-place of Borshom, which (including the Grand Duke's summer

---

[1] This was the same "Mehemet Capitan" who saved Erzeroum from being taken by assault subsequent to the defeat of the Turks on the Denee Boyun.   In the dead of an intensely cold winter night a Russian battalion of picked men (the "forlorn hope" of a strong supporting column), led by a young officer of great courage and perfectly acquainted with the ground, scaled, surprised, and actually (the Turks being as usual unprepared) had possession of a redoubt, which if occupied in force would have given them Erzeroum, being the key of the rest of the works.   Luckily for the inhabitants, Mehemet, who with a weak battalion held a post about 500 yards off, was as usual on the alert.   Hearing some shots in the redoubt he, without a moment's indecision, roused his men, and putting himself at the head of all who were immediately ready made for the spot at the double.   Fortune favoured him ; the supporting column, though close at hand, not being actually "up" when he arrived.   Dashing into the redoubt, a volley from the leading files followed by a bayonet charge, after a short but desperate conflict, in which no quarter was given, dislodged the Russians with severe loss, including that of their brave leader.   This had only just been effected when the Russian column came up, and, after one or two determined but unavailing attempts to escalade, was beaten off, severely punished.   The failure of this attempt was said at the time to have caused a serious personal quarrel between Generals Haiman and Tergukassoff.

palace there) they could have comfortably looted; while four hours' ride more along a first-rate post-road down the river would have brought them to the Poti-Tiflis Railway workshops, and locomotive depot at Michaeloff, the destruction of which would have completely crippled the Russian force in Imeritia and the Black Sea provinces, where they were hardly pressed to prevent invasion. They could have then followed the line of railway down the Koura, towards Tiflis, destroying the bridges and telegraph line, and if opposed or closed with by any superior force could always escape up the wooded gorges on their right, regain the uplands, and return to Turkish territory. Or, collecting all his Kurds, Tcherkess, and Bashi-Bazouks, Mukhtar could have started them, with orders on reaching the centre of the plateau (about the second day) to divide, in the orthodox Tartar or Pindaree style, into two bodies, one taking the above line the other striking north-east, straight for Tiflis, by the old direct Turkish invasion route. Had this operation been briskly carried out and each column taken care to report everywhere that it was the advanced guard of the Turkish army, nothing more would have been required to finish the war. The Tartars and mountain tribes[1] would have risen *en masse*, and even if they did not join the invaders, would have complicated matters and thrown everything into confusion by plundering right and left. Their first idea would probably have been to loot Tiflis, which is an open

---

[1] The Lesghians were already in revolt, and a division employed in opposing them.

H

town, quite defenceless, and was then entirely denuded
of troops.   In fact, there would have been as pretty a
general "smash up" as an invaded country has ever
experienced, and no one knew this better than the
Russian commanders; the one thing they were praying all their gods to avert, from the moment their
invasion of Anatolia was rolled back, being a counter-
invasion of the Turks, which they knew *must* be
disastrous, no matter where it was directed.

Whether Mukhtar had orders to keep strictly on
the defensive it is impossible to say, but there is no
doubt that an invasion would have been a success.
The Russians themselves are, indeed, nowise backward
in owning it, and all their measures and strategic
movements at the time betokened apprehension,
approaching to panic, of this contingency.   It is
probable that Mukhtar could not depend upon his
irregulars, who were certainly a most disorderly lot,
amenable, especially the Kurds, to next to no discipline; yet still, if they had only "gone ahead" for
about a week doing mischief they would have effected
their object, and might have avoided fighting or risk-
ing any engagement as much as they chose.   Under
any circumstances they would have been no loss to
Mukhtar, as they did nothing while with his army but
pillage their own villagers and commit "atrocities."

There would, however, have been really little or no
chance of their "coming to grief," as the Russians, to
effect it, would have had so to weaken their already insufficient force by detaching cavalry and guns in pursuit
of the raiders, that Mukhtar might have defeated the

remainder, or at any rate driven them into the fort
at Alexandropol, and then, joining hands with Ismail
Pacha, have driven Tergukassoff out of the valley of
the Araxes, taken Erivan, and ended the war in that
manner.   If, on the contrary, Mukhtar had determined on acting strictly on the defensive, it is un-
pardonable that a man of his ability should have
allowed himself to be beaten from a strong position,
and half his army taken prisoners, as he did.   He
knew well that towards the end of September the
Russians had received immense reinforcements of
artillery, and that their army, by the arrival of four
fresh divisions, had been raised to 60,000 or 70,000
men.

The fighting of the 2d, 3d, and 4th October, when
the Russians had 150 guns in action, and attempted
in force to turn the Turkish right on the Aladja,
demonstrated that clearly enough.

Having repulsed the enemy with great loss on
that occasion, Mukhtar should (instead of waiting to
be eventually outflanked by the huge force opposed
to him and his thin line cut in two) have quietly
retired into Kars, where he could have stood a
winter's siege very comfortably, leaving the enemy
(as they afterwards did at Erzeroum) to lose 20,000
men by typhus, cold, and want of necessaries, before
the fortress.   In effect, Mukhtar despised his enemy
too much and yet not enough ; while thinking his
position impregnable, which it was not, he thought
taking the offensive rash and impracticable, whereas
it was the one thing requisite for success and victory.

After leaving the Kizil Tepe we had a long, hot,
and dusty ride across rocky ravines and cutcha roads
to Argina, an Armenian village on the new Kars-
Alexandropol post-road.   There are here the ruins of
an ancient church built of lava blocks well squared,
destroyed by Timour in the fourteenth century, as
were all the old ruined churches in this part of the
world. Timour's destructive exploits in Armenia and
Georgia, as narrated by his pious and orthodox
historian, Shereffedin Ali,[1] would, by the way, be instructive reading for our modern "atrocity mongers."
Amongst other feats he buried 20,000 Armenians
alive close to this, at Ani, then the capital of Armenia
and a prosperous city.   Ani is now in Russian territory, and the ruins, which are very fine, are well worth
a visit; they have, however, been often described.

At Argina were two post-houses, with grog-shop
attached, in one of which—the post-house, not the
grog-shop—we got accommodation, and, after the
usual tea and precautions against insects, turned in,
and were early on horseback next morning, in order
to get into Alexandropol with as little sun as possible.
There is no mistake, by the way, about the sun
hereabouts.   From the moment you descend the
southern slope of the Georgian plateau you are
regularly in Asia.   In Georgia the sun, though hot,
is a European sun; and though there is a great
deal of malaria in summer in low-lying localities,
still the heat is softened.   Here, on this side, you
have the baking heat, and the people have the regular

[1] Life of Timour Bek.

dried, blackened look; in fact, you are in Persia, or
Afghanistan, or Mesopotamia, as far as climate goes.
Turbans are common, dust is palpable, high boots in
summer become intolerable; in fact, it is only the
3000 feet or so of elevation that makes the difference
between this and the Punjab frontier.   In winter,
however, the cold is fearful.

We reached Alexandropol about 11 A.M., and,
finding my horse was getting a sore back, I concluded
to stay a couple of days in the caravansary and
doctor him, and while doing so, looked up an Armenian or two whom I knew in the town.   I found
them full of " autonomy " and having their own
government.   " People's eyes were now opened,"
"natives could not be held in subjection, as hereto-
fore," and similar platitudes and dogmas, for much of
which our Radical Liberals are responsible.   I told
them I saw very, very small chance of any such event
as Armenian autonomy coming off.   "In the first place,"
said I (we were sitting in an open shop front), " you'll
have to reckon with these," pointing to a grenadier
patrol—strapping bronzed fellows from Kazan, not
one of them under six feet—who marched past with
sloped arms.   They admitted this was a difficulty,
remarking "that it was extraordinary how brutally
stupid those Russian soldiers are," ignorantly obeying
their officers like dogs, and going *anywhere*, even
through fire and water, if ordered.   One of them
began relating to me how the Turks used to absolutely mow them down during the war, yet they
kept on attacking; and was going on at great length,

evidently quite sorry that the Turks had *not* managed
to whip them.   I was preparing to explain that even
if they got over the Russian soldier difficulty, their
autonomical task would only be commencing, when
some strangers entered, and the treasonable conversation ceased.

Armenian autonomy is in fact nowhere; it might
be *talked about* if the Russians wanted fresh territory in Asia Minor, or more Armenians, which it is
doubtful if they do at present, having other fish to fry
farther east.   Their next big war will probably be
with some nation which can "pay up" well when
beaten, and is not difficult to beat.   They will not fight
the Turks, from whom they can expect nothing but
hard knocks and non-paying annexations, again for
some time to come; indeed, they are more likely to
square the Turk to keep quiet, while they fight
somebody else; but I am digressing.   The effect in
Turkish Armenia of autonomy being set going would
be an immediate massacre of Armenians by the Kurds,
who would naturally regard it as a scheme (which it
would be, *vide* the results of Bulgarian autonomy) to
subjugate them on the part of accursed Giaours and
Kafirs; and there, unless the Russians want to annex,
it would probably end.

In Russian Armenia and the Caucasus we find
half a dozen other native races, any one of which
could thrash the Armenians, and not one of which
would consequently submit for a moment to their
supremacy, especially as the Armenians are very
generally unpopular.   In fact, if the Russians with-

drew from the Caucasus, which they are rather less likely to do than we are to withdraw from Calcutta and Bombay, *i.e.* voluntarily withdraw, the Armenians would be excessively fortunate if they escaped with their lives and, say, one-third of their property. This propensity of subject-races to "get fat and kick" is most astounding. A Parsee or Bengali Baboo must, one would think, know that he could not sit upon Sikhs or Mahrattas; yet he evidently believes that if there were no English in India he would, from his superior civilisation, be somehow at the top of the tree and have matters his own way. As this mania presents itself in an aggravated form only amongst money-making and commercial subject-races, it probably arises from a habitual "besting" and over-reaching the dominant race in pecuniary and mercantile transactions. This produces contempt, which in time transfers itself by reflex action to the warlike races, their former masters, whom the Parsee, etc., cannot help despising for being conquered by people whom he feels to be no match for him in financial smartness and business generally. Such at any rate is, I am convinced, the origin of the feeling as regards Caucasian Armenians, who "do" the Russian at every turn, and have, as I have often remarked, a very hearty contempt for Russian character in consequence. But supposing that there were no Russian Government and no warlike races to interfere with the autonomical experiment, it is even then doubtful if it would answer; for the Armenians are a sort of people who appear to be only able to unite and combine in cases

where some money-making "ring," "plant," or "pull"
is to be organised, so that it is doubtful if they would
submit to be governed by their own people, who
would certainly use the machinery of Government
unscrupulously to promote their private ends.

The Armenian's, *i.e.* the educated Armenian's,
summum bonum of civilisation and freedom appears
to be to dress in European clothes by a decent tailor,
to talk two or three European languages, and yet in
business matters to continue an Asiatic, without being
thought the worse of, or coming to grief for so doing ;
he is at present, in fact, getting to play the "irrepres-
sible nigger" *rôle* in Russia, with the difference that
the nigger is not in society, whereas the Armenian is,
and means to keep there. The Russians, who have
created him, now, like Frankenstein, begin to find
him a nuisance, and do not exactly know what to do
to get rid of him. He *will not* be snubbed, or kept
at a distance ; he goes to Government schools and
colleges, crams steadily and passes examinations ; he
pushes himself into all sorts of good berths, and, once
in, helps others of his race up ; while in commercial
life he monopolises, by combination, every branch of
trade, and beats the careless, easy, slow-going Russian
trader even in his own country.

This, however, is a wide question, this of the
subject-races of the Russian empire ; it is even an
open point if they *are* subject.

One thing is certain, viz. that it is not the Russian
people who govern, or Russians who constitute the
motive-power of the machine ; the empire being a con-

glomeration of different nationalities, each struggling through its representatives to get ahead. Genuine Russians have about as much to say to it as genuine Turks have to say to the Ottoman Government machinery.

Take the army : the mass of the common soldiers are Russians, but the organisation is swayed and directed by officers of almost every nationality in Europe, and half those of Asia. Germans and Poles in very great numbers, and holding the highest posts (both in the military and civil services), Courlanders ditto, Finlanders, Swedes, Italians, French, Austrians, Montenegrins, Greeks, Croats, Hungarians, and some of English and Scotch origin, while of Asiatics, Armenians *en masse*, Tartars of various races, Kalmuks, Kirghiz, etc., Georgians, Persians, some of high rank, to say nothing of the mountain tribes of the Caucasus, Ossetes, Svanetes, etc., who contribute a good few. In fact, anybody who chooses to swear fealty to the Czar can hold a commission in the Russian army, and command Russian soldiers, just as any one who chooses to turn Mahometan can serve, and perhaps obtain high rank under, the Turks.

The Turkoman chiefs are now going in for commissions ; the Usbegs, etc., in Central Asia are already represented ; and when, a few years hence, Russian troops occupy Afghanistan, or perhaps before that, plenty of Afghan captains, majors, etc., will be seen in Russian uniforms.

Departing from the caravansary early on the morning of the third day, after honourably paying

the shot, we got clear of the town shortly after sunrise, and struck along a bridle-track to the right of
the post-road leading directly for the mountains.
After five hours of up and down over barren hills,
with Armenian villages, lately-reaped stubble-fields,
and watercourses in the hollows, we reached the
maidan of Bendivan, a great upland pasture, once
evidently the bed of a lake, about three miles across,
dotted with villages round its margin, all busy harvesting.   Passing this grassy plain, and turning to
the left across some ridges, we at length struck the
Alexandropol-Akhaltzik post-road, at a point where,
about forty miles from Alexandropol, it reaches its
greatest elevation, close to the Dukabor village of
Tropeetshaia, about 5500 or 6000 feet above the sea.
Passing the village and lake on the right, we made
along the post-road to Ephraimofka, a large Dukabor
village about a mile farther on, standing close on the
road, with a double line of substantial houses and
stackyards.   On entering the main street we inquired for the starost, or principal headman, whose
business it is, among other duties, to find accommodation for respectable travellers on their paying
for the same—we inquired, I should have said, as
soon as we could make ourselves heard above the
furious barking of the big dogs from each side of
the roadway as we passed along.[1] Having at length

---

[1] *N.B.*—It is dangerous to enter these upland villages on foot
after dark, especially during winter, when, on account of the cold, the
houses are all carefully closed and no one about, solely on account of
the dogs.

discovered the starost—a big, solemn, puritanical looking man with one eye—we demanded quarters, and getting into the stackyard, dismounted and were introduced to the dogs, whom we propitiated by a "peshkesh" or "nuzzur" of a fid of stale bread each, in case the sagacious animals should fail to recognise us after dark, as they sometimes do if you do not give them anything. We then stowed the horses in the cow-byre, giving them some hay and loosening the girths.

The Dukabors are a sort of respectable and well-behaved communists or socialists; they will not have any clergy, and will not make the sign of the cross—a fearful heresy in Russia; they will not be educated, *i.e.* will not read or write, but are first-rate agriculturists and very industrious; they have their coin in common; they are governed by a *female* head, who is elected and assisted by a council; they always wear one sort of dress, which they never alter; the women even, who dress picturesquely, never change their costume. Nicholas exiled them to the Turkish frontier. They have made many converts even amongst Mahometans, and have always done well since they were settled in the Caucasus in 1840.

We got on first-rate with the starost, who introduced me to his family, his wives, daughters, sons' wives, etc.,—in all, a large roomful of females hard at work, talking, knitting, sewing, butter and cheese making, etc. He wanted me very much to sleep in this apartment, which is also the common dormitory, saying the women would think me "up-

pish" if I did not; but I excused myself on the plea
of being tired, and not wanting to incommode them,
and we took up our abode in a waggon-shed or tool-
house, where we lit the usual fire, and soon had the
copper tea-kettle boiling.

The sons were away harvesting and hay-cutting,
and, with two or three more women and girls, did not
turn up till after dark.

The Dukabor colonists have to work desperately
hard at this season to get their crops in before the
frosts, which, from the great elevation, set in early in
September. I had some talk with the starost, who
seemed a hard-headed sensible man. He told me
the Government had established four new Dukabor
villages between Alexandropol and Kars. He complained of the cold of the climate on the plateau,
which he said was more severe than in Central Russia,
where the barley and wheat were never killed by
frosts while ripening, which here often happened. He
said that they had to work like slaves during the
summer to get in the enormous store of fodder and
fuel necessary for winter consumption. The severity
of the climate on these uplands in winter is, as I have
twice experienced, fearful. There is literally nothing
to be seen but a boundless expanse of snow-covered
mountain and plain. The snow-storms are terrific,
darkening the air so, that if out in them you are certain
to lose your way, and may lose your life. The streams
are frozen to the bottom, and the villages even in fine
weather almost invisible. No one would credit that
4000 feet elevation could make such a difference. You

are usually 1500 to 2000 feet elevation everywhere in
the interior of the Caucasus, and these uplands are
only 6000 to 6500 ; yet the difference between their
climate and that of Tiflis or Kutais is as great in
winter as between Moscow and Marseilles. In summer
one does not feel it so very much cooler than the
low country, and, as I have often noticed, if there
happens to be no wind, the sun is at times almost as
powerful as down below. About 4 A.M. we made
tea, fed and saddled the horses, and paying a rouble
for the night's lodging, milk, fuel, hay, and barley,
about a third of what would have been demanded
near Tiflis, started across the great rolling downs to
the north, passing no end of barley and hay still
uncut, and stupendous quantities, cut and cocked, but
still in the fields. In spite of the early hour, the
Dukabors, women and men, were astir and jogging
off to their work in fourgons. After an hour or two
of riding, the track descended steadily for about a
mile, till we came in sight of a lake and Tartar
village called Toman Geul (mist lake), which we
passed through, and following a valley and clear
stream to the right, came, after another hour's ride,
in sight of the great lake of Taporavan,[1] a fine sheet
of water, some six miles long by two and a half or
three broad, surrounded by lofty mountains on the
gray storm-beaten summits of which patches of winter
snow still lingered. There are here two Armenian and
one large Dukabor village, at opposite corners of the
lake, which is said to be full of fine fish, a kind of trout.

[1] The Turks call it Pervana Geul, or "slave lake."

This place would make a grand sanitarium, and were the country under other (European) hands would have been probably long ago utilised for this purpose, being easily, on account of the very gradual ascent from the north, accessible from Tiflis.

The climate in summer is simply perfection, being almost that of 10,000 feet elevation in the Himalaya, say 9000 feet, but much drier; there are fine open grassy flats of great extent on the margin, and the country round about is excellently adapted for riding, driving, etc., being like the Sussex downs, only on a very much larger scale; while the first-rate boating, fishing, sailing-matches, etc., which might be had on the lake, would afford never-failing recreation and amusement.

In the Caucasus, however, a grand duke or governor-general is required to set the fashion and lay down the law about sanitaria, for without such august example and "hookum" nothing can be done.

It appears that under the old Armenian and Georgian kings the lake was appreciated, as in the middle of the Dukabor village, at the northern end, I on a previous visit discovered the remains of a large ruined edifice, many of the vaulted arches of which, built of solid and squared blocks of stone, were still standing, said to have been a palace, but now used as a sort of stable and courtyard to an adjoining pot-house.

There were, I believe, several Persian or Perso-Armenian monarchs of the name of Taprobanes, and it is probable that some one of these in ancient times

made this a resort in summer and gave his name to
the lake.

At the end of the lake the road rises again, crossing a "ghat" or divide, elevation about 7000 feet,
where is an ancient monolithic stone pillar, and two
or three cairns to mark the track when deep in snow.
From this point a long and very gradual descent of
eighteen miles, over continuous grassy slopes,[1] leads
down to the fertile valley of Psalk, or Trialeti, which one
sees dimly far below, while beyond it range on range
of mountains fill up the horizon.   While trudging
down this long descent we passed numerous Tartar
"aouls" or "yailaks," great flocks of sheep, herds of
cattle, horses, etc., and, just as dusk was closing in,
reached a large village and friendly pot-house (kept
by the inevitable Armenian dukanjee) on the Chram
river.   The dukanjee, who was engaged in an ani-
mated discussion with certain villagers, being at
length unearthed, owned to a samovar, which was
at once ordered to be got under weigh and some eggs
boiled.   This "crib," being in course of construction,
was in a horribly dilapidated state; but there were
some planks, doors off their hinges, and old boxes
lying about, with which we improvised a "tukhta"
or couch, and after tea, and feeding the animals, slept
the sleep of the just.

Rising early, we fed, tea'd, saddled, and paying

[1] I never recollect seeing such a gradual descent anywhere; there
was no road, and hardly even a cattle-track, but one might have
driven a buggy at a trot all the way; a line of railway might be run
up it with hardly any levelling.

the shot,[1] walked the horses to the ford of the Chram
river, 500 yards off, where we mounted and rode over.
Here is a first-rate military position, as the Chram
river above and below this point burrows in a clean
cut and deep chasm through granite rock, impassable except at one or two fords, of which this is
one, for some twenty or twenty-five miles. There is
a Cossack post here, commanding the ford, with a
rocky hill behind it, from which two roads branch off
respectively to Manglis and Bailey Klootch, two large
cantonments and reservist colonies, equidistant from
Tiflis. Passing the ford, we mounted the hill, and taking the western track went for Manglis, distant twenty-
five versts, following the path, which led along a
valley between two rocky grassy ridges for several
hours without any incident worth mention, arriving
about 1 A.M. at Manglis, a fine sanitarium, or rather
"summer resort" and cantonment. Although Manglis, which is at an elevation of 4500 feet, seems quite
cold to people arriving from Tiflis, it was quite hot
to us, who had just descended from the upper regions.
We felt, however, ravenously hungry, and were not
long in despatching a "shislik" or cabob, and a bottle of
wine. It was a great treat to get some good bread.
I insisted on sleeping with all the doors of the ground-
floor apartment they gave us (which looked on the
yard) wide open, to the horror of the proprietor, a fat
Armenian, who sent his boy twice during the night

---

[1] Shot, like many other words supposed to be slang, is merely a
foreign word transposed. "Schott," in Russian, means the bill, the
account.

to implore me to shut them, as there were lots of thieves and robbers about. There was some truth in this, for the last time I travelled this way, in June, I came across some peasants, engaged in burying the body of an unwary traveller (who had been killed by yataghan cuts) by the side of the road, and heard next day of another corpse having been found in a similar condition. The chance of the horses being stolen, however (horse-stealing is a liberal profession in the Caucasus), always alarms me much more than the prospect of burglary with violence, so I preferred to neglect his recommendations, knowing that we could hear the stable-door broken in much easier with our room open than with it shut.

Getting off next morning by 6 A.M. we crossed the ravine, and working up the opposite slope, past a bran new wooden cross erected to the memory of a post-cart traveller who was robbed and murdered there last winter [1] (about 400 yards in a direct line

[1] Amongst other unwary travellers, a young German of the name of S——, whose family I knew in Tiflis, though not murdered, came, while travelling this road, to grief nearly equivalent. He had served through the war as a hospital volunteer (he was a medical student), and had managed, being handy and useful, to accumulate (though penniless at first) £90 in cash by the close of the war, with which, mounted on a good Turkish horse, looted at Kars, and armed with revolver and sabre, he started homewards (about May 1878), reaching Manglis without accident on the afternoon of the fourth day, where he halted for dinner. Manglis is a fifty versts' ride from Tiflis, the greater part of which is along a lofty ridge covered with forest on either side, and the dukanjee advised him to stay over night, but, his horse being tolerably fresh, he determined to push on. Finding, after doing eight or ten miles, that he was getting tired, and that it was getting dark, he concluded to halt for the night, and collecting some

I

from the station—nobody caught of course), got up to the top, from which we had a fine view of the picturesque cantonment, barracks, bazaar, and public buildings, also of the German settlement, and the two large Russian military (reservist) colonies, surrounded by a setting of green mountain and dark pine forest.

The men were out, as they are all the summer, at musketry exercise, and the rattling volleys and file firing added to the animation of the scene. The Russian short-service system merits a word or two (as, indeed, does the Russian musketry system, which is far superior to our black-and-white target absurdities,[1] measured distance, etc., though I have no space for it at present).

A Russian soldier, who is, of course, a conscript, can, after five years' service, marry and join the reserve, when he and his wife have a plot of land given them in one of the numerous military colonies,[2] or rather settlements, which are dotted over the

firewood, after fastening his horse to a tree by the roadside, went down the ridge to a spring to get a drink of water. On returning to where he had left his horse he found it gone, and with it his sword, which he had left fastened to the saddle, his saddlebags, and his money, which latter he had, by way of precaution, sewn up in a corner of his felt cloak, tied as usual behind the cantle; and he walked into Tiflis as he had left it—*sans le sous.* Mistake No. 1—to go on, late in the day, unless you intend to ride all night; mistake No. 2 (the fatal one)—to leave a horse tied within sight of a road.

[1] Being taught to fire at black bull's eyes on a white ground at measured distances is probably the secret of Tom Atkins his "ineffectual fire." In action he has to shoot at dim gray or brown objects at unknown ranges.

[2] The Russians call a village of colonists a colony. They say a German "colony," a Greek "colony," meaning a German settlement, etc.

country, and of which one at least in every favourable locality is attached to each cantonment. There
he can settle down, cultivate his potatoes and cabbages, keep two or three cows and horses, and make
himself comfortable, which, being a peasant born, and
having the advice and example of older settlers, he,
if sober, manages to do. If war breaks out, he is
liable to be called upon to join a regiment, but not
otherwise.

These colonies do well and spread annually, more
and more land being required for the sons of the
colonists, who, as they grow up, are also liable to
conscription, but on easier terms. They of course
materially strengthen Russian occupation, and make
their hold on the country more secure. In fact, everything (*i.e.* every arrangement or institution) of a
serious nature in Russia is connected with military
matters. Though numerically powerful, they are a
poor nation, and must make their army " pay," just as
a poor man must make money by his horses or not
keep them at all.

After a halt half-way in the forest to make a
" shislik " for tiffin, and allow the horses to graze, we
reached Tiflis by moonlight, the heat and closeness
something awful ; in fact, I felt for a couple of days
as if I could not breathe, though everybody left in
town was remarking " how cool it was for the time
of year."

CHAPTER V.

THE road out of Tiflis, or rather the horse-track, which
is the nearest way to the valley of Kakhetia (the ancient
Albania) and the main chain of the Caucasus beyond
it, runs north or north-east across open undulating
downs, by a gradual ascent from the town. You pass
the arsenal and magazines, about a mile to their right,
and cross the commencement of the Baku-Tiflis line of
railway, just outside the town, which, as you gradually
ascend the slope, lies spread in a sort of panorama
behind you. These downs are covered (in spring) with
fresh green grass and are cheerful enough, but, as
summer advances (and the Tiflis climate gets more
and more like Lahore in the month of May), become
adust and burned up, insomuch that a stranger would

hardly believe that green waving oak and beech
forests, cool streams, and verdant mountain-pastures,
existed a morning's ride beyond; but the Caucasus
is a land of contrasts and surprises, and this is one
of them.

After the first five or six miles the road dips down
to a hollow between the hills, forming a magnificent
natural reservoir, a valley five miles long, and a mile
to a mile and a half broad, closed at either end. Into
this hollow, which seems made for the purpose, the
late Mr. Gabb, a clever English C.E., who lived many
years in the Caucasus and planted many public works,
proposed to turn one of the mountain rivers, thus
making it into a fresh-water lake for the supply of the
town; but, as usual, though the town is at present
supplied by puchals and water-carts, there was no
money to be had. From this empty natural reservoir
the track mounts a steep hill, after negotiating which
you arrive at an upland steppe and comparatively cool
climate.

There is a good deal of feathered game about these
downs and steppes in winter—large and small bustard,
coolen, etc.; but all, on account of the number of shikarees always on the prowl round Tiflis, very wild and
wary. Traversing this elevated meadow for a couple
of miles, you come to a small Russian (reservist) military village of the usual type, wooden "frame" houses,
pigs, fowls, dogs, which bay at you all along the street,
untidy stackyards, and rough unkempt men and
women busy about household labours. The downs
all round are mown in summer, and the hay stored

for the requirements of the Grand Duke's stabling; there is a Cossack post on a commanding point to look after the pasturage and haystacks.

Beyond this village the road forks, the left hand branch leading to the blue-roofed monastery of St. Anthony, on a jutting spur of a big wooded range, about two hours' ride off. We took the other, striking across a rolling country, covered with newly-cut wheat and Indian-corn stubble, which we traversed for several miles, passing on the right a large scattered Georgian village built along a stream which comes down from the mountains, whose outskirts we fast approached. Round this village, as round all the old-established villages in this part of the country, square stone towers are dotted here and there, and the village itself contains one or two fortified buildings, remnants of the days, not so long ago either, when the Lesghians harried the country, and Akhaltsik and Akhalkilak were Turkish frontier towns and white slave marts.

Passing the towers, we descended a steep slope to a wide flat bottom, covered with a low jungle of black-berry bushes, with here and there a corn patch, where several mountain streams conjoined, crossing which, we pursued our devious way up a gorge or wooded glen, one of the numerous hollows which ran down the mountain now towering above us. It was blazing hot, there being no wind stirring, and we were not sorry to find ourselves gradually rising into a cool climate and amongst green hazel bushes, with which, and other European forest growth, the hillside was thickly

covered. We met no one but a few peasants in coarse
woollen clothes, as primitive and rude as those of the
heptarchy. After mounting by this ravine for about
2000 feet, sometimes in the almost dry pebbly bed of
the rivulet, sometimes scrambling through dense hazel
coppice and luxuriant fern, we reached pasture slopes,
dotted with beech and oak clumps—the crest of the
range still, though it looked close, 1500 feet above us.
Then we breasted the mountain, along a track which
presently brought us to a rude châlet, where we picketed
the horses and decided to have some lunch.

The herdsman, a fine old man, who told us he had
passed every summer for forty years on the mountain,
welcomed us hospitably, and offered cheese and clotted
milk, which we returned with tobacco and a glass of
brandy. It was noon, the air and water deliciously
cool, altogether a pleasant change from Tiflis, where
the thermometer would now register about 85° Fahrenheit, if not 90°, in the houses. We could see the plain
below glimmering and baking in the heat, and congra-
tulated ourselves on being out of it.

After a chat and a siesta, it being nearly three
o'clock, we remounted, and struggled up the steep
slope towards the crest of the range ; it took us a couple
of hours to get there, some part of which we had to
walk, it being too steep, and the short turf too slippery
for the horses to negotiate without great labour and
difficulty.

Near the summit, the mountain flattened out, and
we remounted, following the ridge towards the north.
The forest had now almost disappeared, and the ground,

which is under snow for six months of the year, was
carpeted with a rich and luxuriant flora, of grasses,
flowers of all descriptions, and aromatic herbs. Horses
are so fond of this mountain herbage that it was difficult to get ours along without using our whips, their
heads being down every moment. The view on the
north was magnificent, an immense extent of the main
"sierra" of the Caucasus, still streaked with snow,
being visible, with a sea of forest-covered mountain
stretching up to it, while on the south and east the
vast arid steppes along the valley of the Koura towards
Elizabethpol and Baku, lay burned up and shimmering
in the haze, 5000 feet below. Following the ridge for
a couple of miles, we came to where it ended, abutting
on a wide valley, or rather expanse of forest-covered
hills and ridges 3000 feet below us (amid which runs
the river Yora, which we could see here and there
winding in the forest), and in a nook or glen of which
lies the little cantonment and military settlement of
Gambor, which, from where we stood, looked like a
white patch in an ocean of green. Resting here for a
space, we prepared to descend, by selecting a likely-
looking ridge, a business requiring consideration and
experience, as you may otherwise come to an impossible
drop of precipitous ground, and have to hark back and
make a fresh cast. This time fortune favoured us; a
blind footpath, which we followed into the dense cover
below, after a deal of scrambling through thickets, high
fern and nettles, and jumping the horses over fallen
logs, led us into an araba track (used to bring down
timber during the winter), which took us to a little

hamlet near the river. Fording the stream, at the
bottom of a very steep and stony descent of 300 yards
from the village, we arrived (after much winding and
turning in the dusk, at the bottom of a gloomy glen)
at Gambor.

Gambor is an artillery cantonment (for convenience
of forage) ; a battery is stationed here ; and there is,
besides, a reservist military settlement, comprising a
long street of wooden thatched houses, gardens, and
the usual untidy stabling, cowhouses, and scrubby
agricultural arrangements. The reservists have patches
of land on the hillsides around in different directions,
where they raise wheat, potatoes, rye, and the inevitable white-headed cabbage, without which a Russian
is nowhere. They also cut and stack large crops of
hay, the surplus of which they are allowed to transport
and sell in Tiflis. Every Russian soldier has a right,
if tolerably well conducted, to demand his discharge
after five years' service, and a plot of land in one of
these communities, where, if hardworking and sober,
he and his wife (he always marries) are often better off
than they would be in Russia. If a big war takes place,
the reserve is called out, and serious grief ensues to
the wives and young families; but a big war only comes
off on an average once in a quarter of a century. We
put up at one of the reservist's houses, housed and off-
saddled the horses in a cowshed, supplying them plentifully with hay, preparatory to the barley, which after
a hard day's work is better given later on.

Our landlady, a stout bustling "Mother Bunch"
sort of old girl, whose husband had been killed in the

war, and who had been left with a houseful of children,
got a samovar under steam, and we were just sitting
down to a tea dinner, or rather supper, for it was between 8 and 9 P.M., when the C.O., whom I had met
at Tiflis at the house of a mutual friend, and who is a
first-rate fellow, sent over to invite us to put up at his
bungalow.

He being a married man, I excused myself, on the
score of being in jungle costume (or rather in Circassian,
which is the Caucasian equivalent); and though they
insisted that that made no difference whatever (which
I knew beforehand) I was resolute; the fact being, that
after a hard day's work Russian hospitality is rather a
formidable affair, for the following reasons:—Russians
do not breakfast; they drink tea about 8 or 9 A.M.,
after which they get through their day's work, dining,
or rather lunching, about 2 or 3 P.M.   After dining
they go to sleep for the afternoon, rousing up about
4 or 5 P.M., and teaing from 6 to 9, after and during
which they play cards and smoke or talk till 11
or 12 P.M., when they have supper, finally retiring
from midnight till 2 A.M.   Consequently, if, after
riding from "morn till dewy eve," you put up with a
Russian gentleman, you will find the family round
the samovar.   They will be thoroughly glad to see
you; acquaintances will drop in, and you will have to
drink tea, smoke, and make yourself agreeable till
supper-time, which, as they are certain to order an
extra good one in your honour, will not appear till midnight.   This is well enough for those who have been
asleep since 3 P.M., but is " rough " on you who have

ridden forty or fifty miles, perhaps with only a scratch
meal and glass of brandy-and-water at mid-day,. and
besides intend being on the road before daybreak, to
say nothing of the probability of your horses being
left untended and unfoddered.   A Russian host, however, "cares for none of these things," and is by no
means pleased at your refusal; in fact, a Russian
traveller would certainly accept (possibly sitting up
with his entertainer till near daybreak and emptying
three or four bottles), leaving next day's journey to
take care of itself.   My excuses, however, passed
muster, and by daybreak we were again *en route*, this
time along a good macadamised post-road, which,
after long circuitous winding from Tiflis, through
steppes and valleys to avoid the mountains, passes
by Gambor, and crossing a high "pereval," "col,"
"kotul," or "ghat," by many zig-zags, descends into
the Kakhetian valley.

This road, which has not been long constructed,
enables the famous wine of the country to get by a
short cut to Tiflis, and we passed shortly after daybreak many arabas groaning and creaking under
huge borachios of the vintage, made of entire buffalo
skins, some of which must have contained nearly a
couple of hogsheads.   About half-way up the ascent
a lofty and picturesque-looking peak juts out from
the range on the right, and in the beetling precipice,
which forms the face fronting the road, are several of
those mysterious caverns or cave - dwellings very
common in Georgia, by some said to be ancient
sepulchres, by others habitations.   They may have

been used as sepulchres in Persia, but in Georgia
were, I suspect, constructed in prehistoric times as
places of refuge, being found everywhere; not only
in the vicinity of populated centres, but in out-of-
the-way forests, where no signs of ancient cultivation
exist.   It is known that they were used as refuges
during Tamerlane's invasion, equally with the
numerous ancient strongholds and rude fortresses
which are constantly met with in the depths of
Georgian forests, miles away from any habitation.   It
is a pity that these caverns, which are very numerous,
are not regularly and scientifically explored.   They
are always cut in rude horizontal tiers or rows, sometimes of three or four openings only, often of six,
eight, or ten, in the face of precipices, and are often
quite inaccessible except by ropes let down from
above.   It seems improbable that the ancient inhabitants of the country should have taken the trouble
to construct such places, often in the remotest jungles,
merely for tombs, besides which *very* ancient tombs of
the bronze and flint periods (often underlying layers of
more modern but still ancient places of interment), have
been unearthed in the Caucasus, always in the ground,
and I have heard of no remains being discovered in the
caves.   If constructed as refuges, they would have
always been useful in time of danger, whether situated
in forests or in populated parts of the country.

Along the grassy crest of the ridge, which we
reached in about an hour, were many Tartar "yailaks"
or summer camps, with sheep and cattle feeding, and
while halting a moment at a stream, down the opposite

slope of the "divide," a tribe of gipsies with their
cattle and paraphernalia passed us. They were, like
all the Caucasian gipsies, evidently genuine Hindo-
stanees, with hardly a trace of foreign admixture, but,
being nominally Mahometans, talked the rough
Turkish of the Kizilbash, or Tartar, as he is usually
here designated. After a long gradual descent from
the pass down a fine wooded valley with open slopes
and meadows here and there, the road suddenly de-
bouches into the valley of Kakhetia, a magnificent
panorama of villages and vineyards, orchards and
cornfields, at the foot of the great Caucasian chain
which towers 10,000 feet immediately above it.

This valley, the richest part of the Caucasus and
perhaps of Asia Minor, is a regular "Land of Goshen,
Capua, and Castle of Indolence." It is about eight
miles in breadth, counting from the foot of the wooded
mountains on each side of it, from which flow hundreds
of rills of water conducted by little canals over the
gradually descending slope (about 3 in 100) to
the river in the centre, and fertilising every yard of
it at pleasure. You ride through a wilderness of
vineyards, fruit orchards, melon patches, cornfields,
and great groves of walnut trees, the nuts on which
are so soft shelled that you can crack them between
your fingers. It is impossible to imagine greater
abundance — you see fruit everywhere ; even the
hedges and surrounding jungles are full of wild grapes,
apples, pears, medlars, and hazel-nuts, and in the
spring, of roses and wild flowers much finer than
their European congeners and varieties. Passing a

large fortified monastery above the road, we came, in
about an hour's ride, to Telav, the principal town of
the western end of the valley, a solid stone-built and
stone-paved street running along a sort of ridge with
a small bazaar and old fortified church in the centre,
vineyards and gardens everywhere, passing through
which we made for the farm of a friend of mine,
about five miles beyond, which we reached at mid-day.
By this time the sun had again made us remember
him, for the valley is not more than 2000 feet above
sea-level, and our twenty miles' ride made us glad to
descend from our horses.   Indeed, I had been watching our progress towards the fine row of poplars
which mark Monsieur Audon's house, with considerable interest for some time, lest we should be too late
for breakfast.

M. Audon, the owner of the farm and vineyard,
came (like most of the French residents) to the
Caucasus just after the Crimean War.   After various
experiences he finally settled down in Kakhetia at his
old trade of vine-growing and farming, and was now,
he told me, making from £300 to £400 per annum.
He had been through the Crimean War, and in Algeria,
and seen a deal of Caucasian life.   The house, an
oblong German-built affair, stood in the middle of a
compound, filled with fruit trees of all sorts, the turf
beneath them being covered with fine apples and
pears, which no one took the trouble to pick up.   The
outbuildings comprised a first-class cellar for storing
wine, filled with huge vats, butts, and hogsheads of
last year's vintage.   The farm itself consisted of

about forty acres of vineyard, wheat, and potato land
of first-rate quality.   The vineyard portion, which
was in full bearing, the grapes just ripening, was a
picture of luxuriance ; grapes of four different varieties
—two French and two native.   The whole land,
house, and garden were surrounded · by a strong and
impenetrable hedge, of great height and thickness, in
which blackberries, cornels, and other wild fruits
flourished in incredible abundance, and was irrigated
by a little canal running from a mountain stream,
which could be turned on or off at pleasure.   Add to
this, magnificent scenery and climate, fair shooting,
consisting of hares and pheasants, close at hand, an
industrious and hardworking wife, whose poultry yard
was a marvel of productiveness, and one would think
all that could be wished for was to hand, but "*Surgit
amari aliquid.*"   He complained of the people of the
country, who, he said, were so intolerably lazy, and
stupidly antiquated and conceited, that he could do
next to nothing with them as labourers, without
infinity of bother and trouble, always recommencing.
They were all too well off, living was too easy, and
would often not work at all, so that he was seriously
thinking of importing men from the Black Sea side
of the country.   In addition, he complained that his
neighbours were perpetually borrowing wine, flour,
tools, etc., which, if not lent, caused ill-will, and if lent
were not returned.   In fact, a general tendency to "best"
foreigners is observable everywhere in the Caucasus.

At about a mile from. Audon's farm is a two-
storied house and demesne belonging to Prince T.,

one of the first, if not the first, family in Georgia, being closely allied both to the hereditary prince of the country and to Prince Nicholas, the hereditary "Dadian," or little King of Mingrelia. One of Schamyl's last feats before his surrender was to abduct the Princess T., her sister, her French governess, and, in fact, the whole of the female part of the family, including servants (as Audon phrased it, *toute la boutique*), from this building, and carry them off to his mountain fastness of Ghonnib in Daghestan, in order to exchange them with his son, then a prisoner in the hands of the Russians. Audon has often pointed me out the gorge in the main chain opposite, by which this "chupao" was effected into the plain, causing a stampede of the entire population into the mountains on the south side of the valley.

A partial stampede took place during the late war, when a mountain tribe in the big range revolted, or rather took up arms, and attacked another tribe who, they considered, had unjustly usurped some of their pastures. Audon told me that he was the only man left in that part of the valley, on this occasion, during a couple of days. It turned out, as he expected, to be a scare, as far as a raid on the valley was concerned. The pious and orthodox Shereffedin Ali, by the by, in his *Life of Timour Beg*, gives a graphic account of the sack of this same fertile valley of Kakhetia by Timour's army in the fifteenth century, since when, as far as one can judge, the manners and customs of the mass of the population have altered very little, if at all. Timour purposely

marched upon it during the winter, knowing that at
that season the unfortunate inhabitants would be unable to take refuge to any great extent in the mountains, which are then usually under deep snow, as,
indeed, is the valley likewise at times. His biographer,
after describing the great hunting-parties organised by
the Tartar army in the Mogan steppe, where Timour
passed the autumn encamped, relates that—" We continued our journey by forced marches, Timour rarely
descending from his saddle, while our troops killed and
plundered (*sic*) every one of a different religion that
they met; for the intention of Timour in this war
being nothing but 'the Glory of God,' it was blessed
of Heaven, and every day we acquired considerable
booty." In recounting the sack of the valley he cheer-
fully remarks—" Very soon the side of the mountain,
which had been a pure white with snow, became 'as
red as a field of tulips' with the blood of these in-
fidels. The execrable chief of these accursed, aban-
doning his goods and family, took to flight. Afterwards we burned all the houses and pillaged all the
villages; and as wine is absolutely necessary to these
people, in order to incommode them still more, and
ruin them entirely, we rooted up all their vineyards,
which they had planted with great trouble, and cut
down or ringed all their fruit trees. We then razed
to the ground all the buildings, especially the churches,
in which they make their *adorations disagreeable to
God.*" He goes on to observe sententiously that—
" What *is* very remarkable, is that only the year
before Timour was occupied at Delhi and on the

K

banks of the Ganges in this very same pious work,
destroying the temples and shrines of the accursed
Hindoo idolaters, so that, as the poet says," etc.

But to return to Prince T. His case is a brilliant
specimen of the way the Russian Government behave
to such of the native nobility as possess enough
territorial and personal influence to make it expedient
to "attach them" firmly to Muscovite rule. Prince
T.'s original rent-roll (from his estates), when he
entered into possession a good many years ago, was
about 50,000 roubles, or, say, £5500 per annum.
He considered, however, that as a prince of the
blood, it behoved him to live up to his title, and
accordingly travelled about, or rather "progressed,"
with an escort of noble retainers, all well mounted
and magnificently armed, keeping the while, on the
"old Irish gentleman" principle, open house perpetually for all-comers. This, however, would not
have damaged his income, to speak of. His ancestors had all kept armed retainers, hawks, and
hounds, and open house, without encumbering their
estates or coming to grief. But the prince, being a
"civilised" prince, found it necessary, and "the
thing" in fact, to give town entertainments and card
parties, and to make expensive journeys to, and expensive sojournings at St. Petersburg, which his
ancestors had *not* done. Consequently he soon found
himself, like all the fashionable "well-received"
Georgian nobility, hard pressed for coin, or rather for
rouble notes, coin not existing in this part of the
world, except in the hoards of certain Armenian money-

changers, and as a curiosity in collections and museums.
He accordingly did what every honest and patriotic
"kniaz" in straitened circumstances does, *i.e.* he applied to the Government Deposit Bank, and received,
at tolerably high interest, an advance of 300,000
roubles (£30,000) on security of his landed property,
effecting at the same time (while he had his hand in)
an "emprunt" from an Armenian capitalist to the
tune of 50,000 roubles more, on the same security.
This £35,000 odd hundred, however, speedily followed
the rest, and the prince was, till lately, harder up than
ever.   Indeed, he and his family had (a sure sign of
impecuniosity with native noblemen, who have been
all carefully trained by a paternal government to
detest country life) to pass most of their time rusti-
cating on the estates, unable, it is whispered, even to
invite visitors to stay with them.   Last year, however,
through the influence of his brother-in-law, the great
Baron N., late chief of the civil administration of the
Caucasus, a post possessing the status (in civil matters)
of a lieutenant-governor of a presidency in India, and
through the interest of his wife's sister, the Princess-
Dowager of Mingrelia, whose son, Prince Nicholas, is
in high favour at the Imperial Court, he was not only
released from the Government debt of £30,000, which,
with arrears of interest, was wiped off the record, but
has received a Government grant of petroleum wells
at Baku, which he has disposed of for 250,000 roubles.
He thus gets back his estates all clear, and finds himself
(after paying off the Armenian banker's 50,000 roubles)
with upwards of £20,000 in his pocket to the good.

After spending a couple of days with Audon,
passed in talking politics — principally French —
smoking, eating, and drinking very superior white
Kakhetian wine, which Audon, just before breakfast
and just before dinner, extracted from the cool depths
of his cellar, we concluded to return, but by a different
route, in order to vary the entertainment.   Accordingly we made straight towards the mountains on the
south flank by a bridle-track leading through any
number of vineyards, and past a couple of villages, each
with little tumble-down gray stone chapels (looking
as if they had been pulled down by Timour's fellows,
and built up again crooked, as they probably had),
crossed a shoulder of the mountain covered with dense
oak forest, and dived down into a ravine or valley,
through whose centre flowed a small river, the sources
of which lay high up in the wooded mountain ranges
in front between us and Tiflis.   After following the
wide shingly bed of the ravine for about a couple of
miles, we passed a great number of cave-dwellings, or
refuges cut in the face of a lofty precipice immediately
overhanging the road to our right.   It would have
been possible to have reached one or two of the lowest
tier of openings by felling a tree where the scarped
face of the precipice joined the steep slope below, and
I should have much liked to explore them ; but the
attempt would have taken a couple of days to effect
properly, and Audon, being engaged in harvesting,
could not spare the time.   As we proceeded, the
valley closed in more and more.   After eight or nine
miles, along a tolerable forest road, through a perfect

jungle of wild fruit of different sorts, the track crossed
the shingly bed of the torrent, and struck up a very
steep muddy incline, which some woodcutters had not
improved by sledging logs down it. It was as much
as the horses could do to keep their footing. Having
got over this, we found ourselves in a lofty beech forest,
the ground beneath full of quagmires, twisted roots,
deep holes, and all sorts of disagreeable riding. The
quagmires, full of gluey mud, are even dangerous.
You never know the depth beforehand; and if your
horse gets in well over his hocks, it is as much as he
can do to extricate himself, the efforts he makes being
liable to send him rolling on the top of you, so that
you are in constant dread of a mud bath. However,
by keeping a sharp look-out, and by careful handling
of the animals, cramming them through thickets,
jumping logs, and taking detours to avoid bad places,
"by wily turns and desperate bounds," we managed
to negotiate the worst part of it without grief. The
first time I came this way (from Tiflis), a wrong turn
on the top of the mountain brought me to a very
wild part of the range, and it was with a good deal
of trouble and danger that I reached the villages at
all. I was alone, and saw no one the whole day, except two or three wild-looking swineherds, who took
me for an abrêk,[1] and wound up by getting "pounded"
at the bottom of a gorge, from which I had some considerable difficulty in extricating myself. After again

---

[1] *Abrêk*, the equivalent for "haiduk" and "yagee" in Turkish and
Persian, "an outlaw," "banished man." There are a "good few" in
the Caucasus.

crossing a torrent through a chaos of piled rocks, and
doing another quagmire beech forest, but not so bad
as the first, we came to good safe riding in a shingly
river-bottom, and after a mile or two of this to a vast
green amphitheatre of fine pasture, dotted with clumps
of beech trees in all the glory of autumn foliage. At
the base of the ascent was a Tartar "yailak" or summer
camp. The men were absent, but some scarlet-dressed
women were hard at work churning butter in goat-
skins. We tried to get some milk or curds from them,
but the barking of the dogs, who sallied out to meet
us in a regular pack, was so furious that we could
hardly make ourselves heard, and it would not have
been safe to alight without shooting two or three of
the brutes as a preliminary.

Tartar dogs are aggravating. You ride up to a
camp to ask your way, and long before you get there
are surrounded by a mob of them, snapping at your
boots and your horse's nose, and barking enough to
deafen you. The leading dog will often catch your
horse's tail in his mouth, and hold on, dodging the
best-directed kicks, and putting everything you were
going to say out of your head, so that the temptation
to commence pistol practice is almost irresistible.
After riding slowly up a grassy ridge of the mountain
for a mile or so, we passed through a hanging forest
of splendid beeches, through which the ancient bridle-
path twisted and wound, presently emerging on to the
summit of the range, an expanse of short sweet grass,
along which we rode for several miles, with magnificent scenery on either hand, passing here and there

Tartar camps and temporary châlets.   We were about
7000 feet elevation.   On arriving at a bend in the
range where the track suddenly quits the crest of the
mountain, we halted to give our horses a feed on the
rich herbage and enjoy the panorama.   Gambor was
out of sight, round a shoulder ; but we could see the
white buildings of the little cantonment of Makravan,
across a sea of forest stretching for miles below us,
with here and there the ruins of some ancient monastery or rude fortress peeping from the trees.

Descending by a very steep path for the first
quarter of a mile, we entered a nearly level stretch
of fine forest, which became denser as we descended,
till the path, which gradually sinks for two or three
miles, turned a shoulder of the mountain, hard by an
open meadow of seven or eight acres, surrounded by
dense and luxuriant hazels, and dotted with wild plum,
apple, and pear trees.   As the grazing looked particularly fine I decided to encamp, if we could find water,
which, as some of the grass had been mown and rudely
stacked, I knew was to be had somewhere.   We set
to work to explore, but though we hunted all over
the lower end of the maidan, could find none ; but on
approaching the upper portion we came upon a scrubby
sort of grass hut, with adjacent barley patch, from
which a ragged evil-looking old ruffian, followed by a
dilapidated woman and four or five children of various
ages, as wild as " lungoors" and much dirtier, presently
emerged.   They were a dreadfully Yahoo-looking lot,
and, of course, did not understand a word of Russian ;
but on Freddy speaking Georgian, the old rascal said

there was water near the road farther down ; asked
why we wanted to encamp at the meadow; and showed
a disposition to be bumptious. However, I took no
notice beyond telling him we would give him a "buck-
sheesh" if he was civil. Making him point out the
exact spot where the water was to be found, we chose
a place near it to encamp in, and took the "khoorjens"
off the saddles. I had just began loosening the girths
when I discovered I had lost my "beshlik," and guessing it must have dropped while we were scrambling
through the high ferns and bushes at the other end
of the maidan in search of water, remounted and went
for it. While returning I heard Freddy fire his revolver, and on galloping back, thinking he had let it
off by accident and perhaps shot himself, found him
surrounded by the group, and the old rascal talking
excitedly. Freddy said he fired to show them it was
loaded, as he did not like the way they were going on
while I was away, examining our things, etc. Dismounting again I began picketing the animals to feed,
when the old man coolly ordered me to clear out, unless we would agree to pay him two roubles for each
horse for a night's grazing. As grass in these out-of-
the-way places is worth about two roubles a stack, and
as I had just as much right to it as he had, it being
Government property, I merely laughed at him; but
the next thing he did was to begin letting the horses
loose, so I dispelled his illusions by a tap on the nape
of the neck with my whip, which nearly knocked him
down. His wife began screaming and dragging him
off, and he went, cursing us heavily in Georgian. I

was just thinking that I ought to have given him some
more, when Freddy told me that, while I was away,
he had threatened that unless we gave him the four
roubles it would be the worse for us, as there were five
abrêks near at hand, as well armed as we were, whom
he would set to steal our horses before morning. This
information rather disgusted me, as I knew for a fact
that there were abrêks in those forests, with whom it
was of course not only possible, but probable, that the
old scoundrel was intimate.   Accordingly, as we had
no dogs, I picketed the horses some distance off, in
order to save the grass nearer the fire till later on, and
concluded to wake up and watch after midnight.
About dusk, as we were boiling the kettle, an individual (not the old man, but some other) hailed us from
the meadow and asked what we were doing, but getting
no answer cleared off without coming nearer ; and
about nine or ten I saw some one else creeping up,
who, however, turned out to be the wife. She told us
that she had advised the old man not to " try it on "
with us without effect, for that ever since he had
bounced a couple of Russians who came there shooting
two months before out of some money, by threatening
to get their horses stolen, he was always for doing it.
She said he was a bad lot, and had given her a beat-
ing when he got back to his hovel, for reminding him
that she had " told him how it would be." She
begged us not to feed our horses on the barley.   I
told her I would have given her husband half a rouble
or so if he had been civil, and gave her forty kopecks
(to convince her that soft sawder was the best policy),

with which she retired.   This might have been a ruse
to put us off our guard, so I kept a look-out at intervals, and the horses hobbled and tied close up, but
we were not disturbed any more, and by daybreak had
saddled up and left.

I had an adventure in this forest on a former
occasion with abrêks while trying to hit off a short
cut to the crest of the mountain from the old Gambor
road.   Having taken a wrong direction, I got led
from one blind trail to another, all ending nowhere,
till I at last took a line of my own and went
straight through the forest, hoping to strike upon a
track which would lead up to the ridge.   After an
hour or two's winding about in dense covert, through
all sorts of difficulties and obstacles, we found a trail
which seemed to lead directly up the mountain, but
was very little used.   There were the fresh tracks of
two or three horses on it, generally a sure sign that a
path leads to the summit of a range.   It became,
however, more and more "blind," winding about,
now in heavy undergrowth, now along precipitous
ground, and up and down ravines and hollows.   The
horse-tracks being still visible I pushed on, till the
trail, after mounting to a very great height over
steep ground, completely disappeared in a little flat
covered with fern and hazel bushes, on the edge of
a deep chasm of many hundred feet.   I had been
so occupied in finding the way as to have quite
forgotten the existence of abrêks, and was just thinking what horses could be possibly doing in such
a place, when I saw a "choga" lying on the ground

close to some newly-cut grass, on which lay a sickle, evidently just dropped; and, looking closely about, was presently aware of the narrow opening to an old half-underground hut, so overgrown with rank grass, nettles, and brambles, as at first to be completely indistinguishable. Indeed, had a few ferns or a green branch of a bush been cleverly placed in front of it no one would have dreamt that a hut existed there, as the opening was not above a couple of feet high, and a little less in width, more of a hole than a doorway. Not a soul was visible, and we called out several times in Georgian and Tartar with no result, though they must have been somewhere close at hand. As the trail ended at the hut, and as further exploration might have resulted in " looking down a gun-barrel and seeing the charge come out," I gracefully went " threes about " and retired. The men could not have been there for any legitimate purpose. There was hardly any grass; what there was was rank and bad. Besides, ordinary junglewallahs, woodcutters, shikarees, etc., are always glad enough to see anybody on the chance of getting a drink or some tobacco, and would have answered our shouts. The horses were probably stolen ones; and, catching a glimpse of us through the bushes, they took us for Cossacks who had tracked them out.

Striking down into the valley through the forest, by devious paths at dewy morn, we hit off the old Gambor post-road and, passing a ruined chapel and monastery in a hollow, crossed the Yora, and worked along the opposite bank, leaving Makravan on the left.

In this valley of the Yora, on a rocky spur overhanging the river half way between Makravan and
Gambor, is a fine specimen of one of the ancient refuge
castles.   It is built on a rocky hill (rising some 500
feet above the valley bottom), the steep, almost precipitous, sides of which, covered with dense forest,
stretch down to the stream.   There being no water in
or near the fortress, they had constructed a high double
wall, or sort of open corridor, with a flight of steps
inside leading down to the stream, protected every
twenty or thirty yards by towers built across it,
which, in turn, were commanded by the castle
above.   Inside the "hold" was an ancient oratory,
and the remains of chambers, passages, and galleries.   It was probably constructed subsequent to
Genghis Khan's invasion.   Near it, in the forest, are
two or three ruined chapels.   Indeed, these wilds are
dotted over with ruined towers, chapels, and monasteries, showing the state of insecurity which formerly prevailed.   The predatory Tartar and Persian
armies, being mainly composed of cavalry, did not care
to follow into mountain fastnesses, by blind footpaths
made still more impassable by fallen trees, through
gloomy defiles often obstinately defended by a hardy
peasantry ; they accordingly, after devastating the
villages and open country, were obliged eventually to
quit even that, there being nothing left to burn or
plunder.   When they had quite gone the population
gradually returned from their towers of refuge in the
mountains, looked up the hidden stores of grain, and
repaired their habitations.   This state of affairs exist-

ing normally all over Western and Central Asia
(strong settled Governments, like our own in India
and the Russians in the Caucasus, being quite exceptional, and, after all, things of yesterday which *may*
disappear to-morrow),—this state of affairs, I say,
though barbarous and perhaps uncomfortable, had its
advantages. The population was kept within due
limits, food and provisions were extraordinarily cheap
because money was scarce. The people, if more rude,
were more hardy, courageous, and warlike, and just
as clever and full of resource as they are now; often
more so, for it is in times of *real* danger and difficulty
that "nous" and presence of mind are most required.

Reaching Gambor about 11 A.M., we halted in a
garden for breakfast and fed the horses, starting again,
after a siesta, down the valley, or rather up. Crossing
the river at a Greek hamlet about six miles from
Gambor, we came, towards evening, to a little Georgian village on the spur of a big mountain. Here we
found the inhabitants, it being harvest-time, all drunk
or stupefied, for Georgians rarely reap while sober.
They do not get " tired with the labour and heat of
the day," and then drink to keep themselves going,
as one might suppose, but regularly prepare themselves by getting drunk before they begin work.
When the corn is judged to be nearly ready they
lay in (if it is not already to hand) enough wine to
make the whole community intoxicated for two or
three days, or as long as they expect the harvest (*i.e.*
cutting and carrying the corn) to last. This being
arranged, they drink hard early on the morning of

the day they intend to begin work, and, as soon
as they feel "fit," seize their sickles and implements,
yoke their oxen, and rush into the corn, yelling,
shouting, singing, dancing, and jumping like a lot of
maniacs, or a mob of Irishmen "going in" at a fac-
tion fight.   This goes on more or less the whole day,
the excitement being kept up by tom-toms, and fresh
supplies of liquor brought to the field in goat-
skins, until by evening they are done up and hoarse
with shouting.   It is noticeable that they have an
air of scrambling and fighting for the crop, snatching
armfuls of it from each other, and rushing towards
the arabas ; while many of them carry daggers, pistols,
etc., on these occasions, though the practice of doing
so, except when on a journey, away from home, is falling out of repute.   It is probable that this way of harvesting is a "survival" from some ancient period when
the crops belonged to the community at large, who actually fought for it, the strongest getting the lion's
share.   There are other indications of a sort of commu-
nism having once extensively prevailed in the Caucasus.

Quitting these drunkards after a short dialogue,
having for its object to discover the nearest cut to
the summit of the range, we kept gradually ascending, always in dense forest, by a good "araba" road,
i.e. good for the mountains, till we had mounted to
about 4000 feet elevation above the river.   It was
getting dusk when we reached an open plateau covered
with fine herbage, some of which had been mown for
hay, and a standing barley-crop, which at this elevation
seldom ripens before the middle or end of September.

There was no hut there, and not a soul to be seen, but we could hear the distant barking of dogs at intervals from some châlet high up the mountain, whose grassy summit loomed above us in the fading daylight. There was plenty of dry wood and water, so we speedily had the "khoorjens" off, a fire lighted, and the kettle suspended, supplying the horses meantime plentifully with cut grass, amongst which I rather fear that Freddy, who is fond of animals, and especially horses, gave them (by mistake; he is *very* short-sighted, and it was nearly dark) some barley as well. Presently the moon rose and we passed a quiet evening ; the widespreading beeches kept off the dew, the fire brightly burning kept off the autumnal chill, while a pipe and glass of grog produced philosophical calmness and tranquillity.

Freddy soon slept the sleep of the just, and after re-picketing the horses on to fresh pasture I also slumbered undisturbed, except by the occasional bark of a roe-deer, until an hour or so before dawn, when we arose perfectly refreshed, made tea, and by daybreak were again *en route.* Crossing the corn-field, which was surrounded on every side by very high forest, we soon struck a cattle-track which led us, after a severe pull of 1000 feet, the ground being too steep to ride the horses without punishing them, to some châlets, passing which, after the usual dog skirmish, we reached the open ground at the summit of the range.

There was a heavy driving mist, however, and cold wind, which did not clear off until we had done several miles, by which time we found ourselves opposite the monastery of Saint Anthony, but, of course, still high

above it.   However, a rapid trudge down the intervening slope brought us to the bottom of a "khud,"
where we mounted, and ten minutes' ride along a
good hill road, through the woods, brought us under
the ancient gray walls, tower, and belfry of the sacred
building.[1]   This old fortified monastery is a favourite
place of resort from Tiflis during the summer months ;
tents are pitched there, picnic parties arranged, a
regular little market held by the villagers every
morning outside, and groups of elegantly-dressed
young ladies may be met promenading in the bosky
woods around.   Their Paris-fashioned costumes and
the black coats, pot hats, and stiff collars of their
admirers, form a curious contrast to the rough "caf-
tans," "chogas," and fur caps of the Georgian villagers
or Tartar horsemen who pass along occasionally ; just
as the fiddling, dancing, card-playing, and scandal of
Tiflis contrast strangely with the gloomy Ishmael-like
life of the Tartars who inhabit the adjacent steppes.

[1] Saint Anthony was a hermit, or "rishi," who ages ago inhabited a
hermitage on a peak of the mountain some 500 feet above the monastery
which, after his death, was built in honour of him. Unlike the Catholic
Saint Anthony, he appears to have lived peacefully and tranquilly.
Several rude oil paintings in the monastery represent him as accompanied by a large stag with branching antlers. His cell, which still exists,
is close under a ruined stone tower of immense antiquity, built on a jutting crag. On the summit of the peak, from which the crag and tower
project, is an ancient "deota" amongst gnarled oaks, to which votive
offerings are still made by the villagers, as to another shrine far below in
a wooded gorge, through which a footpath winds up from the villages in
the valley to the monastery. On a wooded spur a mile or so from
the monastery is an ancient ruined chapel dedicated to Saint George,
with a rude stone carving of Saint George and the Dragon. Saint
George is much reverenced by Eastern Christians, and even by the
Turks.

CHAPTER VI.

THE TARTARS AND THE KARYAS STEPPE.

THE Karyas steppe is an enormous "maidan," or barren plain, lying south of Tiflis, along the left bank of the Cyrus or Koura, extending for scores of miles, destitute for the most part of drinkable water, and surrounded on the north-east by dust hills much resembling those around Attock or Rawal Pindi.

On the plain, however, a good deal of wild shooting of one sort or another is to be picked up by a persevering and adventurous shikaree — curved-horned antelopes, flocks of great bustards, little ditto, hares, quail, sand-grouse, and quantities of wild fowl —along the river, or wherever there is water. Consequently, having acquaintances living on a portion of the steppe, which has been reclaimed and irrigated by means of a small canal, I used, whenever I could find a companion (and sometimes when I could not), to proceed there on horseback, i.e. during the winter and early spring. In the summer, heat, malaria, and

L

mosquitoes make the game not worth the candle. The Karyas steppe, which, like the still more extensive one of Mogan, on the right bank lower down, is almost deserted during the summer, becomes in winter a general rendezvous for the Kizilbash Tartars, who make it their headquarters and general grazing-ground.

These Kizilbash (commonly called Tartars by the Russians and Christian population) form at least two-thirds of the population of the eastern districts of the Caucasus, comprising the valley of the Koura, lower part of Kakhetia, up to the base of the Daghestan Hills, with the tracts around Zanga (Elizabethpol) and Shusha,[1] as far as Nakhetchivan,[2] where the Armenian element begins to predominate; and thence away again by the Mogan[3] and the Caspian to Derbend and Temir Khan Schoura.[4] They are light, well-built, active fellows, very hardy, standing any amount of fatigue and exposure. They shine chiefly as horsemen, forming the very best material for irregular cavalry in the Caucasus, or perhaps in the world, having all the good points of the Tcherkess, Daghestans, and other mountaineers, with the faculty of obeying orders and submitting to discipline and regulation, which the former will not do. Nevertheless,

[1] Shusha, a great Mahometan "centre" in the Karabagh district. There is a fine breed of horses in this part of the country.

[2] Nakhetchivan, in the Araxes valley, close to the Persian frontier. Noah is supposed to have settled here after the deluge.

[3] The Mogan steppe, great plains at the confluence of the Araxes and Cyrus, extending to the Caspian Sea.

[4] Temir Khan Schoura, near Derbend.

though there are plenty of Kizilbash officers, some of high rank, and numbers of Tartar privates scattered about in different corps in the same proportion to Russian soldiers as that of the other numerous nationalities of which the overgrown empire is built up, the Government does not care to raise separate regiments of them. They have a gloomy look, somewhat crabbed and sulky, but like most " good men," hold bumptiousness and servility in equal contempt. You do not get from a Tartar any of the " cheek " which an Armenian, Georgian, or Russian is often ready to display. As to morals, perhaps the less said the better; but here note that, if a Tartar wants any chicanery or rascality of a legal nature " put through," he bribes an Armenian to do it for him. He considers robbery, after a manly cavalier fashion, on the highway or by raiding, as an " art," " disport," or " recreation," which every proper man ought to know something of—a sort of private war; but pilfering, cheating, and larceny are beneath him.

These men formed the mainstay of the Persian armies of former days (almost entirely composed of cavalry), which, under Prince Hamza[1] and his brother Shah Abbas, often defeated the Turks in spite of their artillery. With these men (or rather with their ancestors) Nadir Shah drove the Afghans from Persia, and afterwards invaded India and sacked Delhi; and amongst them almost every important heresy or

[1] Hamza Mirza, a famous Persian prince; he was afterwards poisoned, it is supposed, at the instigation of Shah Abbas, who was jealous of his military renown. He signally defeated the Turks in several battles.

schism, which has set Islamism by the ears, from the time of Babek[1] the Horremite (institutor of the sect of "no-religion-at-all-wallahs" in the eighth century), down to the present day, has arisen. Many of the great "Omrahs" who ruled India under the Moguls came from these provinces, then of course part of Persia—notably Meer Jumlah, the famous Minister of Aurangzeb, whose tomb is still to be seen at Agra, and who is said to have walked (on foot) from his native land to Delhi. There are many Shubias among the Kizilbash, a sect who decry sectarianism, holding that Shiahs should not be preferred to Soonnis, or Soonnis to Shiahs, both being good Mahometans.

During the late war, when the Russians were getting the worst of it, the Tartars used to say openly that "they were waiting to see red caps." Had

[1] Babek was a remarkable "practical politician," a sort of Asiatic John of Leyden, who has been undeservedly forgotten. He undertook to abolish both Islamism and Christianity, as being "phases of thought productive of bloodshed and persecution," and to substitute "nothing." He preached this doctrine vigorously, and got together a large and effective force, with which he completely defeated an orthodox army sent against him by the caliph, killing Ebu Hamid, its commander-in-chief, with his own hand. He was eventually, after much campaigning, in the course of which, if I recollect aright, he got as far as Damascus, betrayed by a Greek, and executed by the caliph's order. He travelled with ten executioners, and committed serious excesses. The chief executioner admitted having himself "operated" on 20,000 people, but could not speak as to the other nine. Mahometanism (like some other religions) was itself not "made with rose water." Hedjaj, governor or satrap of one of the first caliphs, executed 120,000 men to his own score, and had 50,000 others in prison, according to his historians, at the time of his death awaiting execution. The severities exercised by the first caliphs were extraordinary, and these it was which caused Babek's doctrines to "take" readily.

the red caps become visible, what the Persians call a
"kharabi singui" would have probably taken place in
such sort as to make the Bulgarian atrocity business
hide its diminished head.

There is a Tartar proverb which says, "Do not
fear wars and trouble, for that is the time when
impostors are detected."[1]   Another, which would
"bear acclimatisation" (in the Transvaal or Afghanistan), purports that, "He who is fond of eating
guano should always carry a spoon with him," meaning that he will always, when once his tastes have
been ascertained, find plenty of people who will supply
him with the comestible in question.   Unfortunately
some of the best and most epigrammatic are unfit, in
this Grundyish age, for print.

Taking the left bank of the river, and traversing
the Avlabar quarter, you strike the Signac and
Kakhetia road, which you cross at the General Hospital, a huge barrack, or rather series of barracks,
pass the village of Nafluk, and progress along a
cutcha road, with the river on your right, and a
barren rolling desert country on your left.   Some
miles off on your left, situated in the above wilderness, is a tract of partially reclaimed land, which
forms another specimen of the manner in which "resources are developed" by a beneficent Caucasian
administration.   A former "civil governor of the
Caucasus," whom we will call Baron T., conceived

---

[1] Literally, "the season when the harvest of hypocrites is gathered in."
This proverb, by the way, perhaps explains the mysterious "masterly
inactivity," "force no remedy," "blood-guiltiness," etc., theories.

the notion of starting a large model farm and agricultural college. The baron, who was usually quoted as the one thoroughly disinterested man in his department, had matters pretty much his own way; the Grand Duke—notoriously caring for nothing except plenty of shooting abroad, plenty of etiquette at home, and not to be bothered—left all purely civil affairs entirely in his hands. He accordingly was conceded, from a Government fund set apart for these purposes, or rather he conceded himself, a subsidy of 200,000 roubles, an extensive area of land, plus a subvention of 22,000 roubles per annum for general expenses, and set vigorously to work. After the lapse of some years, in which time about 100,000 roubles are computed to have been expended in farm-buildings, tools, wells, irrigation channels, etc., the baron, discovering that the grant of land was unnecessarily extensive for the purpose contemplated, sold half of it to an Armenian capitalist for 100,000 roubles. After a few more years, finding himself on the point of quitting the Caucasus, after a lengthy and laborious term of office, he sold the remainder of the property, building, etc., to the Government again and departed, realising by the sale 150,000 roubles.

His account balanced thus:—

	Roubles.
Original subsidy of	200,000
Portion sold to capitalist	100,000
Remaining portion resold to Government	150,000
	450,000
Deduct expenditure (say 150,000 roubles)	150,000
Total roubles	300,000

or a profit (at their rate of exchange), in pounds sterling, of £35,000.

After a few more years a reforming successor of
the baron found out that little or no agricultural
information was acquired at the college, consequently
the whole establishment, which from first to last
had cost the Government about 700,000 roubles (or
£75,000), was abolished.

A mile or two more along the cutcha road brings
us to some queer little Georgian and Armenian
chapels, and some gardens and vineyards, much frequented during the hot weather, it being considered
meritorious to go there early in the morning, taking
plenty of wine and provisions, pray, hold a picnic,
and return (rather drunk) in the cool of the evening.

There is here a small dukan or grog-shop, where,
there being no other beyond, we used generally to
take a horn of wine, or, if cold, some tea and vodky.
The proprietor, a quiet unassuming Armenian, owned
one or other of the vineyards, and did a little horse-
dealing as well; that is, he received horses (stolen in
Tiflis), worked them privately in the gardens, and
disposed of them eventually to purchasers at moderate
figures for cash. You never *see* horses about these
fellows' places; they have a way of burrowing a
stable out of a bank or hillock, opening in some quiet
corner, the entrance to which is through a cowshed,
which is apparently all there is to be seen. At the
back of the shed, however, with its entrance obscured,
will be a good-sized subterranean apartment, with
two or three " useful quads," which have strayed and
been " taken care of," feeding in security and comfort.
Farther on you come to a wide plain of three or four

miles, on which are a couple of Tartar villages close
together.   These are "kishlak" or winter villages,
and deserted, or next to it, all the summer, at which
season you will find the inhabitants living *al fresco*
on the high ranges described in my last between
Gambor and the Kakhetian valley.

Now, however, they swarm with children, ponies
feeding loose, cattle, and women, gangs of whom, in
wide red pyjamas, loose shirt, red bedgowns (Tartar
women always dress in red), and hair braided with
gold and silver coins, are fetching water, grinding
corn, etc., as in India.   They do not hide their faces,
and have a wild gipsy appearance.   The men, dressed
in chogas and poshteens with great conical bee-hived
shaped fur caps, loaf about, or sit talking and smoking
on the low flat-roofed houses.   They look surly and
repellent; but if you are with any one they know,
they will try to get you to stop an hour or two, feed
your horses, and prepare a shislik or cabob, and some
tea.

A mile or two farther you cross some low hills
overhanging the river, which continue for a mile or
more, and then descend on to the great steppe stretching away on the south to the horizon.   About eight
miles of it brings you to the Karyas canal, crossed by
a little wooden bridge, barred and closed after dark
(with a couple of armed chowkidars and savage
dogs, keeping watch), as some security against the
divers "plants" perpetually being concocted in the
neighbourhood.   The canal makes a circuit of some
fifteen miles from the river, and, though narrow, is

very deep, both in mud and water; indeed, quite
impassable for mounted men; and this is the only
bridge from end to end. This canal was constructed
by an Englishman—the late Mr. S. Gabb, C.E.—and,
owing to neglect of his advice and instructions, is
yearly falling more and more into disrepair, getting
choked by dust and sand from the steppe. Crossing
the bridge, we turn sharply to the right along the canal,
and in another five minutes are at our destination,—
a low flat-roofed, one-story brick house, with a rabbit-
warren of grass-choppers, half-underground huts, and
cowsheds at the back of it, in some of which, after
the usual dog-skirmish is appeased, our horses are
stowed by the attendants. The "estate" consists of
two or three hundred acres of wild-looking forest
and reedy jungle, between the canal and the river;
they are going to make a large fruit garden of part
of it, and have got immense nurseries of fruit
trees of all sorts for the purpose, but overgrown
with grass and weeds, and generally neglected, as the
hands are employed in draining. It belongs to a
Government official in Tiflis, but his nephew (Mr. D.),
who is our host, is the manager. D.'s grandfather
was a French officer of Napoleon's army, who was
taken prisoner and remained in Poland. D. himself
is a smart young fellow of twenty-five or thirty, talks
about seven languages, is a good shot and rider, a good
agriculturist, and a first-rate hand at managing the
heterogeneous lot of men he has under him. He is
also a sort of honorary magistrate, and understands
surveying. In fact, he has had a first-class (Russian)

education, and could have held high and lucrative appointments under Government; but, like many of the best men in the country, he hated the "tchin" from the first, and preferred private life.

He is popular with the Tartars of the steppe, but has been nevertheless four or five times fired at in as many years, and once narrowly escaped from an ambush laid for him; besides being nearly drowned on two occasions in crossing the river by night after cattle-raiders. As the short winter day closes in, D. and his assistant return from their labours, check off their workmen, distribute the rations to the foremen of different gangs, and see all snug for the night. Then, the open fireplace being crammed with blazing billets, and the windows carefully obscured (for a bullet sometimes finds its way in after dark if the lights are too conspicuous), we feed, tea, hot grog, and smoke till a late hour, the piercing wind from the northern mountains, which often blows a gale for days togther down the valley in winter, howling without. Karyas is a "lively" place, and we discuss the latest incidents, in the way of cattle-stealing, murders, affrays, rapes, and robberies which have occurred in the vicinity. I never went there without hearing a fresh case or two, as the Tartars on opposite sides of the river are perpetually rushing each other's cattle across, sometimes to the tune of 700 or 800 sheep or cows at a haul, which practice naturally leads to hard riding across country, ambuscades, night attacks, and other athletic and invigorating exercises. Many of these are "put up" affairs,

under the patronage of the local authorities themselves, who are almost to a man either Armenians or
Tartars (if the latter, often with relatives amongst the
raiders). No Russian or German official cares to live,
i.e. to be in authority in a Tartar district, or, if he
did, he would take care not to interfere too much
with what went on, and for very good reasons. We
used to pass the time at Karyas by day in shooting,
either in the reedy jungle along the river, where
pheasants, an occasional woodcock, ducks, and teal
were to be had; or on the steppe after "giran"[1]
(antelope), bustard, hare, etc. The best shikarees on
the estate were a Georgian named Tarakan and a
Persian of the name of Eli or Elias, Russianised into
Elia, both of whom had queer histories.

Tarakan, as I discovered after I had been several
times out shooting with him, had robbed and murdered
more than one individual, and had been arrested in
Kakhetia and imprisoned in Tiflis for the same. As
he had no money, or means of "squaring" anybody,
he would have certainly gone to the mines. However,
being aware of this, he contrived to creep down a
sewer by night (the Avlabar prison stands on a steep
scarped rock, and is a regular fortification), and by a
desperate leap from the face of the precipice to fall in
the river, which is there very deep, swim down it, and
escape. He was supposed to have been killed, and
his body washed away by the current, so no search

---

[1] "Giran" is the same word as the Indian "hiran;" the northern
Asiatics pronouncing the *h* gutturally, as *g* (as do the Russians). Thus
they say Allagh for Allah, Shagh for Shah, etc.

was made, and he took service at Karyas, where I daresay he is still. Elias, a northern Persian, was strongly built, very muscular, and active; a regular " Haji Baba," full of shifts and dodges, about the very deepest dog I ever met anywhere; at the same time afraid of nothing. He had been up to some curious practices on the frontier about Nakhetchivan and Djulfa, smuggling, complicated with shooting somebody, I believe, and had " travelled " in consequence. He was as "hard as nails," and would have made a splendid soldier in time of war, being worth his weight in gold as a spy, *i.e.* if you could have kept him straight. He would walk day after day, from morning till night—in fact, was indefatigable, and I do not think I ever saw him miss anything he fired at. He once, while flight-shooting, spotted a wolf within sixty yards, and hastily dropping a ball down over a heavy charge of shot, aimed and fired. The ball having rolled half-way down the barrel by the time he pulled the trigger, caused his gun to burst " explosively." He nevertheless killed the wolf. On one occasion, during a hard frost, remarking that the wild-fowl kept alighting in swarms on an unfrozen part near some reeds, in a large lake or jheel, at the other end of the canal, he quietly waded in, and stood in the reeds for several hours, with the water up to his elbows, making an enormous bag. This exposure, which would probably have killed anybody else, gave him a severe cold and touch of rheumatism, which went off in a week.

One of his " proclivities " was poaching in the Grand Duke's preserves lower down, which are very

strictly guarded and watched. In spite of his shifts
he was one day detected by the Cossacks, and, though
he managed to hide his gun before they actually caught
him, was very roughly treated. About a couple of
months afterwards, he and Tarakan, while as usual "on
the prowl" in the jungle, spotted some of these same Cossacks cutting grass in an open to make hay, with their
arms and traps under a tree at some distance, horses
unsaddled, hobbled, and let loose to graze as usual.
Tarakan proposed stalking round to some cover at
the far end, where they would get themselves, the
Cossacks, and their camp, in a line (thus securing
250 or 300 yards start, as the Cossacks would have to
run to the camp for their arms), then firing into them
with slugs and skedaddling. Eli, however, "evolved"
another manœuvre. Strolling quietly up to the
Cossacks (after hiding their guns in the bushes), they
got into conversation, and began helping them in
their work, twisting grass ropes, etc., and generally
aiding and assisting for some time. After a bit, Eli,
taking out and filling his pipe, sauntered off to the
camp to get a light, leaving Tarakan at work with the
Cossacks. When there, he sat down and smoked, and
while, apparently, carelessly looking at the carbines
to pass the time, managed to ram an acorn half-
way down each of the barrels, causing two or three of
them to burst when fired subsequently, and seriously
injure their owners.

They were always playing some scurvy trick or
other. Tarakan being sent one day with an araba
to buy beef at a village, pocketed the coin, and

cutting a lot of meat off a dead horse, which had got drowned in the canal, brought it back loaded on the araba, and palmed it off on the workmen. I one day asked D. why he kept such rascals. "Keep them!" said he, "why, they keep us. If it was not for those devils we should often have nothing to eat. Besides what they shoot, they are always 'foraging,' and rarely come back empty. My uncle sends me precious little coin at times, and I cannot keep killing our own geese, ducks, etc. Those two chaps have stolen, within the last year, three oxen, over thirty sheep, and eight or nine araba loads of cabbages. It's every man for himself at Karyas. Do you think the fellows on the other grants don't steal from me whenever they get the chance?" Karyas, in fact, is a sort of Alsatia, a refuge for hard-up fellows of all sorts from Tiflis; and on this and the neighbouring estates, within the canal boundary, divers queer characters are congregated.

You see a man come in (in rags) who has been an officer of Cossacks or Russian infantry; another who has been an accountant, or bank clerk, or held a berth under Government, but has been kicked out for drink or embezzlement, working with spade or mattock in company with men who have been more than once in gaol and barbarous Georgian peasants. D.'s cowman was a man of about forty-five (and a very quiet, good sort of fellow), who had been a captain, and, in fact, was then, *i.e.* as much so as any retired officer can be. After twenty-five years' service, during which he had been through half a dozen campaigns (including the Crimean War, and endured all sorts of hardships in mountain fighting against the Lesghians, Tcherkess, etc., he found himself, with a number of others, compelled either to retire (without pension) or pass a stiff examination, which at his age he was unable to do. He had excellent testimonials (which I saw myself) from commanding officers under whom he had served; but, having no friends of interest, and being only fitted for army life, had fallen lower and lower, until he was now herding cattle on fourteen roubles a month. In fact, there is always such a glut of officers in the Russian service, from generals downwards, that promotion for any but very highly-gifted men (or men with interest) stagnates fearfully, and would, in time, were not these clearances from time to time effected, cease altogether for the *hoi polloi.* And this is another "reason why" the Russian Government (unless revolutionised) will, or rather must, always be at war, or preparing for war. The army, *i.e.* the chiefs of the army (the Emperor himself one of them), sway the councils of the nation, the ranks become choked by inaction, and war is made to get breathing room amongst other reasons. Captain P—— used to talk of waiting for a chance of throwing himself in his ragged clothes in the way of the Grand Duke, when he came shooting, and when asked who he was, saying, "I was for twenty-five years one of your Highness's officers, but I am now a cowherd."

Another character was D.'s assistant, S—— T——. He was the son of a Polish landowner, and when the rebellion of 1863 broke out (at which time he was about nineteen) he joined the insurgent cavalry. After rushing about for six weeks or so, destroying telegraphs and Government buildings, and taking part in much desultory skirmishing and fighting, his party found themselves surrounded early one fine morning, after having been incessantly on the move for twenty-five or thirty hours, by an immensely superior force of hussars, and Cossacks, five or six of whom, in the confused rout and *mêlée* which ensued, laid into our friend, who, after receiving and giving several severe slashes, was dropped from his horse by a tremendous sabre-cut (in which you can now almost lay your finger) through the front part of his skull.

He lay senseless for some time, and on coming to himself found he was being dragged along the ground, face uppermost, by a Cossack, who was trying to get his boots off. Having a small pistol in an inner breast-pocket of his jacket, he pulled it out and fired into the Cossack, who fell ; whereupon he was at once surrounded by a number of others, who were plundering not far off, and again severely hacked and slashed, receiving to boot a carbine shot in the pit of his stomach, which traversed his body. He told me that, up to the time of this shot, which made torrents of blood rush from his mouth, he did not, in spite of all the hacking, feel done for, but that this seemed to finish him there and then. However, some peasants who came over the field early next morning, finding signs of life, took him to a cottage, where he was shortly afterwards discovered, bundled with other wounded prisoners into a cart, and put first in a barn, and then in prison. Luckily the doctor who attended them was fond of his profession, and, seeing that S.'s was an "extraordinary case," took a great deal of trouble with him. He has three awful cuts on the head, two of which, each over six inches long on the front and back of the cranium, seem to have been originally about an inch in depth; besides twenty-four other wounds on the limbs and body, including the carbine shot. The doctor told him that this latter must have been fatal had not his stomach been completely empty. Luckily for him, as it turned out, he had been nearly forty hours without anything to eat. As soon as he became convalescent, he was sent to Siberia, where he remained eight or ten years,[1] finally receiving, through the exertions of an influential friend, a pardon. On his return he, with other amnestied exiles, had to present himself before Prince Milutin, Minister of War, who, after questioning him as to his experiences of rebellion and exile, wound up by observing: "You ass, had you got half as many wounds in the service of the Emperor, you would have no room on your breast for decorations and crosses." S. answered: "True, your Excellency; but I bear a cross for my country for a long time, and want no other." Milutin is himself a Pole.

[1] His account of Siberian exile was not unfavourable; he said it was a fine country and climate, that political exiles were leniently treated, had plenty of liberty (it is almost impossible to escape without a passport), were allowed to go shooting, to work at trades, etc., and encouraged to settle and remain in the country.

M

CHAPTER VII.

MIKHAILOFF is a big scattered "location" on the
railway, about half-way between Poti and Tiflis.
There are extensive workshops, a locomotive depot,
and resident civil engineers; in fact, from Mikhailoff
the Poti-Tiflis Railway is governed and carried on.

It stands on a wide windy plain, miles in breadth,
dotted with Georgian villages (half underground), and
surrounded with wooded mountain ranges. Being
about 3000 feet elevation above the sea, the place is
always cool, even in the height of summer. In winter
all travelling, including the railway, is often at a
standstill on account of the snow, which, driven by
furious and continuous blasts of wind from the mountains (often lasting for several days), absolutely fills
the air, drifts many feet deep in every hollow, blocks
the line and the roads, and often prevents one seeing
beyond twenty or thirty yards. In fact, you never
really realise what a "snowstorm" is until you come

to travel in winter on the Armenian and Georgian plateaux, or on the steppes north of the Caucasian chain.

From Mikhailoff a good post-road, leaving the railway at a right angle, and traversing the wide plain, enters the mountains by the valley of the Koura, which here bisects the lesser Caucasus, passing through a noted defile, a sort of "Khyber" on a small scale, famous in old times for "adventures," being one of the few difficult and dangerous entries into Georgia. On each side of the rapid river densely-wooded mountain-sides tower for thousands of feet, while the road is dominated, at every point of vantage, by gray stone castles and quaint loop-holed towers, strongholds which, a century or so ago, were in full use as a means of closing the road and levying contributions. It was along this defile that the Lesghians used to run their "industriously-acquired" caravans of handsome slave-girls destined for the Constantinople market; many a well-planned ambuscade and rattling skirmish taking place as they returned with the coin realised at Akhaltsik by disposal of their captives.

After following the picturesque windings and turnings of the lovely valley for some twelve miles, you reach Borjom, the Simla of the Caucasus, where the viceregal staff and *crème de la crème* of the Tiflis administration, civil and military, pass the hot months. At this point the valley widens considerably, forming a fine *emplacement* for a sanitarium. The river is crossed by a good bridge, and clusters of houses line either bank. The station proper, regularly laid out

in streets of garden houses, is on the right bank ; on
the left is a summer palace and grounds, magnificently
laid out, of the Grand Duke Michael's.   There are
mineral baths, a club, a sort of kursaal, and two
or three decent hotels.   Walks and rides are cut
out in the hillsides in many directions, and ruined
chapels, old castles in the woods, etc., form *points
de mire* for picnickers.   All the fashionables pass
the summer here, and gambling, flirting, riding,
and dancing are as perseveringly practised as at
Simla or Monaco.   Borjom, however, possesses the
drawbacks of all sanitaria located in valleys, being
alternately either too hot or too cold and chilly,
according as several still, hot, cloudless days are
succeeded by the heavy rain, fogs, and mists which
invariably follow.   It was, like other Caucasian sanitaria, "built to order."   The Grand Duke Michael,
having first appropriated the surrounding forests, and
converted them into an estate and hunting-ground
(rights of timber-felling reserved), ordained that a
sanitarium and palace should be constructed there,
and "it was done as seemed good to Darius the
King."

As the forests round Borjom (many thousands of
acres in extent) supply all the building necessities of
Tiflis and other towns (the timber being floated down
the river on rafts), considerable grumbling on the part
of certain Georgian "villeins" and "zemindars"
(who, having been accustomed to free warren in these
forests for centuries, had now to pay for it) accompanied the little "improvement."   Nevertheless, the

" transfer" was made, the station and palace built, and an extra £6000 per annum added to H.I.H.'s credit. H.I.H. having now quitted the Caucasus for good, proposes, it is said, to part with this valuable property to a company for a sum of three to four millions cash ; but it is doubtful if he will find a purchaser, *i.e.* a *bond fide* one, on the merits, Armenian capitalists being well aware that considerable difference exists between His Highness realising profits from an estate and private parties doing the same. Leaving Borjom, the road again winds up the valley, by the rapid foaming river, and, after twenty miles of magnificent mountain and forest scenery, every jutting crag occupied by the ruined towers of bygone mountain chieftains, suddenly emerges at a village and post-house called " Atsquooa," on to a rolling open country of villages and cultivation, much resembling that round Kars and Alexandropol.

Atsquooa was, till 1829, a Turkish frontier-post, and there was, up to about that date, a guard of Jannissaries in the picturesque old fortress, which, with crenelated battlements and donjon keep, dominates the ancient bridle-road on the right bank of the river at the opening of the defile.

The road here leaves the river Cyrus (which, by the way, is doubtless the river crossed by the ten thousand Greeks in their wintry march through Armenia, and which they mistook, naturally enough, finding it flowing north-west, as it does in this part of its course, for the Phasis or Rion). A morning's ride from

Atsquooa, across an open undulating country, dotted
with Georgian villages and apple orchards, brings you
to Akhaltsik, once a proud pachalik, and the northern
place d'armes from which the Osmanli dominated
Imeritia, Gouriel, and Mingrelia. It was also the
" mart or depot " from which the seraglios of Anatolia
and Constantinople were supplied with fair Georgian
and other " mountain born " odalisques.

Akhaltsik is now principally inhabited by Armenians, but the surrounding country, though peopled
by a race of pure Georgians, is entirely Mahometan,
the inhabitants having been converted *en masse* to
that religion towards the close of the sixteenth century. They are very quiet, well-behaved people,
good Mahometans, contrasting favourably with their
Christian countrymen; to which latter faith, although
now half a century under Russian rule, and repeatedly
importuned " by authority," they have steadily refused
to revert.

All this country, including the Borjom Pass, was
formerly the " ilaqua " or Government of Manuchiar,
the famous Georgian chieftain, the remains of whose
feudal fortress of Altunchala (Château d'Or) may still
be seen farther down the valley. And thereby hangs
an instructive tale, as what the Georgian princes were
then they are now in inclination, and would have
perhaps played the same *rôle* (had Georgia been
invaded) during the last war, as they did in the
sixteenth century.

When the Turks, in their palmy days, just 300
years ago, in the reign of Sultan Murad III., invaded

the Caucasus with an army of 110,000 men, collected
from all parts of Asia Minor, four princes (Simon,
David, Alexander, and Manuchiar) ruled Georgia,
then tributary to the Persian Shah, against whom the
Turks had declared war, and from whom they intended
to wrest the Caucasian provinces. The eldest (Simon)
had been a political prisoner for some years at Cas-
been, then the Persian capital. His cousin Manuchiar
governed Akhaltsik, Akhalkalak, and the elevated
country south of the lesser Caucasus; while David,
having become a Shiah Mahometan, ruled Tiflis in
his elder brother Simon's stead (who had steadfastly
refused to abandon the faith of his fathers) under
the name of Daoud Khan. Alexander governed
Kakhetia.

Mustapha Pacha, the Seraskier, having assembled
his army[1] at Erzeroum, marched on Kars, and encamped beyond it, on the same battle-ground, well
trodden for ages, below the high plateaux, between
Georgia and Armenia, where the Russians were encamped during the summer of 1877. The Shah had
called out a general levy, but Persia, being as usual in an
anarchic state, distracted by treachery and disaffection,
not more than 20,000 men[2] (Kizilbash and Georgians)
from the provinces immediately menaced turned out,

[1] Consisting of 110,000 men — 14,000 Jannissaries, 10,000
Albanians, 40,000 Spahis (cavalry), the remainder irregulars and
Bashi-Bazouks.

[2] " These twenty thousand were all horsemen, armed with Scimitar
and Bow, with some Arquebuses among, and furnished with very fine
and well-tempered Armour, but above all, courageous they were and
resolute, and well the more for the Valour and Prowess of their
General " (*Knolles*).

who, under Tokmak, a famous Turkoman khan and
wild horseman, marched in the usual *débandade* style
to encounter the invaders, joining issue in the Kars
valley, below Lake Chaldir, where a bloody battle was
fought.   The Caucasians, mostly picked men, well
armed, and equipped in Asiatic fashion, though without artillery and firearms, charging desperately, completely routed the advanced column of the Turks, and
were only eventually repulsed after very severe fighting by the main body and artillery under Mustapha
in person.   They finally retreated with a loss of 5000
killed (having done as much, or more, damage to the
Turks), and 3000 prisoners, who were immediately
decapitated.

Mustapha, next morning, by way of " improving
the occasion," ordered a " Kelle Minar," or tower of
skulls, composed of the heads of the slain, to be constructed in front of the camp, which edifice was in
course of completion when word was brought that
Prince Manuchiar was coming in to make his submission.

A deputation of all the principal chiefs was at
once ordered out to meet and escort him, while the
Jannissaries and Albanians, who, to the number of
20,000 men, formed the *corps d'élite,* were got under
arms, which, being effected, the Georgian and his
bodyguard, escorted by the various Sanjaks, Begler
Begs, etc., who had received him, rode into camp
under the usual salute, descended from his horse,
embraced the Seraskier, said he had long wanted to
learn the art of war with the Osmanli, was prepared

to swear fealty to the Sultan, and would turn Mahometan to prove his good faith.

This scene would have made a good subject for a historical painting. In the background the magnificent " canvas palace " of the Turkish general, with the Jannissaries, Albanians, and Spahis ranged on either side ; in the foreground the Seraskier himself, surrounded by chiefs of every warlike tribe in Asia Minor or Arabia, in different rich and varied costumes and glittering arms. The wild robber prince, surrounded by his still wilder " Asnaours," strangely equipped mountain horsemen, from all parts of the Caucasus, dismounting warily, glancing askance the while at the grisly bulwark of heads adorning the place of meeting, which heads, a day before, had been on the shoulders of his own countrymen.

After being shown round the camp, whose size, regularity, and discipline, together with the numerous artillery, then almost unknown in the Caucasus, surprised him, he was presented with the customary " khillut " of cloth-of-gold, enamelled arms, and train of slaves, and generally made much of.

The Persian forces of those days were composed entirely of horse, supplied by the various " khans " or satraps who ruled the different provinces—Turkomans, Kurds, Kizilbash, Georgians, Khorassans, etc. ; each khan was a sort of separate prince, and kept up a small army, in the ranks of which were numerous Afghan, Belooch, Tartar, and Turkoman adventurers.

As horsemen, the forces of the khans were superior to the Turks, and, being well armed in Asiatic fashion,

with long spears, gauntlets, "chahareineh,"[1] good
steel helmets and coats of mail, usually rode down
the Spahis and Arabs with comparative ease.[2]

It was rare that they went, as on this occasion,
to meet the enemy, their tactics being usually to keep
a day or two's march in advance of an invading army
(devastating their own villages and driving the inhabitants to the mountains, or before them like sheep),
so that it found nothing but deserted ruins on its
line of march. Foragers, even in great force, if
despatched to right or left of the route to search for
supplies, were generally surprised and cut to pieces.
When the invaders, starved out, ultimately retreated,
as commonly happened, they were promptly followed
up by the hitherto invisible enemy, all stragglers cut
off, and the rear harassed by incessant skirmishing,
any opportunity of defeating the entire force (while
crossing a river, or encamping in disorder) by a well-
timed and furious stampede being at once seized.[3]

[1] "Chahareineh," the four plates (lit. four mirrors), were light, but
strong, steel breast, back, and side pieces, joined by thongs, and forming
a sort of cuirass outside the "zirvakt," or coat of mail.

[2] Knolles says : "The Turkish horseman is not to be compared to
the Persian 'man-at-arms,' who comes into the field armed with a
strong cuirass, a sure headpiece, and good target, and 'wearing their
poldrons and gauntlets,' with long spears armed at both ends, fight at
the half staff, 'in the manner of the Numidians,' using both greater
and stronger bows, and making small account of the Turks."

[3] The charging of the Persian cavalry of former days is well
described in the lines of the Shah Nameh—

"As the dust of the march of their army we near'd,
Fierce joy on the face of my warriors appeared ;
With the shock of my onset their centre I broke,
And hewed out a path for my men at one stroke ;

To return to Manuchiar, he and his men accompanied Mustapha on the campaign, marching to Tiflis, which the Seraskier garrisoned; afterwards subduing the Caucasus as far as the Caspian, occupying Derbend, Shumaka, etc., and returning through Kakhetia to Tiflis. Thence, fearfully harassed by the Persians and mountaineers, *viâ* the Borjom Pass, Akhaltsik, Ardahan, and Kars to Erzeroum, whence he despatched the Georgian princes Manuchiar and Alexander to the Sultan with a flaming account of the success of the campaign. This was rather premature, as in the meantime Hamza Mirza, the famous Persian Shahzada, had entered Shirvan with 14,000 horse, smitten Abdul Ghirai, the Crimean Tartar prince (who, with 30,000 men, had come round through the steppes to support the Turks), hip and thigh with great slaughter, cut off the Turkish garrisons, and re-taken the whole valley of the Koura east of Tiflis.

At Constantinople, Manuchiar formally became a Mahometan, taking the name of Mustapha, and entered the Turkish service, holding his government of Akhaltsik for the Turk, and himself in readiness to accompany their armies on the campaign with his contingent.

The Persian war, begun in 1577, had now lasted four years, when Mustapha Seraskier was replaced by

> As firm in the saddle we crashed through the foes,
> The earth seemed to reel with the force of our blows."

As the old Kurdish Aga said to Fraser : "All is changed : no bands of gallant horsemen now." Futty Ali Shah broke up the power of the khans, and the Persians have ever since been stagnating in inefficiency and corruption.

Mehemet Pacha, who, the great object being always to keep Tiflis victualled, usually opened hostilities each year by despatching provisions, stores, and money under convoy of a small army of 10,000 to 15,000 men to that capital.

The state of affairs was much as if we had strong garrisons in Kabul and Kandahar, and had to fight our way up to them, once a year, with supplies from the Punjab, to do which, by the way, would probably come cheaper than subsidising the tribes.   On the occasion in question, Mehemet Pacha, being in command, marched from Kars at the end of August, and, on arriving at Akhalkalak on the direct route to Tiflis, was there met by Manuchiar (now Mustapha) with his mountaineers. Mehemet, after the usual exchange of presents, consulted as to the best method of proceeding to Tiflis, whether by the route across the plateau, and through the defile of Tomanis,[1] or otherwise. Manuchiar strongly recommended a route through his own government, *i.e.* along the valley of the Koura, *viâ* Borjom, which was adopted, the army peaceably marching under his guidance (though by a circuitous route) until they reached Gori, just outside Manuchiar's jurisdiction, when they were suddenly aware of a large force of Georgians and Persians on the opposite side of the river, who, sending heralds, offered them instant battle.

[1] The defile of Tomanis, on the old road from Tiflis to Alexandropol, *viâ* Dzellal Oghli, was a dangerous " pass " in which the Turks were several times beset and discomfited with severe loss.   They subsequently built forts at either end, and regularly garrisoned it till the close of the war.

Mehemet Pacha, hampered with his convoy, and
wishing to avoid an action, dismissed the heralds, saying that negotiations for peace were going on.   Next
day the two armies marched parallel to each other down
the river, on opposite sides of the valley, till the Turks
reached a point where a ford had to be crossed. Here
Mehemet consulted Manuchiar as to whether they
should cross at once, in face of the enemy, or camp and
wait till morning.   Manuchiar advised waiting; but
Mehemet, suspecting collusion and treachery, which,
by the way, was probable enough, resolved to spoil the
plot by crossing then and there, and ordered the convoy, escorted by the Kurds and Arab irregulars, to
ford immediately, which was done; but before these
could form in sufficient force on the opposite bank,
they were attacked with fury and overthrown, and the
greater part of the treasure and provisions captured.
On the arrival of Mehemet's force in Tiflis, minus pay
and supplies, there was a mutiny in the half-starved
garrison, which he had to appease by a forced sub-
scription of 30,000 tomans, thereby much exasperat-
ing his officers.

On the return march, *viâ* the Borjom Pass, Mehemet
Pacha, in order to be able to lay the blame of these
misfortunes to Manuchiar's account (in his despatches
to the Sultan), determined to have him assassinated
at a durbar or divan, which was convoked with the
pretended object of reading orders arrived from Constantinople.   The wary Georgian, however, getting
wind of this treachery, attended the durbar with fifty
picked men, armed to the teeth, whom he left outside

the tent, with orders to rush in if he called for assistance.

The firman was read by Mehemet's secretary, all
the chiefs standing up, as usual. At its termination
they sat down—all but Manuchiar, who, rapidly making his salaam, proposed to retire. The Capijee Bashi,
or master of the ceremonies, catching his sleeve, would,
however, have forced him to sit down, whereupon
Manuchiar, drawing his sword, and tearing off the
turban of the captain of the guard, who sat opposite,
clove him to the shoulders. He then "went" for
the Pacha of Caramania, whose big turban (though
cut through, and one ear and part of a cheek sliced
off) saved his life; then for Mehemet Pacha, whom
he cut down and severely wounded. By this time
the henchmen had rushed in with ready weapons
and borne him off in triumph. The durbar broke up in
confusion; and the whole camp, astonished at such
audacity and pluck, made no opposition to his retiring
to his fortress of Altunchala, which was close by, marching themselves the same day for Kars and Erzeroum.
Manuchiar forthwith sent off a courier with *his* account of the business to the Sultan, and, by the influence of certain fair friends and countrywomen in the
seraglio, managed so well that Murad forwarded him
a khillut and laudatory epistle by return messenger.

The next year (1583), the Persians being internally
in a still worse state from rebellion, etc., did nothing;
and the Turks built two large forts on the road between
Kars and Tiflis, and took and fortified Erivan.

The business of keeping the communications open,

guarding convoys with supplies, and forwarding mes-
sengers between Kars and Tiflis, devolved on Manuchiar; the military routes into Georgia running, as
aforesaid, through his territory; agreeably to which,
in the spring of 1583, some Turkish officers, with a
year's pay of the Tiflis garrison, were sent to Altunchala to be escorted on by Manuchiar, who, at the head
of 500 of his men, went in person.   Unfortunately,
however, for the Turks, they fell in on the way with
the great Simon, now reinstated by the Persians (or
rather allowed to reinstate himself if he could) in his
government, who, at the head of a considerable force
of gentlemen robbers and Bashi-Bazouks, was blockading the road, ambuscading convoys, and plundering
as usual.   There being numerous relatives and old
friends of Manuchiar and his men in Simon's ranks, a
parley was held; and, both sides agreeing that it would
be absurd to fight, a feast and big drink were organised,
in the course of which the two chiefs swore eternal
friendship; and Manuchiar, ordering the heads of the
unfortunate Turkish officials to be taken off, divided
the 30,000 tomans he was convoying with his cousin,
abjured Mahometanism, and joined him in ambuscading,
intercepting supplies, and beleaguering the Tiflis garrison—this last feat completely re-establishing his reputation (already in high renown for the durbar business)
both with his own countrymen and the Persians.

On learning the news of the murder of the Chaoush
and Capijees, and the annexation of the treasure, Ferhad Pacha (the Seraskier at Kars), first sending Hassan
Pacha, a bold partisan warrior, with a picked force,

stores, and money, to the Tiflis garrison,[1] ordered Resvan Aga, a noted Kurdish chief, with 6000 horse, to
ravage Manuchiar's territory, which was performed in
orthodox fashion—everything burned that could be made
to burn, fruit trees and vines destroyed, and every one
who could be captured killed or enslaved. Next spring
(1584) Ferhad Pacha, marching from Kars across the
plateau, with an army of some 40,000 men, halted
beyond the defile of Tomanis, where he constructed
another fort, meantime despatching Resvan Aga, and
the Pacha of Caramania, at the head of 15,000 men,
to revictual and relieve the Tiflis garrison.

During their stay at Tiflis, David (Daoud Khan),
the Georgian prince, disgusted at Simon's being set at
liberty, came in with his men, swore fealty to the
Sultan, and, having previously turned Shiah, now
turned Soonni. With him they returned to headquarters. They were encamped half-way, Resvan and
his Kurds being at the foot of a hill, apart, when Simon
and Manuchiar, who had been hovering about, coming
in sight of Resvan's camp, imagined that this consti-
tuted the whole strength of the column, and, thinking
to surprise, charged them furiously. The Georgians
were only 4000 strong ; and, while hotly engaged with
the Kurds, were suddenly taken in flank and surrounded by the Pacha of Caramania with the rest of
the force. A most desperate *mêlée* ensued, in which

---

[1] Hassan went and returned (with the convoy) in ten days from
Kars, an extraordinary feat, being over forty miles per diem. All the
marches given in the old history are double, sometimes treble, the length
of our modern ones.

Simon and Manuchiar, at the head of a few of the best mounted, succeeded in cutting their way through, the rest of their followers being all slain or made prisoners.   On the return march, Ferhad Pacha again looted Manuchiar's territory, a fortress was built at Akhaltsik, the whole population forcibly converted, and the country made into (as it remained till lately) a Turkish pachalic.   Subsequent to this unfortunate affair Manuchiar does not seem, according to the chronicles, to have performed any notable actions; he is, nevertheless, one of the national " worthies," and many of the Georgian princes are named after him to this day.   At their barbaric festivals wild chants still occasionally recount his exploits, amidst much draining of beakers brimming with ruby Kakhetian wine.

Akhaltsik is a second-rate Asiatic town, a smaller edition of Alexandropol, of flat-roofed, one-story houses, very dirty, lying in a hollow sloping up from the river, which is crossed by a wooden pile bridge, and divides it from the fort.   This latter is merely the old Turkish fortress furbished up and improved, the mosque converted into a powder-magazine, etc., in Russian fashion, and is completely commanded from the high ground opposite, and indeed from other points.

From Akhaltsik a ride of four or five hours, across an undulating country, villages in hollows, surrounded by fruit trees, vineyards, etc., brings us to the opening of the narrow defile, leading across the range by Abbas Tuman, another famous mineral hot spring, watering-place, and summer resort, situated at the foot of the

pass leading into Imeritia. The hot springs of
Abbas Tuman are the most efficient and curative of
the Caucasus—not excepting those of Tiflis. They
are situated at the bottom of a narrow valley or
" khud," with steep fir-clad hills rising on each side
to a great height. The small space round the ·hot
springs, not above 300 yards across, is completely
choked with houses. The "khud" winds up beyond for miles, always narrow, into the heart of
the big range. House accommodation is dear, and
difficult to be got, the place, except in winter, being
always crowded. The springs are *very* hot and sul-
phureous. You can only just bear the temperature
of the water.

From Abbas Tuman a long winding ride of three
hours, always ascending through fir forests, hazel
copses, and beech groves, leads to the summit of the
pass. Abbas Tuman and the surrounding hills and
forests were to have been given as a dowry to the Princess L., the beautiful eldest daughter of the Grand
Duke Michael, on her marriage, *i.e.* as part of the
dowry, but the death of the late Emperor is reported
to have disarranged the proposition, which remains
unauthorised by the Council of the Empire (at any
rate *pro tempore*).

The crest of the great range above Abbas Tuman,
where are much open undulating pasture land, springs
of water, and a glorious view over miles of rock, mountain, and fell, would, in my opinion, make a far finer
sanitarium than the place itself; but Russians love
valleys, and it is improbable that the crest of the

pass, with its magnificent summer climate and capabilities, will ever be utilised.

It was by this pass that, in the old days before Russian domination, the Pacha of Akhaltsik used to send troops across, whenever the Imeritian and Mingrelian princes got too utterly chaotic and unmanageable.

On the northern slopes of the huge barrier are many little Christian villages and hamlets, nestling in secluded "khuds" and wooded valleys, some of which had a bad time of it during the war, plundering parties of Lazes and Kabouletz from the Batoum side occasionally looking them up. I often wondered that the Russians did not attempt a turning movement against the Turkish lines from the crest of the range, which leads right down to Tzikinzeri; but Russians are indifferent mountaineers, and the idea probably appeared, and to them perhaps was, impracticable.[1]

---

[1] On one of my expeditions across this range during the war, when the road was deserted, I found a bridge carried away and progress entirely barred. However, a peasant from a village above, whom I happened to meet, offered, for a rouble, to show me how I could get to an old disused bridle-path, a thousand feet or so higher up, which led to the crest of the range. The hillside we had to negotiate, though covered with short hazel growth, was nearly perpendicular. Luckily my horse, being a mountain animal from Ratcha, was sure-footed, and scrambled like a goat till we reached the old road (believed to be the same as existed in the time of the Roman Empire); but I had not got far along it when, at a turn in the narrow path, I encountered a posse of armed villagers, headed by a white-bearded old "Mamoo Saklis" (Kotwal), who, spotting my Turkish-hilted sabre and crooked dagger,[2]

---

[2] The same equipment, had I met a party of Lazes, would have been a passport and recommendation.

On crossing the crest of the ridge, the road, after traversing a grassy open down for about a mile, suddenly plunges into deep gloomy gorges, dark fir forests, and hanging beech woods, precipices, laurel-clothed steep banks, and damp cold "khuds," with torrents raging at the bottom.   After wandering amongst these for twelve or fourteen miles, you emerge at a place called Baghdad—why I know not ("*quid aranea cum febris*," as Burton says)—into the level valley country of Imeritia.

Here is a complete change of scene from the Anatolian uplands round Akhaltsik ; whitewashed wooden villas, dotted on green hillsides, or amidst clumps of walnut and beech trees, everything green and luxuriant.   Along the road are little streets of wooden houses and "dukans," inhabited by big loafing vagabonds, with beards, chogas, hoods, and long daggers, handsome *dégagée* women in loose trailing gowns, and all the singing lazy "devil-may-care" life of the Rion valley.

Round about Baghdad are extensive forests, some of which belong to Prince S. V.   His family, compromised in the Polish Revolution of 1830, emigrated to France, where Prince S. V. was educated,

---

was very near arresting me, which, as I had already had two or three narrow escapes, would have been inconvenient.   However, answering immediately that I was a Frank, which explains a good many peculiarities in the Caucasus, I pushed right on, and, as no one likes to be the first to stop an armed cavalier in the mountain,[1] got through them and made the best of my way to Abbas Tuman.

---

[1] The Tartars have a proverb "the sowar is 'lord' on the steppe," which applies pretty well all over the Caucasus.

entering the Legion Etrangère as a cadet, and serving for some years in Algeria, where he obtained
the rank of captain. An amnesty being ordained,
he, a short time previous to the Crimean War, returned to Russia, and was appointed aide-de-camp
on the staff of General Mouravieff, the Russian
general who subsequently besieged and captured Kars.
Mouravieff was a rough specimen, even of a Muscovite *militaire*, the expressions he would make use of
when "put out" being still proverbial in the army of
the Caucasus, and at the time frequently commented
upon by his staff, in which served numerous men of
good family, some of whom amused themselves by
writing descriptions of the scenes which took place at
parades and official receptions, where the commander-
in-chief presided, to friends in Moscow and Petersburg. A very clever letter, in dialogue, taking off
Mouravieff on some occasions when he had made use
of unusually frightful language, fell into the general's
hands; but as the writer's name was erased, it was
impossible to bring it home to the author, beyond
the fact that, from certain passages in it (not the
least amusing), it was indisputably the production
of some one who was always at the great man's
elbow. After this discovery, as may be imagined,
the aides-de-camp were "led a life;" Mouravieff,
with the avowed purpose of making them all suffer,
trebling his violence, until (the situation being, unless the perpetrator should hand himself up, recognised as no longer tenable) Prince S. V., confront-
ing the general as boldly as he subsequently did

his former comrades-in-arms at Inkermann and the Tchernaya, owned himself the writer of the epistle.[1]

Mouravieff (after an outburst), observing that, as S. V. was " so clever," he ought to see active service, " had him degraded to the ranks, sent to the Crimea," and put through a " course of sprouts," which was duly, " agreeably to orders," performed. He was desperately wounded at the Tchernaya, and left, with heaps of others, for dead on the field, where K., then a gallant captain of Cossacks (afterwards general, and killed near Kars in the last war), scouting round during the night over the debatable ground, with some of his men, found him lying ; and guessing that, in spite of his coarse soldier's uniform, he was of noble birth,[2] had him removed to his " kibitka," and took such rough care of him as the exigencies of incessant warfare permitted. Prince S. V.'s wounds were, however, terribly dangerous. He was almost dead from loss of blood when discovered, lay for a long time between life and death, and nothing but the strength of his magnificent constitution eventually saved him. In the meantime he had been reported killed, and was, at the seat of war, in the hurry of events, for-

[1] The real author has been very generally suspected *not* to be M. after all, but a clever scion of the house of W., one of the most influential and wealthy in Russia, to whose good offices M. (who lacked everything to ensure success in his profession, except courage and adroitness) wished to recommend himself.

[2] Numbers of young noblemen, especially Poles, were in Nicholas's time serving as common soldiers, for political and military reasons, in the army of the Caucasus. In fact, the Caucasus was then a sort of " swell " military penal settlement.

gotten.   Captain K., being day and night on picket
and outpost duty, had no time to spare, and it was
only on the W. family making strict inquiry that,
some two months afterwards, he was found to be alive.
His incautious removal to the hospital caused a relapse,
which again nearly carried him off, but he eventually
recovered, and, returning with rehabilitation and promotion to the Caucasus, was placed on the staff of the
then ·Viceroy, Prince Bariatinski, who, on his marriage
with an influential Georgian princess, made him
Governor of Kutais.   As governor, he managed
to obtain a large grant of land, plus two valuable
tracts of forest, from which, in conjunction with a
native contractor, he supplied sleepers for the Poti-
Tiflis Railway, then in course of construction, realising
large profits.   He also had the address to get the line
of railway diverged from Kutais through the grant in
question, thereby considerably increasing its intrinsic
value, but, at the same time, half-ruining Kutais and
several large villages on the route originally proposed
by the English engineers, who made the *tracé* of the
line.   It was necessary subsequently to construct a
branch line at considerable expense.

Under the viceroyalty of H.I.H. the Grand
Duke Michael, in whose favour he stood high, the
prince eventually became Military Governor of the
Caucasus, the highest position short of the Viceroyalty.   Being " well posted," in every sense of the
word, he, at the commencement of the late war,
entered, in conjunction with an Armenian capitalist,
into an extensive flour contract, realising, some

accounts say, a profit of a million roubles each.   This
" operation," however, creating scandal, H.I.H. was
unwillingly compelled to advise him to send in his
resignation, which, shortly after the peace, he did.
Prince S. V., who is a handsome, distinguished-look-
ing man, with the " air noble," of affable manners
and address, has great ability and diplomatic *savoir-
faire*.   His French education has made him fond of,
and partial to, Europeans.   He has given ample proof
that he possesses great personal courage ; but his
military talent, like that of most Russian generals,
may be considered mediocre.   The attacks on the
Turkish fortified lines in front of Batoum, both of
which failed, and *might* have produced consequences
still more disastrous, were, it is believed, undertaken
at his advice and recommendation.

Leaving Baghdad, the road passes for several miles
through a fine beech and oak forest, then crosses a
river and approaches the line of railway, overhanging
which is a line of low undulating hills and plateaux,
mostly covered with oak jungle, hazel, etc., on one of
which, overlooking the line, are situate the pretty
rural cottage, vineyard, and outhouses of Count L.,
now, poor fellow, deceased, after many years of hard
struggle, just as his property was beginning to give a
return ; just also when he would have inherited a
considerable fortune left him by a relative.   L., like
most men one meets in the Caucasus, had " a history."
Originally Vicomte ———, owner of a fine landed property in his native country, besides receiving a large
fortune with his wife, he irretrievably crippled his

resources, and, after mortgaging his estate to meet his debts of honour and other liabilities, fled in company with his wife's maid to the Caucasus. As he took care to change his name, his family were for many years completely ignorant of his whereabouts, during which time he had been engaged, assisted by his mistress—a woman, not only of great personal attractions, but of uncommon ability—in endeavouring to create a new home. At length a French working man, who had known him, came to the Caucasus, and, returning, gave his wife and family news of him. They made every possible effort to persuade him to return, but without success. An aunt, with whom he was a favourite, dying during the course of the negotiations, left him a large fortune, which was on the point of being transmitted to him, when he himself died of smallpox, caught from his mistress, who, with her usual unselfishness and devotion, had insisted on visiting and nursing some neighbours whose servants and relations had deserted them during an epidemic of the disease which prevailed in 1881. She recovered, but he died. She now manages the little estate, having been left in undisturbed possession by L.'s heirs, who, recognising her many good qualities, respect the " faith unfaithful " which kept him (one can hardly say " falsely ") true.

CHAPTER VIII.

KUTAIS, the Cotatis of old writers and Colchis of the
ancient Greeks, situated in an unrivalled position on
the sloping hills, where the river Rion issues from the
wooded spurs and mountains composing the *avant-
garde* of the great sierra of the Caucasus, has been often
described by travellers. Like Tiflis and other considerable cantonment towns, it is constantly improving and enlarging, as the Government, by a system of
lending money on security of the site, makes it paying
work to build houses (and house property is always at
least as safe an investment as paper money). Numbers of the inhabitants can recollect it a dirty collection of wooden hovels raised on beams and blocks three
or four feet from the ground—the normal Mingrelian
and Imeritian architecture still observable at Poti,
Zugdidi, and other primitive unsophisticated bourgs;
half-starved pigs, dogs, and buffaloes wandering in
and out. Now the place is for the most part a pretty
brick and stone built town, with numerous villas and
garden-houses dotting its green environs; extensive

schools, churches, and hospitals ; tolerable roads, markets, and hotels—all effected, one may say, in spite of the local administration, bad even for the Caucasus, which is saying a good deal.

The Governor, who is said to have risen to his present position through the good graces of a certain great lady, has travelled, as a matter of course, talks several European languages, is affable, polished, and serene. His manner of governing, however, leaves—*i.e.* as compared, say with the orthodox *kutchery* system in vogue in the North-West Provinces—" something " to be desired. He rises, winter and summer, between noon and 1 P.M., by which time of day a considerable assemblage of grievance-mongers, petitioners, sufferers from " zooloom," and omedwars of all sorts, has collected in the hall of the gubernatorial residence, at the foot of the staircase leading to the " huzoor's " suite of apartments. All the less " eligible " having been eliminated by the retainers, the great man, having duly " tea'd," shaved, dressed, and consumed a cigarette or two, at length deigns to appear on the landing outside his anteroom, thereby producing a thrill or sensation in the " ordinary crowd " below, on whom he gazes supremely for some moments, while a confused whispering murmur (any one who talks above his breath is immediately expelled) and rustling of petitions is heard. Indicating two or three individuals, selected at hazard, to his attendant myrmidons by an authoritative gesture, he finally makes sign that their respective documents in MS. be handed in, which being done, and the same consigned to a clerk, another moment sees the assemblage dismissed, the component parts being hustled outside with scant ceremony.

This *levée*, a little listening to abstracts of reports and much important private confabulation with police masters and " pristoffs,"[1] make up the great man's morning work, lasting till 4 P.M., when dinner and a siesta supervene ; then tea, and a drive if the weather is propitious.   If not, the serious business of the day, or rather night—viz. cards—sets in, at which they stick till well into the small hours, drinking tolerably hard the while.

With reference to these *noctes ambrosianæ* divers anecdotes are current ; also respecting the police master, the great authority of the place, next to, if indeed he is inferior in actual influence to, the Governor.   Tradition asserts that a late police master was himself in prison for some years at the outset of his career for defalcation.   The gaol is, as may be imagined, a small pandemonium, very like Newgate a couple of centuries or so ago, guarded by a detachment of soldiers (relieved once a week) under a lieutenant, who, to dissipate ennui, has the opportunity of making himself agreeable to such of the female prisoners—and there is always a tolerable supply to choose from—as happen to be goodlooking.   In this manner (criminals being often in gaol for two or three years before sentence is given, and the execution of it enforced) several interesting

---

[1] A pristav, or pristoff, meant originally a sort of petty political agent ; it has now got to mean a police inspector.

murderesses have actually added to the population while in durance.

A certain charitable (to Muscovite administration) and benevolent traveller, or perhaps, which is more probable, innocent of the mysteries of what in Indian official parlance is called "eyewash," armed with documents recommending him to all governors, natchalniks, and provincial magnates, has lately travelled (post-haste, of course) over the length and breadth of the Russian Empire, from Dan to Beersheba, *i.e.* from Petersburg to Petropaulovsk on the Pacific, and from Odessa to Orenburg on the Urals, finding (as was to be expected) everything "very good," *especially* the prisons.

His experience, however, does not alter facts in general, or the fact in particular, that Russian gaols (in the Caucasus at any rate), and I have reason to believe in other parts of the empire, are normally pretty much what our gaols were 150 or 200 years ago, when old Minshull wrote his thieves' spelling-book (I say normally, because there *is* such a thing as clearing a place up *pro tem.*, making prisoners wash, giving them clean shirts, and something to eat once in six months, or so ; and the moment selected for doing this is often, in Russia—and indeed elsewhere—found to strangely coincide with the advent of some great man, distinguished foreigner, or traveller who is writing a book) ; in support of which view I will proceed to quote some "modern instances."

Less than three years ago there was in the Kutais

gaol, where he had been over two years without trial
(or awaiting sentence, I forget precisely which), a
young Georgian "noble," an educated man with
"aspirations," herding with barbarous felons. His
crime was having in his possession a work called *En
Avant* criticising the Russian Government rather
sharply, demanding representative institutions, con-
stitutional government, etc., and consequently pro-
scribed by the censorship.

He was finally sentenced to Siberia for life. His
wife, a most amiable and charming lady, who, being
previously engaged to him, had insisted on marrying
him (against the wishes of all her relations) while
actually in prison, sharing his exile. He was certainly *no* Nihilist or conspirator, and seemed, from
what I saw of him, to be a well-meaning, rather
enthusiastic young man. Many other prisoners were
then in gaol who had been there months without
trial.

The sanitary arrangements of the gaol were of the
very worst description; and I repeatedly heard that
the funds allotted by Government, both for the
above purpose and for supplying the miserable
rations allowed the prisoners, were diverted to other
"purposes."

This gaol is also used (or was, when I was there)
as a "bedlam," or lunatic asylum, spare cells being
devoted to this purpose, thus adding to the other
horrors of the place.

The gaol superintendent, whose dilapidated habitation (unrepaired for years) was inside the prison-

yard, or rather the *enceinte,* was an old officer (lieutenant) of over thirty years' service, in the course of
which he had seen much hard campaigning. A better
fellow I never met. I believe that he frequently
alleviated the misery of the more unfortunate
détenus who had no friends, or whose friends (outside) had abandoned them, out of his own pocket ;
though he was, of course, powerless against the
Augean corruption which underlay the evil, and, I
have reason to believe, eventually lost his place by
speaking too freely concerning it. His salary, all in-
cluded, was, after thirty-five years' service (in the
army and in the prison) £100 per annum. He had
a wife and large family to support entirely from this.
After losing his appointment in the prison, he had
nothing to live upon except his lieutenant's pay (£3
per mensem). Such is Russian military life for those
without family interest and connections. But I am
digressing.

As a contrast to the case above cited, and as
showing that when a crime is not political, and when
the accused has "resources," Russian tribunals can
be lenient, and Russian gaols polite "houses of
detention," rivalling the old Fleet prison as regards
"accommodation" for "gentlemen as *is* gentlemen,"
I will relate an anecdote of the Tiflis "penal arrangements."

The year before last a tradesman of the colony,
condemned to eight months' imprisonment for falsi-
fying accounts, and thereby cheating the Russian
Government (while employed by it to purchase

machinery in England) out of considerable sums, had, though he contrived, by demurrers, appeals, and legal chicanery of all sorts, put in motion by his solicitor, to avert execution of his sentence for *eight years* (during the whole of which period he went about his business as usual), finally to undergo it, and went quietly into "quod." The evidence against him being perfectly clear and convincing, he might just as well have done so at first, and saved his money, instead of, as he did, spending several thousands of roubles in vain endeavours to avert the consequences of his "mistake." But this is neither here nor there.

While incarcerated, being a man of substance, he was treated with consideration and respect ; he had a room to himself neatly furnished, his friends had access to him, and whatever he chose to order for his meals was provided. He was even let out at night (on parole), and used to drive to his house in the suburbs, after dusk, and visit his family.

These two examples of the "working of the system" are, I presume, sufficient ; if not, plenty more can be given.

I may remark, in conclusion, that well-meaning travellers, ignorant of the language, who fly about the country with letters of introduction, and are preceded by cipher telegrams, indicating what they are to see, what conclusions to draw, etc., though "convenient" for the official (if a bore), stink exceedingly in the nostrils of the liberal and progressive portion of the Russian non-official public.

It was at Kutais, after the war, that I first met
Captain C., whose lively "eccentricities" were just
then a standing fund of amusement for his intimates
and polite society in general. A dragoon captain, he
had distinguished himself generally throughout the
operations in Turkish Armenia by active outpost duty,
scouting, foraging, and obtaining intelligence and
supplies. He, however, during the "heat and hurry"
of the campaign, somehow not only indented on
the villagers for hay and barley, but for "girls"
for himself and subalterns, which practice being
carried out wherever his troop happened to be
quartered, the inhabitants, though long - suffering
(being used to a great deal of that sort of thing
from the Bashi-Bazouks and Kurds), sent in such
complaints against him to headquarters that he was
tried by court-martial towards the end of the war,
only being pardoned by the commander-in-chief on
the score of meritorious and efficient service. Finding
himself, shortly after this event in his career, stationed
at Alexandropol, C., ever restlessly eager to contribute to, and promote public amusement and recreation, got up a grand ball, to which he and his
intimates invited nearly all the ladies of the station,
most of whom accepted. A large hall having been
prepared and duly adorned, a good supper and plenty
of potables laid in, the festivities were commenced
on the appointed evening, and continued till about
3 A.M., by which time champagne and excitement
having begun to tell, a previously concerted " practical joke" of the confederates (by which, at a given

o

signal, access to, and egress from, the ballroom were cut off by certain troopers posted for the purpose) was put in execution, the lights were turned off, and—the rest must be imagined. The audacity of the escapade naturally saved its perpetrators. Too many were compromised, and there was no individualising or selection possible. Besides, the whole affair was voted "too exquisitely ludicrous" to make a serious business out of.

This jest, however, C. being well known as the sole contriver, got him to be considered "rather too clever by half," even by his comrades (when tolerably sober), and he was consequently, as a sort of penance, relegated with his troop to an out-station on the high plateau, where, far from clubs, baccarat, *petit soupers*, etc., he prepared to pass the long and dreary winter months as best he could.

To kill time and keep his hand in, he took to visiting the Armenian tradesmen of the place, and their wives, many or all of whom talked Russian, and some of whom, having enriched themselves by contracts during the war, now and then gave small entertainments. At one of these reunions he made the acquaintance of an Armenian girl, who, having a good dowry and tolerable education, was engaged, and shortly to be married. To her did C. "seriously incline," making love in real hussar fashion, on every possible (or impossible) opportunity, utterly careless of the effect produced on the bridegroom and the young lady's relations, who naturally looked upon such behaviour as *inconvenable* to the last degree, and consequently hurried on the preparations for the wedding, to which they took care that that gallant officer should not receive an invitation.

Now the manner of Armenian and Russian weddings is, that they take place in the afternoon, and are followed by a feast, which is followed by a dance and supper, the happy couple retiring to their apartment about midnight; while the guests, with much dancing and joviality, "keep it up" till daybreak. Our hero, though, as aforesaid, he had received no invitation, nevertheless, accompanied by two athletic subalterns, all three in uniform, presented himself at the dance, and politely but firmly demanded admittance, which, as he was second in command of the station, to avoid unpleasantness and scandal, was conceded by the company assembled, consisting of the relations and friends of the bride and bridegroom, and the bridesmaids, selected, as usual, from the best-looking girls in the neighbourhood. Once in, the trio, after helping themselves liberally to drinks, began to "put on side." C., marching up to the bride with a resolute air, claimed a dance, while his companions paired with the two best-looking bridesmaids. This passed off, but when the next dance, and the next, and the next were monopolised, the "harmony of the evening" became somewhat overclouded and dimmed. Liquors of various descriptions having been freely partaken of by the Armenians, as well as by C. & Co., the cloud presently burst in a furious verbal shindy, followed by a well-meant attempt to eject the intruders from a window, which would doubtless have succeeded had not C., like a prudent and experienced officer, provided against such a contingency by posting a dozen of his men outside, who, smashing in the door, and plunging into the fray, very soon turned the tables on the "Armiashkas." [1]

While this reinforcement was actively engaged in clearing the field of the enemy, bundling them down staircases, and generally "mopping the floor" with them, the Captain, constituting himself protector of the bride, took her "out of harm's way," and did his best to soothe her alarm and supply the place of a husband, while his subs paid similar attentions to their partners; after which, and another bottle or two of "fiz," they crowned their exploits by "having in" such of the Armenians as could be found on the premises, "et milites suos in ordine ponens, braccas descendere mandavit, et Armenios nudos eorum posteriores osculare jussit, quod, sine morâ factum quia, et ense suo minando compulsit eos," they returned, rather drunk, but covered with glory, to their quarters.

It was, of course, hopeless to expect that this last freak (coming, as it did, on the heels of the Agapemone ball business), though admittedly the *sublime du genre*, could be passed over, and C. was accordingly brought to trial—seriously this time—by court-martial, for conduct unbecoming, etc., prejudicial to, etc. (the charges were a perfect curiosity of military jurisprudence), and after over a year's proceedings and open arrest, was, with his two subalterns, at

[1] The Russian diminutive for "Armian" (Armenian), applied contemptuously, as one would say "le petit Arménien."

length condemned to dismissal from the service, and, in addition, himself to fifteen, and his subs to seven, years' transportation (or rather exile) to Siberia.

He was not, however (his family being a firm of lawyers, long established, and knowing how to pull the wires), at the end of his resources, for, though his unfortunate subalterns went to Siberia, C. somehow or other never got farther than Tiflis, where, and at Kutais, he used to roam about openly enough, well known by his numerous friends and acquaintances to have "bilked" his sentence, and to be contemplating a trip to Paris, with which object in view he was, when I last saw him, studying French under a fat professor of that and other languages, whom he was in the habit of galvanising with Rabelaisian chaff and jokes.

Kutais, amongst other notabilities who have sojourned there, was at one time the headquarters of Prince W. S., nearly related to some very exalted personages, whose military career it would be no exaggeration to describe as in one sense the most extraordinary in Europe, having been, according to universal report, for the last twenty-five years or so, an almost unbroken series of escapades, debts (usually paid by Government), indiscipline, neglect of duty, and extravagant exploits of all sorts.

Prince S. turned up in the Caucasus shortly after the Crimean War, being immediately appointed to command a fine regiment of irregular horse, recruited from different districts which K. (the

same officer who found Prince V. lying wounded
on the field of the Tchernaya) had raised and reduced to exact discipline, and with whom he had
performed excellent service. Under Prince S. this
fine corps speedily went to the dogs, becoming
notorious for highway robbery and other irregu-
larities, which the Prince is said to have actually
abetted and encouraged, telling the men when they
applied for pay, which, for particularly good reasons,
was not forthcoming, that they were soldiers, had
arms, and should know how to live, etc. It was while
in command of this corps, then cantoned in the Araxes
valley, that the Prince privately invaded Persia,
crossing the frontier with his regiment, and burning a
village, the inhabitants of which had retaliated on
his men for looting, or some such freak. Prince S.
served through the late war, *i.e.*, he was present at
the headquarters, and " assisted," as the French say,
at various engagements, while not occupied in holding certain eccentric entertainments at Alexandropol,
concerning which, and the means adopted by the
Prince and his cronies for "raising the wind," I have
heard some curious and instructive anecdotes.

Prince S., and some of his intimates, including
Count B., commanded the first expedition against the
Turkomans, which, as might be expected, came to
grief, and was nearly annihilated. Shortly after his
arrival in the Caucasus he married a Georgian princess
of high family, who is considered his legitimate wife.
He is said, however, to possess twelve or fourteen others
in different parts of the country, most of whom are

Tartar ladies, married during his intervals of professing Mahometanism, which religion he is said to adopt when on the Mogan steppes, the Terek, and such localities, where it prevails extensively. He has lately for "distinguished" services received a grant of petroleum land near Baku, disposed of for, I believe, £25,000, with which, after settling some debts, he, I have heard, proceeded on furlough to Europe.

Kutais is, for a traveller proposing to explore the western, or, indeed, any part of the Caucasus, a good "centre" from which to commence operations. Arriving there in a few hours by rail from Poti (or now from Batoum), he can, after purchasing or hiring horses for self and guide, or by post-cart, start up the valley of the Rion (a lovely route in spring and summer) to "Ony," on the head-waters of the river, previous to reaching which place he can diverge, if adventurous, visit Mount Elborouz, and, resuming his route to Ony, cross the snowy chain, and descend on Wladikavkas at its northern base, thence by rail, or on horseback, across the steppes at the foot of the chain to Petigorsk, a great summer resort and watering-place. Thence again by railway and post-cart to Maikopp and Ekaterinodar, to view the Cossack settlements, etc. From Ekaterinodar again cross the sierra, here much lower, arriving at Novo Rassisk on the Black Sea, thence by steamer along the coast of Circassia to Sookhoom Kaleh or Batoum, or home *viâ* Odessa and the Crimea, Constantinople, etc. Or following the "route militaire de Georgie" from Wladikavkas, he can recross the great chain by the Dariel Pass, past Mount Kasbek, and reaching Tiflis, visit Kars and the Armenian highlands.

Or proceeding south instead of north from Kutais, he can traverse the Elborouz range facing the town, arriving at Abbas Tuman in two days' ride, thence to Akhaltsik, Ardahan, Olti, Kars, the Araxes valley and Ararat to Erivan, returning to Tiflis by the post-road, past the great Lake Sivan, which is well worth seeing, as, indeed, is the whole neighbourhood of the late war in Asia Minor to any one interested in the Eastern question, Russian " progress," our Indian possessions, and Asiatic history.

CHAPTER IX.

To proceed to Gouriel, or Gouri, from Kutais, you cross the Rion by an iron bridge, and, passing the great military hospital and barracks on the left, emerge through a long straggling suburb and Russian reservist settlement, on to the flat alluvial plain of Imeritia, dotted with scattered hamlets, nestling amongst fruit groves, patches of Indian corn, woods and copses, while the greater and lesser Caucasus tower on either side, clothed with sombre forest, above which their snow-streaked summits appear at an altitude of 8000 or 9000 feet perpendicular above the valley.

The barracks and military hospital situated on the right bank of the river, just below the bridge, are fine stone buildings kept in excellent order. They were, towards the close of the war, at which period I was often in Kutais, filled (as well as all the hotels) with wounded and sick officers, or rather with officers who *had* been wounded or sick, but who being, although now convalescent, in a chronic state of impecuniosity, found drawing subsistence allowance in hospital, in addition to their pay, with nothing to do, pleasanter work than regimental duty (on pay alone), and consequently hung on as long as possible, as, the medicoes being indulgent good fellows enough, they had no difficulty in doing. Among these gentlemen figured a certain Captain K., of the Russian navy, a man of considerable talent and varied information, who had travelled and read much, but dissipated, and with a perfect mania for the duello.

Cards, smoking, and the consumption of inordinate quantities of wine and spirits being often the order of the day, and always of the night, disputes frequently arose, which would not have much mattered, for Russians rarely bear malice, and are, as a rule, ready to patch up the most serious quarrel next morning, had it not been for the presence of the said naval officer, who, though he preferred figuring as principal, would condescend to act as second, sometimes in both capacities on the same occasion.

As K. was often the aggressor, either by making use of violent language, throwing packs of cards, tumblers, or candlesticks when in liquor, or knocking somebody down (for he prided himself much on his boxing, which he had learned in England), I was astonished at his not being put under arrest, more especially as, even when by his own admission in the wrong, he invariably refused to apologise. Russian commandants, however, will rarely trouble themselves about those not under their immediate authority (properly enough), and the gentlemen in hospital came under this category, not being under any one in particular, except perhaps the divisional surgeon, who naturally thought affairs of honour no business of his.

The " affairs," which usually came off near a church or monastery outside the town (much, no doubt, to the edification of the ecclesiastics belonging to it), were not conducted with any particular secrecy. They used to charter a couple of cabs or phaetons and drive off, taking a gun or two as if going shooting. If anybody was hit, an obliging doctor would certify that it was "an accident" which had happened while sporting, which satisfied all parties.

They were posted at twenty to twenty-five paces, tossed up for first shot, twenty seconds being allowed to take aim, and usually missed each other dead; indeed I do not think any one was hit all the time except by K., who was a good pistol-shot, and would pink his opponent in the leg or arm, if he thought he had tried to hit him. · K. seemed to think it quite twenty to one against any one hitting his man when fighting for the first time, and often said so. He told me he had fought three duels before he succeeded in "making an example" of an antagonist. He hailed from Courland, in the Baltic provinces, where, according to his account, affairs were as common and as easily arranged, "without any fuss," as in Ireland during the last century, or, as formerly, in India. He talked with contempt of the degeneracy of the Caucasus in this respect.

K. was a tall thin man, with a stoop (slight) in the shoulders, deep-sunk black eyes, and a sallow complexion much marked with smallpox, giving him a hard determined look. To see him "in position," grasping a long duelling pistol, with just enough vodky inside to steady his nerve (he never drank the evening before fighting), was an instructive sight. He was a grandson of Admiral K., the friend of Nelson, and first Russian navigator who sailed round the world, and a nephew of the general mentioned in my former letter killed during the campaign, who on finding that he was mortally wounded, called for champagne, and, as K. would relate with pride, "died like a gentleman," pledging his comrades-in-arms.

It is probably the respectable distance—usually twenty-five paces—at which Russians place their men in a duel which makes these combats generally harmless; though it is, by the by, well known that at the short distances of ten or fifteen paces, adopted formerly by English amateurs, quite a small percentage of hits took place, and a very small ditto of *fatal* duels (I forget the proportion), in comparison to the number of shots exchanged.

The road to Orpiri (twenty-seven versts) from Kutais goes nearly straight (past a few hamlets of wooden houses, village greens, and a great deal of jungle, in which good woodcock-shooting is to be had in autumn and winter) to a place on the Poti and Tiflis railroad

called Samtrede, whence the new branch line to
Batoum leads off. Samtrede is a large "bourg" of
scattered houses densely inhabited.

Entering one of the numerous wooden "dukans"
or wine-shops, with which the place abounds, for the
usual drink, we find ourselves amidst a crowd of un-
lettered "villeins" of the Gurth and Wamba type, in
hoods, chogas, and breeches of "rugged woollen,"
with the inevitable long dagger at girdle, the better
sort being represented by an occasional Armenian
trader, or a kniaz, with wooden trencher containing a fat capon or pullet before him (which he
dissects with a knife out of his belt), store of white
manchet bread, and a jug of sack; his silver-hilted
falchion, long dagger and pistol, hung on a peg behind him as he tucks in "provant" at what is literally
the hospitable "board" of the posada,—as wild a
one, by the way, as ever Don Quixote or Gil Blas de
Santillane adventured themselves in.

A ride of four miles from Samtrede brings one to
a wooden pile bridge across the Rion (here running
between muddy alluvial banks on its way to the
Black Sea) at the bourg of Orpiri, once the point to
which steamers ran from Poti, now, since the making
of the railway, nearly deserted. Crossing the river
here, you ascend the small outer range, *i.e.* comparatively small, dividing Imeritia from the Gouriel
country (as the Sewalick hills divide Saharanpore
from the Dhoon), and after much winding through
wooded ravines and glens, reach the summit of
the little pass leading into a beautiful upland,

dominated in its turn by the huge range of the lesser
Caucasus towering 8000 feet above it.   Old gray
towers and ancient chapels peep here and there from
the wooded slopes of the valley, down the centre of
which a clear river runs, bordered by green meadows
and Indian-corn patches.   On right and left of the
road, as we descend to the level of the river, the
white country-houses of the local nobility are conspicuous.   The first on the left belongs to Prince
D., whose history, or rather that of his wife, Princess B., well known in St. Petersburg, is rather
curious and instructive.   Prince D., with his troop
of mounted volunteers, all frontier men, served
through the war, and towards the close of it often
pressed me to accompany him.   Had I done so, I
should have witnessed the closing incident of the
campaign—namely, the bloody repulse of the Russians
from before Batoum on the 12th January.   And
I should certainly have accepted his offer, had I not
already been arrested four or five times for proceeding to the front without permission (which was
never accorded to any Englishman),— on the last
occasion narrowly escaping execution; so that the
risk, in addition to that of being shot by the enemy,
or by D.'s men, some of whom, though fine fellows,
were not particular, was too great.

A little farther on, on the right, is the house of
D——g, another prince, who, in the days of the
empire, made an excursion to Paris; and finding
himself short of cash, applied successfully to Louis
Napoleon to pay his hotel bill and return journey,—

a fact which says something for the late Emperor's generosity.

Five or six miles farther on, at the foot of a bluff on which is perched a solid stone tower of refuge, is another demesne, and country-house with farm and garden, where I once put up for the evening, and was hospitably received by the owner, Prince E., a tall handsome man, with a gloomy expression of countenance. Next day, however, I was told in Ozurget, on relating my experiences, " that I had better not have done so ;" and on closer inquiry as to the reason why, learned that my entertainer, being tolerably well known to have recently assassinated his father (suspected on good grounds of intending to form a second marriage), people were rather shy of him, especially as the old prince had been very popular, having done a great deal in various ways for the neighbourhood.

A fifteen miles' ride along the picturesque valley brings us, after passing several villages and crossing a forest-covered ridge of hills, to Ozurget, the former Turkish frontier station. Ozurget is a long "bourg" of antique wooden "dukans" and shops, built in a hollow with a stream running through it—a perfect specimen of old Mingrelia ; houses and gardens of "kniazes" dotting the ridges and slopes around, while the immense chain of steep mountain, wooded nearly to its summit, towers miles above. A more romantic locality is inconceivable ; and the history of the men of the valley, which up to this day has been a series of fierce frontier fighting, domestic treachery, robbery, assassination, and feudal skirmishes, is of a piece with the sombre wildness of the scenery.

The women are, now that the Circassians have left, the handsomest race of females in the Caucasus. Old Mar, an Englishman, who came to Gouriel in the days when the Western Caucasus was independent, and the Turks had fortresses along the coast as far as Anapa, and who had passed near fifty years in the valley, used to relate some interesting stories of the "goings on" of certain princesses in former days; reminding one rather closely of Brantom's *Dames Galantes.* One of these turned upon the manner in which a certain lady revenged herself upon Mar's wife for a slight she had experienced; and, though striking and characteristic, has, I fear, too much "local colour" in it for print.

In his day the old-world life of "excursions and alarums" was in full swing. His house and property were twice destroyed in clan fights; for, though on excellent terms with the chiefs and people, he steadily refused to take a side in their warlike operations, which was considered in those times most inexcusable conduct.

As the men of Gouriel are intimately connected by ties of race, language, relationship, and descent with the Kabouletz, Afshars, and Lazes across the late frontier-line in the mountain, and along the Black Sea shore, which latter became Mahometans while the Gouriels remained Christians, the greatest emulation and hostility naturally prevails, or rather prevailed, in war-time.

In the late campaigning, barring the attacks in force on the Turkish lines, both of which failed disastrously, and the usual artillery long-bowl duelling, the fighting at this point was a series of skirmishes between the Lazes and the men of Gouriel. Both sides being practised mountaineers, acquainted with the ground, dressed alike, and well armed, the Gouriels with the Berdan rifle and the Lazes with the Martini, the finest available bush-fighting went on throughout.

The theatre on which this portion of the " War in Asia" was fought out is most picturesque. Imagine a section of the sub-Himalaya, or of the Alps, where tolerably lofty, planted on the seashore, with, immediately below it, a sort of undulating park-like country three or four miles in breadth, consisting of wooded ridges and valleys, stretching down from the lofty mountains above to the sea; here and there a high peak or abrupt crag. Suppose one of these low spurs extending in an unbroken forest-covered ridge, nearly level, from the base of the big mountain to the beach, and ending above it in a steep over-hanging cliff. Parallel to this wooded ridge in the little valley in front of it is a largish mountain stream, unfordable when swollen by heavy rain or melting snow. Imagine the ridge fortified at every available point and coign of vantage, with mountain batteries, field ditto, and shelter-trenches (especially near the end resting on the sea, where the natural defences are weaker and the ground more undulating), and further covered and protected by an ironclad anchored a mile or so from the shore, with its

P

guns bent on the strip of sand below the cliff. You will then be able to form a correct "mind's-eye" picture of the Tzikinzeri lines about six miles from Batoum, so gallantly held by Dervish Pacha throughout the campaign.

The Russians, marching from Ozurget (about 3000 regulars and artillery), preceded by swarms of native levies, horse and foot, Cossacks, Imeritians, and Gouriel men, attacked and captured an advanced post of the Turks in the forest (held by the Lazes and a battalion of Nizams, who fell back), about ten miles from the boundary-line; after which they encamped at a place called Mookestat, whence they advanced to Kootsebani, five versts beyond, an elevated peak, overlooking, but at a great distance, the Tzikinzeri ridge and enemy's lines, between which and their camp (*i.e.* the Russian) intervened a confused landscape of forest-covered ranges, and valleys trending down to the sea; a dangerous debatable ground, occupied in force by experienced mountaineers thoroughly acquainted with partisan warfare, and to whom, living as most of them did, actually on the ground, every nook of it had been, as the Russians speedily to their cost discovered, familiar from childhood.

The plan of General Oglubjee, a Montenegrin or Dalmate, who commanded the Russian column, was naturally to turn the right of the Turkish position, which rested on the big mountain range; their left, resting on the sea, being, from the concentrated fire of the batteries, rifle-trenches, and anchored ironclads, justly considered impregnable.

Reconnaisances, skilfully effected by Gouriel men, having demonstrated that the artificial defences of the enemy's right were inconsiderable, and that a lodgment in force, once effected on the ridge at its junction with the big mountain, would take the batteries *au revers*, it was determined to make a move in that direction.

Had this decision been immediately carried out by a *coup de main*, pushing the whole of the native levies forward, following them up closely by the regulars, through the dense jungle of laurel, rhododendron, and hazel covert, which clothed the ravines and hollows between the Russian left and the ridge, it is possible that the operation, though a difficult one, would have succeeded. But General Oglubjee considering his guns indispensable, and it being of course next to impossible to transport even mountain pieces over such ground without some kind of road, orders were issued to commence the construction of one practicable for field artillery—a task not easy, even had there been no opposition to encounter.

To effect it, the sappers and pioneers were set to work, reinforced by numerous volunteers from the line regiments, the whole guarded by strong supports and pickets, of mountaineers and foot Cossacks, thrown out on front and flanks of the working parties; but the Kabouletz and Lazes, armed with Martinis, excellent shots, and on their own ground, availing themselves of every " coign of vantage," harassed the outposts and workmen day and night to such purpose that the Russian commanders speedily found that they were losing from forty to fifty men killed and wounded daily, without inflicting any adequate loss on the enemy. The road meantime was advancing so slowly that it was clear they would, at that rate, lose half their men before completing it to the ridge; the final success of the operation being of course even then problematical. This being the state of affairs, it was determined to traverse the space intervening between Kootsebani and the Turkish position by a route practicable for artillery existing lower down, towards the sea, where the covert was less dense, and to attack the centre of the fortified line, trusting to luck, resolution, and the chapter of accidents for success; but this turned out badly.

The Kabouletz and Laz irregulars, all mountain shikarees and frontier men, accustomed to the use of arms from their childhood, and, from their thorough knowledge of the ground, cool and confident, falling back across the jungly ridges and hollows as the Russians advanced, kept up a deadly fire, and by the time the scattered column reached the Kintrish river, they had already lost many men, chiefly irregulars. When there, the concentrated fire from the batteries and rifle trenches along the ridge mowed them down by scores without their being able to inflict any loss worth speaking of on the enemy, and, joined to the big guns from the ironclads, completely demoralised the force, they finally retreating in great disorder, with a loss of 1800 killed and wounded, many of whom were abandoned to the enemy, and narrowly escaping losing their artillery, actually cap-

tured for a time by a rush of the Kabouletz, but re-
taken by a rally.

After this bloody repulse, the whole force retreated
upon the first position occupied, viz. Mookestat, a
broad flat-topped ridge, the Turks advancing and
occupying Kootsebani, which dominated Mookestat,
at a distance of some 4000 yards. Here the Russians
(after despatching their superfluous artillery and regulars to reinforce the army of the Grand Duke in the
Kars valley, then with difficulty holding its own
against Mukhtar Pacha) entrenched themselves, formed
a standing camp, and passed the rest of the summer
and autumn in long bowls with the Krupp guns of
the Turks on Kootsebani, and in outpost and picket
affairs with the Lazes and Kabouletz, until near
the close of the war, when, on New Year's Day[1] (old
style), the armistice having been actually agreed to
and proclaimed at Constantinople, they insidiously
attempted to catch Dervish Pacha napping, seize Batoum (which they were by no means confident they
would get by treaty), and hold it, on the *beati possi-
dentes* principle ; but in this expectation they were
miserably (and justly) deceived.

A theory, supported in high quarters, prevailed
amongst some of the staff, that the former attack had
failed in consequence of the denseness of the covert
clothing the ridges and ravines of the debatable
ground, causing the leading battalions to lose touch
of their supports to right and left, to scatter and miss
their bearings, and while thus confused and be-

[1] 12th January 1878.

wildered, to be overcome and shot down by the
mountaineers. This indeed was partially true, it
being notorious that the Russian soldier, though doggedly brave on open maidans and steppes, is, like
some other regulars, an inferior bush fighter, being
extremely liable to panic in woods and mountains,
to which he has a natural aversion. It was consequently insisted that an attack made in winter,
when the leaves were off the trees, would have every
chance of success, the advocates of this strategy
forgetting that the same conditions would be equally
advantageous to the enemy, as the result proved ; for
the Russians, reinforced since the retreat of the Turks
from Sookhoom, had no sooner reached, as on the
previous occasion, the Kintrish river, than they found
their column crowded together in a disorderly mass in
the narrow valley, and exposed to perhaps as heavy
and deadly a fire as ever, in all the bloody annals of
their ill-conducted Turkish campaigns, has been poured
upon them.

The wooden bridge they had contrived to throw
over the Kintrish river, which was swollen by melted
snow from the surrounding ridges and mountain sides,
broke down after part of the force had crossed, and
these, unable to face the fire, had to recross by swimming, drowning each other in the attempt, or shot down
by the Lazes and Kabouletz who crowned the ridge,
and were swarming over the slopes within 100 or 150
yards of the mob of fugitives, adding to the confusion
and panic by shouts of " Allah " delivered with start-
ling emphasis. The stream was choked with corpses,

and the opposite maidan and slope strewed with them, the Russian loss on this occasion (officially stated at 1000 killed and wounded) being known to have been in reality something like 2500. Artistically considered, this fight was by far the most glorious episode (excepting perhaps the march of Suliman Pacha through Montenegro) of the whole war. The scene itself was magnificent, and would have made a grand battle picture. Lofty mountains, capped with snow, towering in the background above the leafless ridges and dark glens, in and on which, partly concealed by clouds of white smoke from the batteries, the contest was being fought out; in the foreground the dark blue sea, with an ironclad or two firing. A gallant population victoriously fighting *pro aris et focis* against despotism and corruption; soon, alas! in spite of their successful heroism, to lose them for ever, and, abandoned by Europe, to suffer more severely than if they had basely allowed themselves to be vanquished. Such was the panic attendant on this defeat that had Dervish Pacha advanced, he might, after exterminating or capturing the *débris* of the Russian regulars, have occupied the Ozurget valley and perhaps Kutais.[1]

I am, however, all this time forgetting Prince Gregory Gouriel, now vice-governor of Batoum, the most perfect gentleman of the Western Caucasus, of whom I have been three times the guest. Tall, affable, and aristocratic, hospitable to excess, fond of conversa-

---

[1] A general and some of the best officers of the army of the Caucasus lost their lives in this action.

tional anecdote and the society of foreigners, Prince
Gregory was the principal personage in the valley.
His local influence and knowledge of local politics on
each side of the frontier were unlimited, and his judg-
ment assured.   I heard him, just previous to the opening of the campaign, when every one imagined that
the Russian army, having been reorganised, remodelled,
and infinitely improved since the Crimean War, would,
unless the Western Powers intervened in favour of
the Turks, carry all before them, hold quite a different
opinion, and indeed prophesy almost exactly what
afterwards actually took place.   "We shall be lucky
in my opinion," said he, "if we can manage to keep
the Turks from paying *us* a visit, far from being in
Constantinople in six weeks, as most of them expect
to be."

It was at Prince Gregory's hospitable mansion
that I made the acquaintance of Captain G., whose
history, typical of the intellectual Russian officer
with free aspirations, deserves some notice.   G. was
of good family, and received an excellent education;
but being turbulent and insubordinate as a subaltern
—a line of conduct often mistaken by Russian youths
for independence and manly freedom—was ordered to
do duty in Siberia, where he passed several years,
making a name in society at Irkutsk.   While here,
his father dying, he came in for considerable property,
and, applying at once for leave of absence, sent in his
resignation in true Russian style, leaving Irkutsk with
such precipitation as to abandon his furnished apartments, containing, amongst other property, a valuable

collection of arms and other articles of vertu, which,
it is believed, he never afterwards heard of. On
arriving at home and receiving possession, he at once
turned his paternal heritage into cash, and settling
half the sum thus acquired on his two sisters, thereby
providing for them, departed with the remainder to
Paris, where, in a few years, he ran through the whole
of it, eventually turning up completely penniless in
Tiflis. Finding his applications to the staff for military employment—the only thing he was fit for—unsuccessful, and being entirely without resources, he
quietly exchanged his European clothes for a rough
choga and Asiatic suit, in which guise he hired himself
out as a coolie to a road contractor, and commenced
work with the usual gang of Tartars and refugee Persian labourers in the streets, breaking stones, sweeping
up mud, etc. Being a tall man of striking appearance,
it was not long before some of his staff corps acquaintances recognised him in spite of his disguise, whereupon G., on their expressing considerable surprise
at seeing him in such a plight, coolly told them: "You
should be surprised at the cursed Government which
permits honest men who have worn its uniform to
starve unless they do such work."

Soon after this he received a communication
requesting his attendance from the Adjutant-General,
which he complied with, haughtily entering the recep-
tion-room (through a brilliant crowd of uniformed
swells) in his choga, begrimed with dust and dirt. The
first thing he did was to ask, as a preliminary, for a
drink of whisky, which being supplied and promptly

disposed of, his requirements were entered into, the result being that he was appointed to a Cossack corps, afterwards made inspector of the Frontier Militia, on which duty he was travelling when I first met him, and ultimately commanded a battalion of "platoons," or foot Cossacks, during the operations against Batoum. G. is a poet, and an ardently patriotic Russian. A Pole having on one occasion incautiously remarked in his presence, *apropos* of an anecdote illustrative of the shabbiness of a certain official, "that no one but a Russian could have done it," G., who was in Cossack uniform, solemnly drawing his enormous khinjal,[1] fetched a blow (without saying a word) at the Pole, which, if he had not rapidly vacated his chair and the room, would have probably "done his business." The last time I saw G. was at Poti, where he and some friends were fêting a Hungarian officer *en route*, I believe, to Persia.

Having already given the reader a tolerable idea

---

[1] A Caucasian khinjal or dagger is always fifteen to eighteen inches long, sometimes a couple of feet or more.

Apropos of fetching blows with khinjals, a common enough way of settling disputes in the Caucasus, where everybody more or less goes about armed, a Cossack officer, not long ago, at a "big drink" in the Mogan, as often happens at such *séances*, drew his sabre and began flourishing it about. He was told by one of the convives, a "quiet sort of man," to put up his iron, "as he could do no good with it ;" whereupon the Cossack maintained that he could cut off the interlocutor's head at a blow, and offered to back his opinion by a bet of fifty roubles. This wager being promptly accepted, the quiet man knelt down (nobody interfering), bared his neck, and was decapitated there and then, to the astonishment of the company, who now began to recover their senses. The Cossack was, I believe, cashiered for this feat, and relegated for some years to Siberia.

of the landscape lying along the seashore between
Ozurget and Batoum in my sketch of the military
operations which took place there, I will not trouble
him with a detailed description of the ride, but go on
at once to Batoum itself and the surroundings of the
same. In effect, from Ozurget to Batoum is a day's
journey on horseback over an undulating country of
hill and dale, more or less wooded; lofty mountains on
the left, the sea on the right.

Batoum itself is a Turkish town, with a small
harbour, now in process of " Russification," and
the inevitable hideous barracks and Government
custom - house, where *" voi che entrate, lasciate,"*
etc.; for though a free port, they have contrived to
levy duties of some sort, under, I believe, the excuse of an octroi. There is a cordon of Cossacks all
round at a distance of four miles from the town,
where the regular business of customs blackmailing
goes on.

Most of the Mahometan residents have been de-
spoiled of their land and property by the methods
already described, and have left the country. The
comparatively few country-people and mountaineers
who remain in the villages of the interior have
many of them turned brigands, in consequence of
which a severe system of dragooning, or rather Cos-
sacking, has lately been instituted, and is now in
progress. Russian annexation apparently demoralises
both those who remain under it, and those who, like
the Circassians, emigrate to avoid it.

Batoum itself is being regularly fortified: an arsenal

and depot for military stores has been constructed up a valley behind the place, heavy artillery landed, and earthworks run up, which, by means of the circular railway now constructed, can be armed with 18 and 25 ton guns in a few hours.

Batoum will, within a few months, be connected by railway with the Poti-Tiflis line at Samtrede.

CHAPTER X.

LEAVING Kutais by the western post-road as before,
we follow the same for a few miles, then strike off
to the right, and approach the base of the gloomy
Ratcha and Lesghoom ranges (spurs of the main chain),
which shut in Imeritia to the north. We now enter
upon some hours of rather intricate riding, along bridle-
paths, through dense hazel coppices, and patches of
wood, remnants of the primeval forest which doubtless
once covered the whole wide valley.

The scattered hamlets we pass consist of square
wooden-frame houses (the normal Rion valley architecture), raised from the ground on thick beams and
logs, and situated each in a separate " compound,"
carefully fenced in (to keep out the droves of half-
starved pigs which get their living how they can), and
containing apple, pear, walnut, and other fruit trees.
After much skirting of maize patches, negotiating of

rude gates and primitive unsafe bridges, we arrive, towards the afternoon, at the Tskeni-Skali (horse river), one of the principal affluents of the Rion, rising in Svanetia, and reported dangerous, on account of its rapid current and sudden floods.

Fording this obstacle, by judiciously directing our course down stream to minimise the force of the water, we again traverse a pleasant country of groves, woods, and corn patches, till, towards evening, when, after crossing another large river, this time by a ferry-boat, we approach an isolated mountain, on a jutting spur of which stands one of the ancient fortresses before mentioned, and below which lies the " bourg " or street of tumble-down wooden boxes composing Old Senakh.

As this place, formerly an important village, was completely ruined by the railway taking another line, we proceed five or six miles farther on, to a location hight New Senakh, where are the railway station and a bran new wooden town, on an improved principle, containing not only numerous taverns and groggeries (all houses of entertainment for man and beast), but an actual " hotel," patronised by the local nobility, Senakh being to some extent a " centre."

The " public in general " stick to the dukans, as do we, having horses to look after, for which animals (every one of consequence being supposed to travel by post-cart) there is rarely accommodation in such new-fangled establishments. As aforesaid, a Mingrelian town of the orthodox type is a long straight street of wooden one-story houses or cottages on each or either

side of a public road. These houses are in reality
nothing more nor less than huge wooden packing-cases,
roofed in, elevated upon joists or beams laid hori-
zontally, and raised from the ground to a height of
two or three feet by blocks of wood, squared, and
placed over each other at the corners. By this arrangement a vacant space is left underneath the building,
where pigs and dogs habitually congregate (especially
in rainy weather), grunting, squeaking, barking, and
biting each other at intervals, all which is more than
distinctly audible, and sometimes visible through the
wide chinks of the planking forming the floor.[1] Pigs
and pariah dogs, but above all pigs, are everywhere.
The sheds which form the stables usually contain pigs
occupied in rummaging in the straw with a view to
picking up the grain which falls from the rude mangers
(always full of holes and cracks) in which, if you are
green enough not to carry a nose-bag, your horses
will have to be fed.[2]

Pigs of all sizes will frequently "drop" from time
to time into the verandah, the bar, or the "keeping
room" of the hostelry, their visits passing unnoticed
unless they venture to attack any "provisions" belonging to the establishment, when they are driven out

[1] The jocose traveller can, while drinking tea, abate this nuisance,
and amuse himself at the same time, by baptizing them, through the
chinks aforesaid, with boiling water from the kettle.

[2] *N.B.*—It is as well to remain with your animals until they have
finished their feed, as Mingrelian travellers, though they will not
actually steal the corn themselves, have a way, if you leave the stable
(after pouring a peck or two of maize or barley into the manger), of
letting their horses loose. The sagacious animals immediately go for
the provender, probably getting more than their share,

with blows and execrations, to reappear " proximo
intervallo."

Each of the buildings composing the street has a
" balkhan " or verandah, made by prolonging the broad
shingled roof in front on the side facing the street,
creating, as the houses are set close together, a covered
raised " promenade " or *trottoir* down the whole
length of the roadway, in which, and in the open shop
fronts, groups of the inhabitants, reinforced by detachments from the villages and hamlets around, are loafing, smoking, drinking, haggling, and quarrelling from
morning to night, their unfortunate animals remaining
tied meanwhile to the posts supporting the verandah,
with, as a rule, nothing whatever to eat. A Mingrelian
will not waste money *en voyage* on feeding his horse,
his idea being that all animals should be, as much as
possible, self-supporting ; on which principle they are,
when not actually in work, turned out to graze and
stray all over the country, a lively horse-stealing business going on in consequence.   Horses are worse treated
in Mingrelia than in any country in the world.   No
other breed could support the abuses and privations to
which they are subjected, just as no other race of men
(except perhaps Irish, whom, by the way, in many
respects they much resemble) could live as the Mingrelian peasant does.   But I am digressing.

The houses comprising a Mingrelian street are
shut in in rear by rude enclosures of split logs set
on end in the mud.   Here are wooden stables and
cowhouses, perhaps also an unwholesome jungle of a
garden containing a few vines, cucumbers, gourds, and

neglected fruit trees.   They sometimes leave a narrow
entry between a couple of houses leading to the stables
and sheds in rear; but this is unusual, disturbing, as
it does, the continuity of the verandah promenade, and
thereby deranging loafing, gossiping, and trade privilege from end to end of the town.

It is besides unsafe, offering increased facilities for
procuring horses gratis, to say nothing of astute customers (after keeping the host up late over a bottle)
getting up very early, going into the yard, and
" vamosing" without inquiring for the bill.

The general practice is therefore for travellers, on
taking up their quarters for the night, to bring their
steeds into the verandah (reached from the street by
an inclined plane of planks, with battens nailed across
them to prevent slipping in wet weather), thence right
through the house into the back settlements.

They are generally led through; but a sporting
kniaz, who has just had a drink, will often *ride* in,
making his screw " curvet and rebound " up the planks,
and appearing suddenly "as large as life" in the
middle of the loafers at the bar, a feat which sometimes literally " brings down the house," or next to it.
The weary traveller, after seeing to his animals, getting his supper, and retiring to his " virtuous couch "
(his immoral plank, by the way, would often be nearer
the precise definition), must not calculate on uninter-
rupted repose, being liable at any moment to be
roused out of his first sleep by the advent of a party
of belated cavaliers,[1] booted, hooded, and armed at all

---

[1] " Owls fly late," as the Tartars say.

Q

points, just off some ungodly errand (abduction, or
horse-stealing probably, highway robbery possibly),
who, with much loud talking, thwacking of whips,
banging of silver-hilted weapons against partitions,
and trampling of hoofs on wooden floors, are travelling across the house with a view to stowing away their
horses for the night, preparatory to supper and a drink,
which latter, if there happens to be a "wandering min-
strel" on the premises with a sackbut, accordion, or
concertina (as is often the case), will be prolonged with
shouts and choruses far into the small hours.

In spite, however, of these drawbacks, the dukan
offers to archæologic or philosophic sojourners a certain interest, being, as it is, a glimpse into the past rude
life of Europe in the fourteenth or fifteenth century.

The dukan boys, shockheaded unkempt varlets,
often barefooted, skip about and serve jugs of wine,
as the tavern boy or "drawer" served "sack" to
Prince Hal and Falstaff. You see fat capons and
other meats ranged literally "on the board," or piled
on great wooden trenchers ready for customers, flanked
by flat loaves of white and brown bread. Forks are
spurned as effeminate inventions, the "drawer" dis-
secting a fowl or roast pig when ordered with a knife
(which he takes from his girdle and wipes on his
greasy jerkin) and his fingers.

The roystering kniazes who dismount and swagger in, booted, spurred, and muddy, are knights,
équités, and armigers ; the peasants in their rugged
woollen gaberdines, hose, and sandals, are villeins,
churls, and *adscripti glebæ*, who but the other day

followed their lords to battle when ordered. Every one who can afford it is armed in some way or other; even the peasants carry long daggers. It is plain that they all think and feel much as people thought and felt in Chaucer's time. These old-world customs and costumes are, however, already rapidly disappearing in the towns, for railways Europeanise a country *a vue d'œil.* It is probable that the end of the century will see the picturesque homespun of the lower classes replaced (except in remote localities) by the shabby black coat, pot hat, and dirty shirt, which, to the Asiatic Christian, denote civilisation.

The road into Mingrelia from Novi Senakh follows the railway for two or three miles. It then strikes off to the right, coasting the "great dismal swamp," morass, and wild forest, which, stretching far and wide on both banks of the Rion for a distance of twenty miles from the sea, forms a most effective barrier against hostile invasion of the coast from Nicolaieff to Anaklia. After eighteen versts, a considerable river, crossed by a strong plank bridge, is reached, on the far side of which is a post-station and hamlet with dukans. Some people pass the night here when leaving Senakh late in the day. Beyond this, along the road, are some scattered country-houses with enclosed gardens and orchards, a noticeable feature being the large "wych gates" at the entrances, *de rigeur* all over Mingrelia. This practice of roofing in gateways I could never ascertain the precise object of. It obtains, I believe, extensively in Western

China, where it probably originated; and was formerly customary in many parts of Europe. I have heard that the churchyard gates in some secluded parts of England are thus roofed in to this day; whether with a view to preserve the gate from the action of the weather, or of preserving visitors on a rainy day while somebody comes to open it, I am ignorant. It can hardly be the latter, at least in Mingrelia, for no people are more indifferent to a wetting, and few less likely to wait if they find a gate locked.

A few miles farther on, facing a wooded range on the right of the road, are the ruins of a curious fortress or castle, probably Roman, very ancient; the thick wall is now crumbled down, and almost hidden by a luxuriant growth of ivy. A mile beyond this the road dips down into a little valley, crosses a small river, and ascends again for a mile to a plateau, where are a hamlet and Cossack post, from which you can see the white buildings and garden houses of Zugdidi, the capital of Mingrelia, on the woody plain four miles off, and to which a gradual descent from this point brings you.

Zugdidi is a specimen Mingrelian town. A double row of wooden one-story houses and shops, with a continuous verandah, as previously described, along each front, constitutes the bazaar, and encloses a " place " or " maidan," over 100 yards in breadth, and some 300 in length, down the centre of which, shaded by a double row of fine plane trees, runs a stream of water, on either side of which is a promenade or walk. Beyond and behind the double row of shops extend, for a considerable distance, pleasant garden houses with enclosed compounds full of fruit trees, while at the lower end the "place" opens on the aristocratic quarter, where are situated the fine palace and "demesne" of Prince Nicholas Dadian, the hereditary ruler of the country, the house of Prince Murat, and the residences of other kniazes and notables connected with the royal family. Prince Nicholas, who is comparatively rarely at Zugdidi since his marriage, is extremely and deservedly popular. In addition to his palace at Zugdidi he has a beautifully-situated shooting-box and summer retreat in the mountains at Gordi, where he usually resides during the hot months, and where ibex and bear shooting parties are organised. The time to see Zugdidi to best advantage is while the Prince is there, surrounded by his retainers, relations, and court of kniazes, who form, when mounted *à la* Tcherkess with costly arms and trappings, a striking cavalcade. Prince Murat (related to Prince Nicholas's family by marriage) has lived at Zugdidi in retirement since the misfortunes which overtook the imperial dynasty in 1870. He is a good sportsman, good shot, and good rider, and besides a thoroughly accomplished gentleman. Zugdidi is situated in an undulating country, intersected with rivers running down towards the coast. On all sides, except towards the sea, are wooded mountains, green in the spring and summer, in the autumn of brilliant scarlet and orange tints. In many directions are ancient castles and refuges; one in particular (reached by a good road) about five miles off on the ford of the Ingour, is well worth a visit, this being the ancient stronghold mentioned by Sir John Chardin, to which the people hurried from the double invasion of the Turks and Abkhasians, which occurred during his memorable experiences of the Caucasus. A more picturesque country than Mingrelia would be hard to find. The people in their dress, accoutrements, manners, and customs very much resemble the ancient Irish, as any one who has perused old chronicles treating of the Milesians of former days, and will take the trouble to compare them with Sir John Chardin's description of the people of Mingrelia, may convince himself, without actually sojourning in the country. If he does, however, he will find the common resemblance so striking as to make him conclude that the two nations must have originally had one origin ; unless, indeed, both are (or were) " survivals " from a prehistoric period when all European races were in a similar stage.

From Zugdidi the traveller can, if he chooses, proceed on horseback to Sookhoom Kaleh (the port of Abkhasia) through a lovely country, perhaps the very finest part of the Caucasus, lying between the noble ranges of Otchem Tcheri and the seashores, densely wooded, but very thinly inhabited, and supposed to be unsafe.

Crossing the ford of the Ingour by the old castle above mentioned, two long days' ride (the first to a place called Ookhoom) through the forests, brings you to Sookhoom Kaleh. Several extensive ruins of churches and monasteries, which no one seems to

know anything about, are met with on this road, or
rather "trail," proving that the country must at some
former period have been occupied by a more civilised
and advanced race than the present inhabitants, who
are hardly equal apparently to the construction of a
boarded shanty. There is good shooting to be had
in this direction in autumn, but dogs are required.
With a couple of good spaniels, a fair bag of
pheasants may be made, or of woodcocks after
October.

Roedeer, boars, and bears are also to be met with,
and there is good trout-fishing in the rivers. From
Zugdidi there is a short cut direct to Poti, through
the forests and morasses of the "great dismal;" but
to negotiate it successfully you require the services
of an experienced bog-trotter; and it is even then
dangerous, unless the season happen to be a dry one.
The regular route is first to Anaklia, a quiet ride of
four or five hours, distance twenty miles, through a
country much the same as that between Senakh and
Zugdidi, previously described. The track for the last
two miles or so runs along the left bank of the Ingour.
As this part of the country was the scene of Omar
Pacha's invasion during the Crimean War, and of
divers "alarums and excursions" during the late
campaign, it requires some comment.

When General Kratchenkoff, without firing a
shot, disgracefully abandoned Sookhoom Kaleh, on
the news of the Turks having landed some distance
up the coast,[1] matters at Zugdidi began to look

---

[1] A sort of "forlorn hope" of 300 or 400 ragged Abkhasians, armed

serious, especially as this descent of the Turks came
on the heels of the bloody repulse of the Russians in
their attack upon Tzikinzeri, on the defeat at Zivin
(in its march towards Erzeroum), and retreat of the
headquarters column under Loris Melikoff and the
Grand Duke, and on the raising of the siege of Kars.

Every available man and gun of the reserve at
Kutais, regular and irregular, was hurried to Zugdidi,
new levies called out, and measures taken to transport
a column across the Ingour with as little delay as
possible, in order to meet and check the enemy
supposed to be already advancing along the coast,
through the forests of Otchem Tcheri and Samourza
Khan.

The Turks having entire command of the sea, had
it of course in their power to land at any non-fortified
point (a privilege of which they made little or no
effective use), and General Alkhasoff's column had no
sooner crossed the Ingour than the Turks made one
of their futile naval "demonstrations" at Anaklia
with the ironclads, firing some shots at the place,
and landing a few men, who as usual returned to the
ships in the evening.

The news of this incident being telegraphed to

with muzzle-loaders, were the first to land, at a place some thirty
miles above Sookhoom. They attacked the Cossacks at Godaout, who
stampeded into Sookhoom with the news that the Turks had "landed
in force." The Abkhasian villagers in the hamlets around finding
that the Cossacks had bolted, flew to arms and joined the invaders.
Kratchenkoff, after hesitating for a day or two, destroyed his stores,
and retreated through the mountains to Zugdidi. He had 6000 men
of all arms and provisions for a year. The Turks, finding the coast
clear, then landed, and occupied Sookhoom Kaleh.

General Oglubjee, who was fronting Dervish Pacha at Mookestat, between Ozurget and Batoum, and being mistaken by him for a descent in force, he counter-telegraphed to Zugdidi that "they were to hold out as long as possible," and that he would send assistance; which being taken at Zugdidi to mean that something very serious was going to happen, produced a tremendous "scare," the whole population deserting the town, and bolting for Senakh, leaving their shops, goods, etc.

As before mentioned, the Turks having landed at Sookhoom Kaleh, General Alkhasoff (with a column of regular infantry and artillery, reinforced by strong levies of mounted irregulars) marched to and encamped on the Ingour, an extremely rapid river, the only means of crossing which was by some wretched caique ferry-boats,[1] holding ten or a dozen people, and which were carried down 200 or 300 yards at each "trajet," and only reached the other side at all with extreme difficulty and danger.

All the horses, mules, etc., had to be dragged or pushed in, and compelled to swim across, the riders stripping naked and "stampeding" them through by shouts, yells, and whipping: many men and horses were drowned, though every precaution was taken. It took more than a fortnight to transport the column and baggage across.

The General then proceeded unopposed *viâ* Ookhoom to Otchem Tcheri, where he took up a position,

---

[1] These are a sort of long punts, flat bottomed, constructed rudely of boards and planks.

or rather formed a line of posts, in the woods along the river Mokva, in order to check the advance of the invaders towards Zugdidi and Kutais. Here he passed the time in skirmishing across the river with the Abkhasian irregulars in his front; his left, which was close on the seashore, being occasionally shelled by the Turkish ironclads and gunboats.

Had the Turks upon landing at Sookhoom marched without delay upon the Ingour, they could have reached it unopposed, and prevented the Russians from crossing at all, for which purpose one battalion would have been amply sufficient; and it is said that this course was repeatedly urged upon the Pacha by the Abkhasian chiefs, who, knowing the country well, were for at once taking the offensive. This chance having been let slip, another, and I am inclined to think better, one presented itself, as follows.

From Alkhasoff's position on the river Mokva, fronting the Turks and Abkhasians, to the ford of the Ingour is at least fifty miles (or two very long marches), so that it is quite certain that he could not have countermarched, crossed the river, and reached Zugdidi with even a portion of the column in less than a week.

On the other hand, nothing prevented the Turks (the Black Sea being like a lake all through the summer), who had plenty of shipping, from embarking a force at Sookhoom, either openly or secretly, and arriving at Anaklia *in four hours;* from disembarking it, under the fire of the ironclads, marching, and reaching Zugdidi next morning, or at any rate next day (where they would have found nothing except a weak battalion and half a battery of guns to oppose them), and thus by occupying the ford of the Ingour on the left bank, to cut Alkhasoff's column off altogether from its base, in a deserted jungle country between the mountains and the sea, without supplies of any kind.

From the description I have given of the fording of the Ingour, which is absolutely correct, as I was there at the time and crossed myself, it will be seen that a battalion and a mountain battery would have been amply sufficient to prevent the Russian force recrossing, leaving which at the ford, the rest of the expedition might have marched on Senakh and Kutais, where there were absolutely no troops available to oppose them (the reserve as aforesaid being employed with Alkhasoff in fronting the Turks and Abkhasians on the Mokva),—unless, indeed, the Gouriel column facing Dervish Pacha (already repulsed with heavy loss in its attack on Tzikinzeri, and weakened by reinforcements sent to the assistance of the head-quarters column in face of Mukhtar) had been with-drawn, in which case Dervish Pacha would have occupied the Gouriel valley, or could have even followed their march to Kutais.

The Turks having undisputed command of the sea, and plenty of transport, might, once the incredible good luck of an unopposed landing at Sookhoom Kaleh had fallen to them, have of themselves done great things. Had England sent a fleet to the Black Sea when the Turks were on the winning hand, with half the force on board sent the other day to Egypt, the Russians would have been compelled either to finish the war on our terms, or to abandon the Caucasus.

Given capable commanders, 10,000 or 15,000 men landed between Batoum and Sookhoom Kaleh would have finished the war; nay, it is probable that the mere presence of the transports and fleet in the Black Sea would have been amply sufficient.

So long as the Turks are to the fore and remain friendly, Mingrelia will be a weak point in the Russian line of defence; unfortunately, it is now the only one.

CHAPTER XI.

CONSIDERABLE facilities for the disposal of stolen
horses existing in Mingrelia, and some of the best
"professors" of the science residing in the neighbourhood of Zugdidi, it is advisable for the traveller to
keep an eye on his "quads" during his stay.

Betting is supposed to be about twenty to one
against any stolen animal being recovered, the same
odds against the thief being arrested, and the same,
if arrested, against his being convicted and punished.

On leaving Zugdidi, a ride of four or five hours
through a picturesque wooded country, much the same
as that traversed from Senakh, brings the traveller to
Anaklia, situated at the embouchure of the Ingour,
which river you strike two or three miles before reaching the place.

Anaklia is the usual Black Sea shore location,—
" doghole," some people would call it. Plenty of

mud, some barn-like dukans, some fishermen, a great
deal of dried fish, and a strong greasy smell of stur-
geon, some Turkish feluccas and sandalls, some Greeks,
some Armenians, some Cossacks, and numerous specimens of the Mingrelian loafer.   It *is* improved since
Sir John Chardin landed there from the Genoese
slaver, but not very much improved.

On that auspicious occasion, the first question put
to Sir John by the missionary friar (whose acquaintance
he, very luckily as it turned out, happened to make
almost directly he got on shore) was: " What enemy
have you got who has advised you to come to Mingrelia ? "

This was towards the close of the seventeenth
century, but the same question might be put almost
as reasonably at the present day.

At that time Sookhoom Kaleh, Anaklia, Redout
Kaleh, Poti, etc., were mere Turkish " scalas " or land-
ing-places and trading depots, visited periodically by
large European vessels, most of them Genoese, which,
loaded with every possible necessary that the natives
required, arms, clothes, liquor, gunpowder, crockery,
etc., made the tour of the Black Sea, bartering their
freight in Circassia, Abkhasia, Mingrelia, and all down
the western coast of the Caucasus, which then almost
exclusively supplied Constantinople with white slaves
of both sexes, obtained in the perpetual raids and
petty wars that went on in the interior, as they do now
with the same object in Central Africa.

The Turkish policy seems to have been directed,
not to annexation of Mingrelia, the Western Caucasus,

and the Colchide, but to establish a mild kind of
suzerainty, keeping it as a nursery for slaves and
women, the outlets of which by sea and land were in
their hands.   Whereby (taking into consideration
that orthodox Mahometans had always considered it,
on account of the barbarous and uncleanly habits of
the people, and the high estimation in which they
held pork and wine, as an impossible country for a
true believer to reside in) they gained far more than
they could expect to do by taking absolute possession.
They therefore left the turbulent princes pretty much
to themselves, allowing them to settle their quarrels
in their own way; unless, getting too insupportably
chaotic, they brought trade to a standstill, on which
not infrequent occasions the Pacha of Akhaltsik would
enter with troops, loot the country moderately, suppress some too energetic prince, and, by setting his
brother or cousin in his place, put things temporarily
to rights,—taking good care, of course, to make the
new chief pay expenses before he left.   This state of
affairs went on well into the present century; I have
talked with old Mingrelians and Imeritians who recollected it, and rather seemed to lament its discontinu-
ance.   They did not seem so much to regret the old
feudal *régime* of their own chiefs (though Russian rule
is by no means popular), but laid great stress on the
extreme cheapness of provisions in former days as
compared with present quotations.   Being sold into
slavery did not seem to be considered by any means
the unmixed evil insisted upon by Exeter Hall (and
here note that the opinions of men who have lived

under a system may be taken as at least equivalent as evidence to the declamations, however violent, of those who have not); they, in fact, averred that not a few of these slaves, both male and female, if clever, intelligent, and handsome, as many of them were, attained high positions,—the women in the seraglios of pachas, and the men in their households, not infrequently from poor serfs in their own country, becoming great men, sending money and presents to their homes, and assisting relatives who emigrated to Constantinople or Asia Minor to lucrative posts.

To return, however, to our traveller. One of these Turkish "putting-to-rights invasions" was in full swing at the time of Chardin's arrival, matters being complicated by the Abkhasian mountaineers, who were briskly plundering, slave-hunting, and burning villages at one end of the country, while the Turks were advancing and amusing themselves in the same manner at the other. The ruling princess of Mingrelia, whose husband's head had just been cut off by some of his relations at Kutais, occupied herself, in this distracted position of affairs, in endeavouring to plunder Chardin (under pretence of hospitality) of his valuables and merchandise, in which she very nearly succeeded.

Sir John soon found out (what many a traveller has since discovered) that landing in Mingrelia means falling among thieves; nevertheless, through good management, luck in meeting the friar soon after his arrival, and prudence in taking the "tip" the worthy missionary promptly gave him, he got out of the scrape much better than might have been expected,—not losing very much, after all, in actual money value, which is more than can be said of many an unfortunate new arrival of late years.

If the "Princes Gueux" (as Sir John calls them) of the present day do not rob by seizing openly on your property, they have nevertheless contrived to plunder such strangers with coin as have been rash enough to land effectually enough,—the *modus operandi* by which they have successively and successfully "done" French, English, Greek, German, Belgian, Italian, and American speculators, being, like everything clever, simple enough.

It consists of pretended sales of timber, effected on the principle of the pea and thimble, the three card, the confidence trick, etc.; the secret of all which is usually based on the victim being what cardsharpers, betting-men, etc., call a "fly flat," thereby meaning a man who thinks himself too clever to be cheated, the art lying in encouraging him to think himself so, and thereby causing him to "let himself in." The foreign speculator believes, or is induced to believe, that the natives are simple unsophisticated people, and that immense quantities of valuable timber exist unexploited in the forests which line the coast, the right of cutting and felling which is obtainable at a very low figure.

He accordingly goes, or sends a trustworthy agent, on a voyage of exploration ; is shown over a great extent of forest containing fine timber; is introduced to the proprietor, and after some palavering, is informed that the right of felling is purchasable

R

at a certain figure, of which perhaps half, perhaps the whole, is to be paid in advance.

He has no sooner concluded his bargain, chartered vessels, engaged workmen, perhaps brought a foreman and machinery from Europe, and set energetically to work, than his troubles commence; his woodcutters are arrested, and he receives "injunctions" through the local courts warning him against trespassing or felling trees in the forests belonging to Kniaz G. S., or Kniaz T. P. Thinking there must be a mistake somewhere (which there is), he applies to the local authorities, and is blandly informed that the individual who sold him the right of felling is not the owner, having sold or transferred his title some years ago to another person, or that he has mortgaged it, or that he is only part proprietor, or prospective heir, or one of half a dozen heirs, none of whom are consenting parties. The "individual," meanwhile, has, after "sharing the swag" with the part proprietors, co-heirs, etc., disappeared.

The number of times this swindle has been successfully perpetrated on "enterprising business men" of different nationalities is incredible. One would think it would become "played out," but the game appears still to be alive. The victimised probably do not care to mention their experiences, feeling, as the French say, "Honteux comme un renard qu'un poule avait pris" at being done by people so *arriéré* as Mingrelians. It is, as I have myself noticed, difficult to warn them beforehand. They are mostly in a hurry to do a good stroke of business, and it is

always easy for the swindlers, the victim being a
new arrival, to represent such advice as that of a
rival purchaser wishing to mislead outsiders for his
own interest.

The fact of having to do business through inter-
preters is also to some extent against the foreigner,
though not anything like what it is generally held
to be.   A little reflection will convince any man of experience that comparatively very few words of any
language are used in the operations of purchasing
or selling. Consequently a moderate knowledge of
the language principally in use, and there is always
one, is all that is really requisite for bargaining.
Knowledge of character, patience, observation, and
experience of business will do all the rest ; and these
acquirements have nothing whatever to do with linguistic accomplishments, as any person of insight,
after a short acquaintance with Russian employés and
"men of affairs," may speedily convince himself.

Not, however, that, with all these requisites, I
would be understood to encourage any one to commence business in Mingrelia "Astaffer oollah." It is
now very much what the friar described it to be to
Sir John Chardin, and is expressly to be avoided by
any one wishing to lead a quiet life.

From Anaklia to Poti, by land, is a ride of fourteen
miles along the seashore, over swamps, mudflats, and
nullahs, crossed by dilapidated plank bridges. The
best way of going is by a Turkish felucca, some of
which, if the wind is fair, are always available. You
drink your morning coffee, embark yourself and

effects in the clean roomy boat, the big lateen sail is
hoisted, and, catching the morning breeze, you find
yourself, after a rapid spin of a couple of hours
(perhaps less) moored in the river by breakfast-time.
The maritime Turks who own these feluccas, are a
fine set of men, all Anatolians from Copa, Trebizond,
Samsoun, etc., and the best seamen in the Black Sea.
They are extremely sober and temperate (many of
them do not even smoke). Knowing, as they do,
every yard of the eastern coast, from Batoum to
Novo Russisk and Anapa, they would be invaluable
auxiliaries in time of war to a hostile fleet.

During the last campaign some of them did
good service by picking up torpedoes; though,
from the want of enterprise displayed by the Turkish
navy, their local knowledge was scarcely utilised, to
speak of.

Poti is what Americans call "a hard place,"
vividly recalling the "Eden" of Martin Chuzzlewit.
It is built on a large swamp at the embouchure of the
Rion, the ancient Phasis, which here discharges itself
into the sea, discolouring the water for miles, across a
dangerous bar of shifting mud and sand deposited by
its rapid current.

In consequence of this bar the shipping has to lie
at anchor some miles from the shore, in an exposed
roadstead, dangerous during south-west winds, which
often blow with extreme violence. Loading and dis-
charging cargo is effected by means of large lighters
"sandalls" manned by Turks, and owned by
ek, French, and Armenian shipbrokers and agents.

The Poti bazaar, which has been burned down on an average every two or three years since the place came into Russian possession in 1829, is now mainly constructed of brick; but many of the houses composing the streets of the town, which radiate from their common centre, the quays, like the spokes of a wheel, are of the old wooden tumble-down type already described, as was the bazaar itself till quite recently.

The place was entirely abandoned by the population during the war, as it was considered probable that the Turks would land and destroy it. The Cossacks and militia, however, who garrisoned it during that stirring period, though they did not burn it down, did considerable mischief to private property; and when I visited it in the spring of 1878, it had much the appearance of a place that had been bombarded and looted.

Poti society is curiously composed, comprising as it does specimens of most Eastern Europeans, Greeks, Turks, Dalmates, etc., in addition to Armenians, Persians, French, Russians, and the people of the country.

There is a Poti club, at which, as at all Russian clubs, considerable card-playing used to take place. I never belonged to it; but it did not strike me as an *exigeante* institution, judging from what I heard a member remark one morning, when the style of gambling that went on there was under discussion. One man (said he) may possess more "skill" at cards than another, and such men will take every advantage; this I do not object to. What I do not consider fair play is when a man (as I saw —— do last night) pockets a couple of fifty-rouble notes that a friend, excited by argument, had forgotten that he had placed on the table at his elbow.

Another institution is the Poti custom-house, standing in pretty much the same relation to foreign commerce as the Spanish Inquisition did to religious opinion, and treating strangers and outsiders in much the same manner whenever the least informality places them within its clutches ; notwithstanding which, smuggling goes on briskly, extensive frauds on the Government in that line being of normal occurrence.

Next come the Poti police. They may be backed to run down a robber or catch a private thief against any police in the world. Where they fail is in recovering the stolen property (*i.e.* if of more value than an old coat or worn-out pair of pantaloons) and in convicting criminals. A year or two ago a couple of Americans, who had made the tour of the country and were leaving, took up their quarters in Jacquot's Hotel (a great Poti centre now unfortunately destroyed—1882—by fire) to await the departure of the steamer. Jacquot's Hotel is, or rather was, a long, rambling ground-floor building, running round the corner of a street facing the public garden, one room of which, looking on the roadway, the travellers occupied. It being very hot they, after turning in, rashly opened the window. One of them went to sleep at once, the other commenced reading in bed by a candle, subsequently falling asleep and leaving it burning.

The situation being remarked by certain *indus-*

triels, as the French call them, from outside, who in
Poti are always on the watch, one or more of these,
promptly and noiselessly entering by the aperture,
conveyed away, not only their portmanteaus, containing coin and valuables to a very considerable amount,
but every scrap of clothes except what they had on
(consisting of a flannel shirt each), so that they, awak-
ing in the morning, had to send for the English Vice-
Consul and borrow garments, being unable *pro tem.*
to get out of bed. Every exertion was used, of course,
by the local officials; but the Americans soon found
it would not pay to await the *dénouement*, and one of
them having some circular notes which he had luckily
put under his pillow, they, after temporarily rigging
themselves out, proceeded on their voyage homewards.
Some months afterwards the police recaptured the
portmanteaus, containing old clothes, showing clearly
that they had traced down the thieves; but none of
the valuables had up to the date of my leaving been
forthcoming, or are ever likely to be.

Then there was S.'s case. S. was an English
engineer who had been employed for some years on
the Poti-Tiflis Railway and other "surveys" in the
Caucasus, and had accumulated some property. Liking
the country, he determined to settle there, with which
view he built a shanty on the seashore about three
miles out of Poti, and occupied himself in plans for
the amelioration and desiccation of the town, in which
object he was seconded by the then Governor and
others of the Russian authorities. All went well till,
in an evil hour, thinking, probably, to ingratiate him-

self with the powers that be, he lent some £250 to
the Poti "policemaster" or superintendent of police
on a bond, which he kept in his possession.   Shortly
afterwards he was, while driving into Poti as usual
one evening in a low pony-carriage alone and un-
armed, brutally murdered.[1]

The policemaster, immediately on the news of the
murder, proceeded to S.'s house by the sea, where he
made the usual "investigations," and sealed up S.'s
papers, which were subsequently handed to the English
Vice-Consul.   When, however, these documents came
to be handled by the latter official, an inventory
made, and his friends informed of his decease, etc.,
according to regulations, the bond for £250 (which
was perfectly well known to have been previously in
S.'s safe keeping) had disappeared.

This fact naturally caused strong suspicions among
the community of the policemaster himself being at
the bottom of the whole affair, more especially as S.,
a most honourable and benevolent young man, had,
from his kindly manners and disposition, always been
extremely popular among all classes of the natives.
It was, besides, clear enough that the actual assassins
could have gained little or nothing by his death, as
he was merely driving into Poti in his usual manner
'n the evening, and, beyond perhaps a few roubles, had
o money about him.   Had the object of the mur-

---

[1] It is supposed that while one individual, making signs that he
wished to speak to S. from the roadside, attracted his attention and
caused him to pull up, another, slipping up behind the trap, felled him
by a club. He was then dragged out and his throat cut, in which
state he was found.

derers been plunder, they would have broken into his house, which, being a wooden shanty by the seaside, remote from other buildings, and three miles from Poti, it would have been perfectly easy for them to do directly after the crime. The result of this affair was that some suspected individuals were arrested and, after much delay, procrastination, and verbose correspondence, tried, and one of them sentenced to transportation to Siberia for a term of years. I have heard rumours that he was known to have returned from exile. The others got off.

These two anecdotes, amongst scores of similar ones that could be given, will suffice to explain the repressive power of the police authorities and Caucasian executive. I may remark that they are often credited with being in league with criminals, especially so in the western provinces, where they are believed to exploit the industry of the dangerous classes more unblushingly (if half one hears is true) than was ever practised by Fielding's favourite hero, the great Jonathan Wild. This is not surprising : the police officials are usually natives of the country, Armenians, or Mingrelians, badly paid, and accustomed to see people who act honourably almost invariably go to the wall. I do not mean to assert that Orientals are universally unprincipled ; but I believe that upright disinterested native officials are just as few and far between in the Caucasus as they are in the North-West Provinces, if not fewer and farther (I should be inclined to say the latter), and could, if I chose, give plenty of "modern instances" to support my opinion.

But I am at my old lunes—digression. Poti, since
the annexation of Batoum (which lies at a distance of
six hours' easy steaming across a sort of indentation
of the coast, overhung by the magnificent Gouriel
mountains, their summits 8000 feet above the sea,
and usually capped with snow), has been in a lan-
guishing, unsettled state. There was, as happens after
every new accession of territory, a rush, fostered by
Government, to the promised land, where everything
was to be had cheap, where a town as big as Odessa,
which would monopolise the Black Sea trade, etc., was
to be built in no time ; sites for houses and locations in
which were going for nothing, with divers others the
like shams, greedily for a time swallowed by the
uninitiated.   Precisely similar statements had been
set going after the Crimean War respecting Poti itself.
A magnificent harbour of refuge was to be constructed,
a railway run down to it, the swamp and marshes
drained, the ground-level raised several feet,—in fact,
a second Amsterdam and Venice created. Hardly any
of these grand imaginings have, in the course of the
thirty years which have nearly elapsed since they
were first floated, been realised. Poti is as swampy as
ever. I have myself seen large fish caught in the
streets during moderate rises of the river, and have
an remarked snipe, woodcocks, and even wild ducks
iting in front of the custom-house, post-office, and
er public offices. It still, in fact, bears about as
se a resemblance to Eden as can be found.

The object of the Russian Government being to
'float" such acquisitions at the most economical and

speedy rate, its policy is to attract capitalists and
settlers by hook or by crook. The most approved
plan is to promise "golden mountains," and when once
the place has been got populated, *tant bien que mal,*
to allow the population to realise the golden mountains (if they can) by their own unassisted enterprise
and energy. Most of them are, after the bubble has
burst, obliged to stick there, having expended their
little capital in purchasing a plot of land (or rather of
morass), sold during the excitement at a tolerably high
figure, in squaring officials to secure a title to it, and
in erecting a tumble-down wooden shanty, and consequently have to contrive (if they do not die of fever
during the first year or two) to acclimatise and get
along somehow or other, generally badly.

It is probable that the Government will, after
buoying up Batoum, which is now "all the go" (Poti
being nowhere in the betting), discover after a year or
two that Poti possesses "advantages of position with
regard to commercial enterprise which have been over-
looked, only requiring improving and developing to
make it a first-class trading port," and that Batoum
is only suitable for military purposes. In fact, Poti
is undoubtedly the natural commercial outlet of the
Western Caucasus, situated as it is in the centre of
the valley of the Rion, and at the mouth of a large
and deep river.

The same operations as were successfully undertaken by the Austrians and our own engineers at the
Sulina mouth of the Danube would make it an excellent harbour of refuge for vessels of heavy tonnage.

Batoum, on the contrary, being situated at the farthest
corner of the country to be commercially tapped, viz.
Mingrelia and Imeritia, is therefore naturally " out of
the swim ;" the country immediately behind it, instead of a wide alluvial plain enormously fertile, which
with industry could be made into a Lombardy (as the
Rion valley behind Poti is), being nothing but wild and
precipitous mountains, only good for sheep pastures.
That the Russian Government, in their obstinate way
(impelled, in reality, more by strategic and aggressive
considerations than anything else, as they invariably
are, often to their great commercial loss), will insist
on artificially forcing Batoum, perhaps for several
years to come, is highly probable ; but if they ever do
seriously turn their attention to developing the commercial resources of the country, draining its swamps,
promoting its trade, etc., the advantages of Poti from
a commercial point of view must inevitably force
themselves into notice.

CHAPTER XII.

Environs of Poti — The Paleostrom — The Molt Acqua—Scenery
round it—Aquatic Sports: Boating, Fishing, Shooting, the Poti
Hunt, Wild Fowling.

POTI, though as may be supposed an indifferent place
for riding, driving, or walking, possesses great resources for aquatics, including wild fowling and fishing. Any one fond of boating alone, indeed, can find
plenty of recreation. The Molt Acqua, a deep and
broad channel (supposed to be an old bed of the
Rion), runs round the north-eastern part of the town,
falling into the sea some six miles to the south, and
communicating at its northern extremity with the
" Paleostrom," a noble sheet of water five or six miles
square, from which a magnificent view of the lofty
chain of Elborouz mountains to the east (overhanging
the Gouriel country, already described), covered with
sombre forest, as well as of the main chain of the
Caucasus to the north, the latter, though more distant, yet equally grand, is always, except in cloudy
weather, which in the winter is exceptional, attain-
able, in addition to the excitement of sport. Indeed,
to a lover of romantic scenery a sail on a fine day in

autumn or winter on the Paleostrom is, to my mind, in itself worth a visit to the Caucasus. Or you can, to vary the business, enjoy the same unequalled scenery from the sea by sailing from the mouth of the Rion across the wide indentation of coast between Poti and Batoum,—selecting, of course, clear weather, with the wind off shore, and the bar consequently quiescent.

Into the Paleostrom flow several deep and sluggish rivers, intersecting the wide morasses and swampy forests, which extend for miles and miles on every side of the lagoon but the western one (facing the sea). These channels, and the lagoon itself, are full of fish: immense pike, perch, carp, roach, mullet, etc., and in the winter swarm with wild-fowl of all kinds, from swans and geese to pintail, teal, and widgeon. The swampy forests and reed beds which surround the lake also contain occasional roe-deer and wild pigs, which are more numerous, however, in the forest to the north across the river, where red-deer are also not uncommon.

There is a sort of "hunt" at Poti, consisting of several couple of rough hounds of uncertain breed, with which once or twice a week the custom-house employés, and any one else who likes to "assist," are in the habit of sallying forth, and, having taken up positions in the woods, the dogs are laid on and shots obtained at big game, which are sure to pass one or other of the stands. They rarely return without a pig or a roebuck, sometimes a couple, and occasionally kill a stag.

While on this topic I may make some allusion
to the sport obtainable in the Caucasus, as far as my
experience of it during a residence of eight years—in
which I visited most of the provinces—extends, more
especially as considerable difference of opinion prevails, some people representing the country as swarming with game of all descriptions, big and small, while
others are equally positive that none worth going
after is obtainable.

The Caucasus is, I am of opinion, as regards
the greater part of the area (with the exception of
birds of passage), a case of "*fuit Ilium.*" It no doubt
has been (and not very long ago) a sportsman's para-
dise; but now, generally speaking, the contrary is the
case; and the reasons why are not far to seek. The
nobles in the old days preserved the game strictly,
the peasants not only not being allowed to shoot or
hunt, except in company with the chiefs, but forbidden
to disturb the game in many of the forests by pastur-
ing their cattle therein. Since Russian ascendency all
this has been done away with. Any one who chooses
can shoot all the year round (for the fence laws are a
mere farce), the consequence being that except in a
few out-of-the-way, almost uninhabited parts of the
country, game, large and small, has been either exterminated, or is in a fair way of being so. I have heard
Prince Gregor Gouriel say that when he was young he
rarely went out without killing a couple of stags, pigs,
or roedeer, and both he and old Mar the Englishman
told me that at that period (some forty years ago) you
could kick pheasants or hares out of any clump of

brambles in the valley. Now you may walk all day there without seeing a hare or pheasant, and, except in very severe winters, when the roedeer, pigs, etc., are forced down from their retreats in the high ranges by the snow, they are never seen in the valley at all.

The large game of the Caucasus consist of red-deer, the same as the European (the "hangal" of Cashmere); roedeer, the European variety; ibex (the "bonquetin" of Europe); wild sheep (the "oorial" of the Punjab); chamois, the European; gazelles (*Antilope pallas*); the Asiatic brown bear (the "snow" bear of the Himalayas and Cashmere); and wild pigs. There are also wolves, foxes, jackals, badgers, martens, lynxes, wild-cats, otters, etc. Leopards and tigers are met with occasionally in the mountains on the Persian frontier, near Lenkoran on the Caspian, but are very scarce even there.

Red-deer, except in remote, almost uninhabited, portions of the main chain, are scarce. They were formerly numerous in the mountains close to Tiflis, described in my journey to Kakhetia; but, from being greatly hunted down by the peasantry during severe winters, and "driven" with hounds by Russian officers cantoned in the out-stations, have now become almost extinct there. During my frequent peregrinations in those forests, often camping out by night in the most likely spots for large game, and resuming my journey at break of day, I only met altogether with three, a stag and two hinds, disturbed by a spaniel I had with me in some dense covert above the old monastery of Saint Anthony. I believe that these were the only

three deer on the range. I never saw them afterwards, nor did I observe any tracks or deer signs.

Though I was often about the mountains in
all directions, I saw very few roedeer. They are,
however, tolerably numerous in Circassia, as are pigs,
chamois, and brown bears; but it is necessary to
ascend very high ranges to find the chamois.

Ibex and wild sheep (oorial) are also to be found
along the crests of the higher ranges, but in most
places are wild and scarce.

The shepherds who graze their flocks at these
altitudes during the. summer months are, I suspect,
mainly accountable for the scarcity and disappearance
of these and other large game. Nothing strikes a
sportsman accustomed to the Himalayas or Cashmere
more than the sparseness and often complete absence
of game, large and small, over immense tracts of
mountain which ought to abound with it; in fact,
the animals *were* there not long ago, but are now
exterminated.

The same process which has extinguished the
large game of the Caucasus has now been going
on for many years in India, with the same results;
and if . no prohibitory measures are taken, large
game, at any rate in British territory and Cashmere,
will, by the end of the century, have probably disappeared.

More large game are, I believe, to be found in Circassia than anywhere else; but it is difficult to get
about there, as even within a few miles of the coast
all the old paths and tracks are choked up with thorns

and dense undergrowth, on account of the country being uninhabited. For this latter reason also, one must carry stores and supplies as if for a voyage of exploration. It is often rather difficult to find attendants who will accompany the shooter any distance inland.

The best plan of operations for Circassia would be to purchase a felucca at Trebizond or Batoum, and, after hiring a Turk or two to man it, to transport it by steamer or sail in it to a place called Sochu, about half-way up the coast, where are a small German colony and cantonment; and from this point, where you can lay in, if you have not previously done so, your store of tea, sugar, coffee, flour, and other necessaries to commence a coasting voyage, putting in to shore, encamping for a week at a time, and exploring.

You will find everywhere plenty of wood, water, and picturesque sheltered camping-places, the best trout-fishing in the clear rivers on shore, and any amount of sea-fishing afloat.

Wild pigs are to be found everywhere, as are roe-deer; bears are more numerous in the interior.

At every few miles along the shore are small Cossack posts; many of the Cossacks are good large game shikarees, and will accompany the traveller as guides, or assist him with information.

The best season to make such a trip would be the spring or early autumn, according as the fishing or shooting offers most attraction. The first is better in the spring.

The climate of Circassia during June, July, and

August, even close to the sea, is *very* hot, so much so as often to make one wonder how the vegetation, which is exclusively European, can flourish so luxuriantly.

A good felucca, with sails, oars, etc., complete, will cost, according to tonnage, from £10 to £40 or £50. They have a lateen rig, and sail at a great pace "on a wind," but, possessing little or no keel (for convenience of getting through the surf and rapidly hauling up on the beach), will not beat.

For an inland expedition, four or five horses, with native saddles, should be purchased, and loaded up with necessaries. They can be got in the Kuban, near Kertch, from the Cossacks and Circassians for £4 or £5 per animal; are strong hardy brutes, though small; will cost little or nothing to keep, there being plenty of grass everywhere, on which (and water) they will work for weeks. They can be resold afterwards, if taken care of, for about what they cost. A couple of Circassians should be hired for an inland expedition.

On the Kuban steppes, north of the main chain, are plenty of small game (hares, pheasants, bustard, houbara, etc.); and in the mountains overhanging them are bears, roedeer, and wild boars, as in Circassia. Ibex and chamois exist along the higher crests; but are rare, and very wild and shy.

I have no doubt that there are out-of-the-way nooks and valleys in these ranges where, especially since the expulsion of the Circassians and Lesghians, tolerable and even good sport in the way of large game shooting is available; but such places are difficult to "hit off."

In general, in the Caucasus, wherever the local

officials or others tell you that there is " any amount"
of game to be had, you find, on trial, little or none.
On close inquiry on the spot itself you will generally
discover that there once (thirty years ago) *was really*
plenty of game, the reputation of which has outlived
its disappearance.

Exploring remote and out-of-the-way localities in
these mountains on the *chance* of finding sport is difficult and expensive work, your guides and servants will
make all sorts of covert opposition to your leaving the
beaten tracks, and will ask high wages for their services,
while the task of procuring supplies and carriage for
the camp is often so troublesome that only first-rate
sport would compensate one, and this, the odds are,
you never get.

The feathered game of the Caucasus consist of the
European pheasant, the European partridge, the black
partridge or francolin, the French partridge or chikore,
the black-cock, the Indian snow-partridge, the snow-
cock or snow-pheasant, the teesee or Persian partridge,
the large sand grouse, the great bustard, the houbara or
small bustard, woodcock, snipe, double snipe, wild-fowl
of all sorts, golden plover, curlew, etc.

This seems on paper a promising list, but the sportsman will only, under exceptional circumstances and
in remote localities, find *many* of the birds comprised
in it.

The best wild mixed shooting that I have encountered was in the valley of the Araxes, above Erivan,
near the northern base of Mount Ararat, where, in the
course of a day's walk in November—the best time of

year for Caucasian shooting—I have met with great bustard, coolen, hares, sand grouse, chikore, ducks, and
snipe. There were also teesee or Persian partridge about.
Of these, only the bustard, coolen, and ducks were
numerous. This style of "shikar" may be got all the
way down the Koura and Araxes valleys, and throughout the Mogan steppe, with the addition of black partridge and houbara,[1] which latter are very numerous
about the lower part of the Mogan during the winter
season. The sport met with throughout the steppes
of Georgia very much resembles that of the Northern
Punjab, as does the scenery; much the same climate
and country prevail also, extending from Georgia
through Persia, Khorassan, and Seistan to the Punjab,
ranges of, for the most part, arid mountains enclosing
dry salt steppes (Kevir) of varying area, the soil a hard
clay, very sticky after rain, vegetation usually burned
up in summer and frozen during winter, the landscape
appearing for three-fourths of the year from the alternate influences of heat and cold like a desert. Much
of the soil, however, is, whenever irrigation can be
brought to bear upon it (for without irrigation nothing
will grow), of extraordinary fertility.

The European pheasant is most numerous north
of the main sierra of the Caucasus, on the prairies
towards the embouchure of the Terek river, about
Kislar, etc., as is the European partridge. Both are
met with here and there throughout Georgia, but
pheasants are *never* found on the wooded mountain
ranges where the dense coverts of hazel, beech, and

---

[1] Called by the Russians streppit.

every kind of European underwood, would lead one
to expect them to be plentiful. Pheasants in the
Caucasus and in Khorassan, etc., inhabit low scrub
jungle and reeds, on plains and flat valleys, away from
mountains, and forests; in fact, precisely the localities
where in India you would expect hares and gray or
black partridges.

I have often *kicked* pheasants out of stuff half the
height of my knees, in which they ran and squatted
like quail; and, when new to the country, have hunted
over thousands of acres of magnificent covert on the
hillsides without seeing a head of anything,—except,
of course, woodcocks (in the season), and perhaps a
hare or two.

The European partridge, which is rather scarce, is
found almost exclusively amongst low covert of bar-
berry bushes, brambles, whitethorn, etc.; at the foot
of the mountains. I never saw them in the cultivation.

The francolin (or black partridge) and chikore
frequent the same sort of ground as in India,—the
black amongst tamarisk jungle near rivers, the chikore
on barren stony slopes and mountain sides.

The black-cock is scarce, and only found on very
high ranges, like the snow-cock and snow-partridge.
There are hardly enough of these birds on any given
range to make it worth while to go up and encamp
there for the sake of shooting them.

The best plan to ensure tolerable sport is (unless
you prefer wild-fowling at such places as Lenkoran on
the Caspian, or Poti, Kertch, etc., on the Black Sea)

to stick to the steppes, where, from October to March or April, the wild shooting is good; and the sport can be varied by coursing hares and stalking gazelles.

The best arrangement for this latter " shikar " is for a couple of sportsmen, each tolerably mounted on animals accustomed to graze quietly, with a servant, also mounted, and some lunch, to sally out before dawn, getting as far into the steppe by daybreak as possible, then, leaving the man in charge of the animals, to start in different directions on foot, acting according to circumstances.

The gazelles are always to be found somewhere on the steppe; but, as every Indian sportsman is aware, walking after them is useless; the only way is to work by manœuvring and circumvention, taking up positions here and there (under cover of nullahs, etc.), and sitting or standing about until a herd, in avoiding parties of mounted Tartars crossing the steppe, herds of cattle, or other shikarees, some of whom are sure to be about, comes your way. A light gray or whity-brown " puttoo " costume is best; anything dark, being conspicuous at an immense distance on the steppe, is to be avoided.

While waiting about for giran, you may often get a chance at bustard or coolen flying over, for which reason a Cape double-gun, one barrel smooth and one small-bore rifled, is a good weapon to carry, with slugs in the smooth barrel. Indeed, an ordinary 12-bore, with slugs in both barrels, is as good as anything, as giran, when unconscious of your vicinity, will come very close, and you often have to fire at

them while running.   You can sometimes get a shot
from horseback by galloping hard to a point.

Large flights of wild-fowl often pass to and fro
across the steppe.

The Tartars who inhabit these steppes during
winter are many of them good shikarees, and hunt
a great deal, always mounted. After heavy snow-
storms they kill many giran with greyhounds of the
Persian breed.   They sometimes sew white cotton
cloth round the dogs, to enable them to run up
unobserved close to a herd over the snow, while
they distract their attention by galloping round, and
are up to numerous dodges of circumventing and
driving.

It is great fun being out with the Tartars; the
rapid firing from different points as antelopes tear past
with the dogs in chase, the galloping, shouting, and
singing of bullets (the object being to confuse the
deer by making as much noise as possible), remind
one of a cavalry skirmish.

The Tartars are commonly accused of all sorts of
atrocities.   There is no doubt they *are* fond of a little
" vendetta," and will " raise hair" on slight provoca-
tion ; but for all that *I* have always found them good
fellows, ready to be hospitable to the extent of their
means, especially to a foreigner, infinitely preferable to
certain " civilised " Armenians I have been acquainted
with.

It is as well never to approach a Tartar camp,
" aoul," or sheepfold, on foot, as you will infallibly
be attacked by the dogs, who are as large as wolves,

and more ferocious, and will force you, unless you have considerable tact with dogs, to shoot in order to avoid being pulled down.   If you do, you run a chance of being fired at yourself in the hurry of the moment by the Tartars.   On horseback, though the dogs will "bait" you, jump at your boots, bite your horse's tail and legs, make him kick, etc., you can get through in comfort, and as soon as the Tartars receive you they quiet down.   It is best to avoid going outside after dark, as once twenty or thirty yards from the camp the dogs will treat you as an enemy, and you will have a *mauvaise quart d'heure.*

Piercing north winds often prevail on the steppes, penetrating the warmest clothing, and making camping out, unless in a regular "kibitka," miserable work; but in the Tartar "aouls," which are partly underground, it is warm enough.

The Tartars will give you plenty of mutton and flat bread, but they have no liquor of any sort.   They are very fond of tea, and if you want to make them a present it is as well to be supplied with plenty of it, also tobacco.   Many of them are well off, and possess good horses and handsome arms.   They are not the least bigoted or fanatical.

Next to the universal poaching which goes on at all seasons, the scarcity of both feathered and ground game in the Caucasus is attributable to the numbers of birds of prey of all sorts and species, which none of the natives, unless they interfere very seriously with their poultry, will take the trouble to fire at.   Gentlemen who, in the columns of the *Field* and other

natural history chronicles, lament the destruction of
eagles, hawks, buzzards, etc., in Great Britain, would
moderate their complaints if they visited Asia Minor.
Here things are the other way ; it being, as in India,
game birds and animals that are in danger of
extinction.

The rarer birds of prey, such as falcons, eagles,
buzzards, etc., or rather those that are rare in England,
fly enormous distances, and often change their country,
one reason being that in regions like the Caucasus,
Central Asia, Turkey in Asia, etc., where they are
unmolested, they become too numerous. It is probable that nearly all the falcons killed of late years
in Britain have been immigrants, and that if the
keepers and collectors slackened their operations for
a few years they would become numerous. It is un-
likely they will ever become extinct.

In the Caucasus the lammergeyer, golden eagle,
and other eagles, buzzards, falcons, etc., also the
merlin, hobby, and smaller hawks, may be met with
daily. The blue jay, the hoopoe, bee-eater, and
many other birds considered rare in England are
also common.

Circassia, though rich in birds of prey, hawks of
all sorts, hawk-eagles, the osprey, European vultures,
etc., is not—perhaps for this very reason, joined to the
abundance of ground vermin, such as martens and
weasels—much of a country for the ornithologist. All
the European song-birds, including nightingales, are,
however, represented.

The river fishing is excellent ; there are salmon,

and quantities of fine trout, besides other fish.   I
have caught trout, after a freshet, almost as quickly
as I could throw in the line.   Having no reel or
spinning-tackle, and no swivels to rig any up, I could
not use minnow or spoon bait, or I have no doubt I
could have landed some very heavy fish.

On the larger rivers, which are quite undisturbed,
you have many miles of fishing, consisting of rapids,
deep pools, etc., where a well-equipped angler would
enjoy great sport.

I fished with a horsehair line twisted by myself, a
hazel rod, cut in the forest, dried in the sun, and a
butt spliced on to it, topped with a switch of cornel.
I had no gut, but bent my hooks on three or four
horsehairs, and baited with a well-scoured red worm.
I caught trout up to a pound with this tackle, and
lost very few hooks.   I never saw fish in finer
condition.

The Russians know nothing of the piscatorial art
(*i.e.* rod-fishing); at least I have never met any who
did, or heard them talk of it, though they are very
fond of " gassing" about shooting.

Mingrelians can throw a casting-net, but never
use rod and line.   Their nets are not very deadly
engines, being small in circumference, and used only
in shallow water.

The "take" consisted of bleak, chub, roach, etc.,
up to half a pound, occasionally a small trout.   They
murder numbers of small fish by night in shallow
streams and rivulets with torches and hatchets ;
but this poaching can only be perpetrated when

the water is low, and cannot be done at all in the rivers.

Nothing can be more delightful than the climate of Circassia during April, May, and June, when the fishing is at its best. On any of the larger rivers, such as the Zimta, the Sochu river, or the Shacke, the angler will find miles of undisturbed range.

During the spring and early summer the weather is invariably fine, except for occasional showers, which cool the air and improve the sport. It is also a magnificent country for sketching, botanising, and landscape painting.

CHAPTER XIII.

Russian Character, Civil and Military—Militaryism in Russia—Russian Statesmen—Political Designs—The Russian Soldier—Russian Aggression.

EDUCATED Russians are usually polite, courteous, and affable, without hauteur, exclusiveness, or reticence. With some of them these good manners are merely a veneer, covering Asiatic insincerity and falseness; but with the majority it is, I believe, genuine. They are all, however, rather given to talk largely and loosely, and say whatever comes uppermost,—to *blague*, in fact.

It is noticeable that they are fond of new faces, being always more civil to foreigners who are birds of passage than to such as remain in the country. On the whole, they are good-natured and kindly, fond of society, conversation, and anecdote. They may be said to be really hospitable without ostentation, guests and visitors being always, as a rule, welcome. At the same time, their friendships are rarely "solid;" many of them are very fickle and changeable, careless of obligations, etc.

They are inclined to be procrastinating and indolent, with plenty of excuses always ready. Time is no object with them.

They dislike methodical work or exertion. If you arrange with a Russian to go shooting or riding, or to travel somewhere and fix a day, the chances are that he will not come at all ; he is certain to be five or six hours late in keeping his appointment ; yet the same man will often propose starting off somewhere, withany preparation, on the spur of the moment. They dislike moving, but, once got under weigh, will go a great distance in order to get the journey over. They are luxurious and lazy, but will rough it on occasions like Tartars, do without food or liquor for days, and perform wonders of endurance.

Russian educated men, military or civil, often, as youths, work very hard for years, getting up a variety of literary subjects, and foreign languages. This early cramming results in all but those of really superior powers of application getting sickened of books, and rarely or never opening one (even a novel) after leaving college.

Another result is that many of them, though (practically) ignorant, are very self-sufficient, and imagine that no one can teach them anything.

They attach extraordinary value to foreign languages, and consequently acquire a contempt for people who are without linguistic accomplishments, doubting their capacity in all other respects. In fact, they gauge people pretty much according to their proficiency in foreign tongues, which they look upon (which they *are* with them) as the "open sesame" to everything. Many Russians seem to believe that not only any subject, but any business, trade, or profession, can be mastered merely by reading or talking it over. They resemble a man who should, after studying navigation and geography for a year or two (without ever having been on board ship), undertake to command a vessel and sail round the world. And many a Russian *would* probably undertake and accomplish such a voyage (if allowed *carte blanche* as to time and money), by finding men who would do it for him, he taking the credit to himself.

With Russians, generally speaking, speech is golden, and silence copper. They cannot believe in a man who is not talkative and amusing. With them the great thing is to talk (as superficially as you choose) on a given subject.

Your practical quiet man, who knows his business, is a bore. If a man cannot " gas," build castles in the air, and blow his own trumpet vigorously, he is considered an impostor.[1] The fact is, that not only are they usually too shallow to distinguish a good man from a pretender, but, being naturally indolent and unbusiness-like, they require much talking (over a bottle) to enable them to grapple with a subject at all.

A great command of words and linguistic talent, joined to unscrupulous shiftiness and sharp practice, is probably the secret of their success as diplomatists, joined to an unchanging home and foreign policy, and the fact that their press, being gagged, cannot criticise great men, foreign policy, or ventilate public matters.

---

[1] This is the secret of the success of many foreigners in Russia, who have taken the trouble to acquire the language, often without knowing anything else.

Russian social hierarchy is the antipodes of British. In England, civilian opinion, through the press, rules supreme. Military opinion is non-existent, or at a discount. Officers are even more or less unwilling to wear uniform in public, unless on duty, which notion has probably originated in unpleasant comments made by civilians, and accusations of "swagger."

In England, public opinion is very powerful; it prevents or causes wars, changes of ministry, etc.

In Russia, civilian public opinion is, though not non-existent, of no account, and the press dares not comment upon public questions unless as directed by authority.

In Russia, military men and military opinion govern *everything*, including the Emperor himself, who is strictly a military man. Not that the military are obtrusive; officers do not affect to "sit on" civilians (this not being the *consigne* nowadays), but they "govern," and will govern, so long as the country remains unrevolutionised. Civilian opinion exists, and is heard behind closed doors or in private *séances*, but without influencing measures of Government.

It follows, therefore, that any person endeavouring to forecast what turn Russian policy is likely to take should consult the motives that influence and direct the *militaires*, who, in reality, sway the councils. With many clever, enlightened, and humane men among them, the majority of Russian military men (certainly those at the top of the tree) are unscrupulous, ambitious, and daring. They have always, and will always, devote all their energy and activity to furtherance of schemes of aggression and conquest —first, because by these means they gain riches, honours, and advancement ; secondly, because successful war is absolutely necessary to keep the patriotic steam at high pressure, without which there would be considerable danger of the imperial machine stopping. It may be argued that with so many opposing interests, conflicting elements, etc., the machine must stop sooner or later ; but this is by no means a certainty, or even a probability, the Russian people, *i.e.* the civilians, educated or uneducated, are helpless and powerless *per se;* and though the military machinery may not always, and does not, work smoothly, there is safety from this very fact, in the impossibility of confidence and co-operation, added to which, the divers races of which the officers are composed, whether Asiatic or European, know that by supporting the Empire they have all individually an equal chance of reaching the highest rank and honours.

Nay, paradoxical as it may appear, the very insubordination and cliquism, resulting from the composite nature of the officer element, has often pulled a Russian force *out* of difficulties, as related in the case of the siege of Bayazid by the Kurds, when the Asiatic officers mutinied in consequence of their local knowledge and experience, and thereby saved the detachment from destruction. A British force (in which insubordination and disobedience of orders are considered · heinous crimes) would in all

T

probability (in fact, certainly) have been massacred under similar circumstances, just as our brigade was in Kabul in 1842; and probably, if the truth was known, those at Cawnpore in 1857. In effect, as any officer of experience is aware, blind obedience and subordination, though of the highest value when exhibited by troops commanded by capable and efficient leaders, are by no means always an element of success and safety when these latter are not to the fore; especially blind obedience on the part of the officers, amongst whom with us it is perhaps stronger than with the men, whereas with the Russians it is the contrary.

It is thus extremely improbable that the officers of the Russian army will ever join in any revolutionary movement, well knowing that individually, and as a body, they have all to lose and nothing to gain by the business. They are more likely, in fact, to depose any Emperor who should insist upon reforms and progressive measures, foreseeing their own downfall if such are carried out. The only chance for revolution would lie in some popular and victorious general like Suvarrow or Skobeleff (who appears about once in a century) heading a revolutionary demonstration. Such men, however, are always the last to do anything of the sort anywhere, and in Russia would certainly be the last.

Skobeleff "died suddenly," not because he was too popular and advocated reform, but because he was too popular and advocated war with Germany.

Another chance would lie in an unsuccessful war, in which the army got severely defeated. But the Russian Government is far too cautious to quarrel single-handed with any strong power, unless that power were in difficulties through rebellion or civil war, or that rebellion could be provoked easily in her territory.

The Russian soldier, who is a Russian peasant, is rather of an Asiatic turn of mind, with much religious veneration or superstition, capable of being roused into fanaticism. He is quietly disposed, good-natured, though rather barbarous and brutal as to his outer manners; patient and long-suffering. He has been carefully educated in a general suspicion of outside nations, both European and Asiatic, whom he has been taught to consider from childhood as only watching for an opportunity to despoil the country, and suppress his religion, which view is plausibly enough maintained by his instructors, the priests, pointing out the centuries of subjugation under the Tartars, the horrors of their invasions, and the frightful ravages they used to commit; also of their narrow escapes from the same fate at the hands of the Poles and Swedes (and, later on, of the French); the conclusion always enforced being that the national, and even personal, existence depends solely on strict submission to discipline and obedience to the Emperor. The Russian soldier is perfectly aware of the shortcomings of his administration; but the majority think these evils prevail in other countries, and all think that the only alternative being foreign despotism, they must be endured.

It is doubtful if what Europeans call loyalty, as distinct from compulsory duty, is a sentiment with them, also if they are warlike in our sense of the word. They are patriotic and self-reliant, will march coolly and doggedly under a heavy fire, or stand and be shot down, telling you composedly that the business must be done—that it matters little to poor devils like them whether they are killed or not; but have little enthusiasm. It is for this reason that, when an important attack is contemplated, large quantities of liquor are often served out to the men, not so much to give them courage, which they do not lack, as to rouse them from their habitual torpor.

However, the military qualities of the Russian soldier are too well known to need description. Hardy, brave, and submissive to discipline, they have, though worse rationed and looked after on service than any other European army, proved their efficiency in many severely-contested battles; and if better fed and commanded would probably equal, if they did not surpass, any troops in the world. I may, however, remark that the Russian army would never have become what it is—probably never have been heard of—without the example and guidance of the numbers of experienced military adventurers and foreign officers who, from the time of its first formation by Peter the Great, together with Courlanders, Finlanders, Poles, and other non-Russians, have commanded and inspired it.

It has often been advanced that, "money being
the sinews of war," the Russians, who are notoriously
financially badly off, are not likely to attempt to carry
out an aggressive policy, etc. ; but this view is not at
all borne out by their history up to date, or indeed by
the history of plenty of other "poor" nations, which
will suggest themselves to historical readers.

It is certain that want of money has never yet
prevented their statesmen from making war; and
the reason is not far to seek. Though poor in coin,
Russians are rich in all the "raw material" of war,
possessing men, horses, and land transport in abundance. Raising troops costs them nothing: the men
when raised get no pay, and will march anywhere
on biscuit and water.

The provisions their armies enforce contribution
of in war-time, on annexed or occupied territories, are
paid for in paper money, which immediately becomes
legal tender,[1] and is never redeemed. They can thus
always make war upon credit, reserving their actual
bullion for laying in stores of such improved arms,
cannon, and war material as they cannot yet manufacture cheaply at home.

The best proof (if any were required) that their
want of coin does *not* prevent aggression, is that they
are constantly annexing fresh territory. Their army,
which is yearly being improved and enlarged, advances steadily, acting on a comprehensive plan, the
ultimate aim of which may be taken to be universal

---

[1] Loris Melikoff made the late campaign in Asia Minor *entirely*
with paper money.

dominion (or domination at any rate) in Asia, of
which continent they already possess more than half,
as any one can see by consulting a map. While
they are pushing on, and while every parcel of territory they annex from the Pacific to the Black Sea
becomes identified with their empire, we are sitting
in a rich corner of the continent, the civilian viceroys
and governors of which, being compelled nowadays,
if they want to attain success in life, to " trim and
veer," to shape their "opinions" not with reference
to actual political facts and future dangers in Asia,
but according to the exigencies of political factions
and changes of ministry in England,[1] are sitting
quiet, too "cautious" even to hold the mountain
frontier, which, if fortified, might afford some prospect of checking invasion, and too happy to be left
undisturbed by the wild tribes, the imperial garrison
being barely sufficient to keep the peace in our own
territories.

Even the chance of checking Russian advance by
a counter-invasion on their flank and rear from the
Black Sea (the Baltic being now pretty well allowed
to be out of the question), is (unless we can patch up
our misunderstanding with the Turks) likely to slip
out of our hands. Should this door also be closed—
and the Russian advance in Armenia would be a
sign that it was—we shall be reduced to depend for
the preservation of our Indian Empire not on defence
ˑned with attack, which is the best defence, but

t the bottom of which is perhaps Bradlaugh or some Irish

on defence alone, and our naval superiority, with which in the Black Sea we could do much, would be thrown away.

It would then be a question whether we could, at short notice, occupy Kandahar, and forward enough men from England through Egypt to hold that part of Afghanistan against such an army as the Russians, reinforced by Afghans, Turkomans, and perhaps Persians, could bring down. Even then they might complicate matters badly for us by sending a force (*viâ* Balk and Bamean, through the northern passes, by which route large armies *have* penetrated in former days, in spite of its difficulties) upon Kabul and Peshawur, while the regular invasion took place from Herat.

I frequently observed, just previous to the breaking out of the late Russo-Turkish war, at which period, and for some years previously, I was in the Caucasus, that a characteristic of Russian policy was " caution." All the cosmopolitan and reasonably well-informed Russians with whom I conversed, accustomed to weigh the chances of the political situation and divine the motives of their rulers, appeared to be of opinion that if we had declared to back the Turks no war would have taken place. Their leading men, military and diplomatic, only *act* when they think the road clear and everything arranged to ensure success, and will leave nothing to chance, if possible. At the same time, once action is *taken* and war commenced, they become *entêté*, and even should they meet with great and unexpected difficulties and discomfitures, will strain every effort and make every sacrifice to get victoriously through it.

It would be advisable for us to take a leaf out of their book as to prudence. We have, it is true, opened a door in Egypt, but this may close another on the Black Sea, while our Indian door *vid* Kandahar is still wide open, with our "friends" not far off. It would perhaps be better not to tempt them by a show of so much confidence.

THE END.

Printed by R. & R. CLARK, *Edinburgh.*

Lightning Source UK Ltd.
Milton Keynes UK
UKHW020735150922
408910UK00005B/528

9 780469 052017